SANDOZ STUDIES, VOLUME 2

publication supported by a grant from
The Community Foundation for Greater New Haven
as part of the Urban Haven Project

SANDOZ *General Series Editor*
STUDIES Renée M. Laegreid

Editorial Advisory Board
Shannon D. Smith
Leisl Carr Childers

Founding Editor
John Wunder

SANDOZ STUDIES, VOLUME 2

Sandoz and the Battle of the Little Bighorn

Edited by RENÉE M. LAEGREID,
LEISL CARR CHILDERS, and MARGARET HUETTL

Foreword by JOHN WUNDER

University of Nebraska Press | Lincoln

© 2024 by the Board of Regents of the University of Nebraska

An earlier version of chapter 1 was previously published in *Great Plains Quarterly* 39, no. 2 (Spring 2019): 131–58. Reprinted courtesy of the University of Nebraska Press.

All rights reserved

The University of Nebraska Press is part of a land-grant institution with campuses and programs on the past, present, and future homelands of the Pawnee, Ponca, Otoe-Missouria, Omaha, Dakota, Lakota, Kaw, Cheyenne, and Arapaho Peoples, as well as those of the relocated Ho-Chunk, Sac and Fox, and Iowa Peoples.

Library of Congress Cataloging-in-Publication Data
Names: Laegreid, Renee M., editor. | Carr Childers, Leisl, editor. | Huettl, Margaret, editor. | Wunder, John R., writer of foreword.
Title: Sandoz and the Battle of the Little Bighorn / edited by Renée M. Laegreid, Leisl Carr Childers, and Margaret Huettl; foreword by John Wunder.
Description: Lincoln: University of Nebraska Press, 2024. | Series: Sandoz studies; volume 2 | Includes bibliographical references and index.
Identifiers: LCCN 2024008370
ISBN 9781496240972 (paperback)
ISBN 9781496241603 (epub)
ISBN 9781496241610 (pdf)
Subjects: LCSH: Sandoz, Mari, 1896–1966. Battle of the Little Bighorn. | Little Bighorn, Battle of the, Mont., 1876, in literature. | BISAC: LITERARY CRITICISM / American / General | HISTORY / United States / State & Local / West (AK, CA, CO, HI, ID, MT, NV, UT, WY) | LCGFT: Literary criticism. | Essays.
Classification: LCC PS3537.A667 B3837 2024 | DDC 973.8/2—dc23/eng/20240725
LC record available at https://lccn.loc.gov/2024008370

Set in New Baskerville ITC Pro by A. Shahan.
Designed by L. Auten.

Dedicated to

RON E. HULL (May 30, 1930–April 20, 2023) and

JOHN R. WUNDER (January 7, 1945–June 25, 2023)

This book is dedicated to Ron E. Hull and John R. Wunder, two men who made an incomparable impact on expanding knowledge and understanding of Nebraska and the American West. Both Hull and Wunder devoted their careers to preserving and sharing the history, literature, culture, and heritage of the high plains, and their legacies live on through their works and through the vast diaspora of scholars and professionals they mentored. Their passion and discipline shaped the many cultural organizations they led. Each earned the prestigious Sower Award from Humanities Nebraska for their contributions to the state's cultural ecosystem, and they both affirmed that their favorite organization was the Mari Sandoz Society. Truly, without Ron Hull and John Wunder, the Mari Sandoz Society would not be what it is today.

—SHANNON D. SMITH, president, Mari Sandoz Society

Contents

List of Illustrations   xi
Foreword, by John Wunder   xiii
Acknowledgments   xv
Introduction   xvii
PAUL ANDREW HUTTON

1. Draft by Draft: The Battle of Sandoz and Her Bighorn Manuscript   1
   ELAINE MARIE NELSON

2. Mari Sandoz, Sensory Conjuror, and *The Battle of the Little Bighorn*   45
   CHERYL A. WELLS

3. "Such a Jolly Family": Mari Sandoz Rewrites Elizabeth Bacon Custer   71
   CATHRYN HALVERSON

4. Recentering Custer: Mari Sandoz and the Battle of the Little Bighorn   91
   TAYLOR G. HENSEL

5. Writing against Empire: Mari Sandoz and the Fog of War   111
   KENT BLANSETT

6. All That We Cannot See: The Little Bighorn Battlefield Then and Now   155
   LEISL CARR CHILDERS

Contributors   179
Index   183

Illustrations

1. Mari Sandoz, circa 1957   5
2. Sandoz at a book signing in Lincoln, 1959   6
3. Sandoz, circa 1939   7
4. Sandoz, Sylvester Vigilante, and a friend at the New York Strawberry Festival, 1957   9
5. Sandoz in her New York apartment on Barrow Street, 1956   10
6. Portrait of Sandoz in her Hudson Street apartment in New York, circa 1960   11
7. Sandoz during her proofreading of *The Cattlemen*, 1958   12
8. Sandoz likely during a book tour, circa 1961   16
9. Sandoz in the office of her New York apartment, circa 1965   20
10. Sandoz's books, cabinets, and drawers of files, circa 1965   20
11. Eleanor Hinman and Sandoz's camp on White Clay Creek   23
12. Sandoz by the mantel in her New York apartment, 1965   26
13. Sandoz with the Levi Strauss Golden Saddleman Award, circa 1965 or 1966   34
14. Album covers for Floyd Westerman, *Custer Died for Your Sins* and *Indian Country*   124

15. Album covers for Peter La Farge, *Iron Mountain and Other Songs* and *On the Warpath*   124

16. Slogans and graffiti referencing Custer   128

17. Custer posters   129

18. T. C. Cannon, *Soldiers*   131

19. T. C. Cannon, *Zero Hero*, woodcut   133

20. T. C. Cannon, *Zero Hero*, oil   135

21. Edgar S. Paxson, *Custer's Last Stand*; William de la Montagne Cary, *The Battle on the Little Big Horn River*   137

22. American Indian Movement scenes of activism, 1976   143

23. Major E. S. Luce and Sandoz, 1949   144

24. Memorial markers at the Little Bighorn National Battlefield, 2011   161

25. Memorial and tombstones at the Little Bighorn National Battlefield, 2016   162

26. Last Stand Hill, 1984   162

27. Site of General Custer's Last Stand, circa 1960   165

28. "The battle of Custer's last charge," circa 1880–1910   171

29. Last Stand Hill, 1926   171

Foreword

JOHN WUNDER

Welcome to Sandoz Studies, a series of thematically grouped essays either by Mari Sandoz or about Mari Sandoz and her work, published by the University of Nebraska Press in collaboration with the Mari Sandoz Society.

The series expands interest and research into Mari Sandoz with the hope of bringing her work to a broader audience.

The purpose of Sandoz Studies is threefold: (1) to encourage new and innovative scholarly approaches to understanding Sandoz and her writings; (2) to make available in published form a collection of essays either previously unpublished or published in dispersed publications that are not easily accessible; and (3) to provide society members and the reading public with information and available scholarship on Mari Sandoz.

This series and the volumes that compose it are a labor of love and dedication by the editorial board and the Mari Sandoz Society. We hope you enjoy this volume as much as we have enjoyed its preparation. Turn the page and discover ideas and new information about the works of Mari Sandoz.

For this volume, the editors want to clarify that the language we use to talk about Indigenous people in North America continues to evolve. Where Sandoz wrote "Sioux Indians," Indigenous people and scholars today might prefer the "Lakota nation" or "Oceti Sakowin Oyate." Reflecting their own backgrounds and perspectives, the authors in this volume interchangeably use "American Indian," "Indian," "Native American," "Native," and "Indigenous." Whenever possible, they refer to nations by the name(s) they use for themselves.

Acknowledgments

The editors are grateful for the mutual support and energy they each gave to this project. Coediting anthologies takes a talent for collaboration and cooperation, which Renée Laegreid, Leisl Carr Childers, and Margaret Huettl most certainly provided. This volume is loosely based on presentations given at past Mari Sandoz Symposia hosted by the Mari Sandoz Society. The editors thank the presenters for the time and effort they put into revising their essays. The editors also thank the authors who contributed original works to the volume. Finally, the editorial board would like to thank *Great Plains Quarterly* for permission to reprint the chapter by Elaine Marie Nelson.

Introduction

PAUL ANDREW HUTTON

Mari Sandoz is best remembered as an American literary titan, but she was also an influential historian who helped to redefine the place of Native Americans in both literary and historical circles. In this she was well ahead of the times in which she lived, and as a result she suffered severe criticism from some members of the western history establishment. With *Crazy Horse* in 1942, *Cheyenne Autumn* in 1953, *These Were the Sioux* in 1961, and finally with her last book, *The Battle of the Little Bighorn*, published in 1966, she anticipated, as well as encouraged, a sea change in the American view of Native peoples, the Indian Wars, and George Armstrong Custer. By 1969, with the simultaneous commercial and critical success of Vine Deloria Jr.'s *Custer Died for Your Sins* and Dee Brown's *Bury My Heart at Wounded Knee*, almost the entire nation had undergone a conversion experience and had come to accept the Sandoz point of view.

The Battle of the Little Bighorn is on one hand a beautifully crafted and poetic literary work—and can be read as such—and is on the other hand a compelling work of history that proved to have a decisive influence on the image of Custer, his famed "last stand," and the Native people who fought him. Although it received decidedly mixed reviews upon publication—with critics quick to point out its casual blend of history with what they called literary fiction—in 1966 it still could claim to be the best book on the battle. Other titles have since contended for that honor, but it most certainly remains the finest literary treatment of the Little Bighorn fight.

In casting Custer in a negative light, Sandoz was attacking a well-established international icon. George Armstrong Custer, who was already a celebrated national hero as a result of his exploits as the "Boy General" of the Civil War, had quickly entered the pantheon of America's greatest heroes after his death at Little Bighorn thanks to a series of hagiographic books by Frederick Whittaker, J. W. Buel, D. M. Kelsey, and others, as well as the work of dime novelists, poets, and numerous artists of varying degrees of talent. Whitman, Longfellow, and John Greenleaf Whittier all published poetic tributes to the fallen hero. Popular novelists such as Cyrus Townsend Brady and Randall Parrish added to the Custer canon. Both Brady's and Parrish's novels were in turn adapted to the new medium of motion pictures (*Britton of the Seventh* in 1916 and *Bob Hampton of Placer* in 1921, respectively). By the fiftieth anniversary of the Little Bighorn, nearly twenty silent films on Custer and his last battle had been released. The grandest of these, Universal's *The Flaming Frontier*, came out in 1926 and featured Dustin Farnum as the heroic leader of the doomed Seventh Cavalry—"see his sublime courage in *The Flaming Frontier*" ran the breathless ad copy.[1] Farnum's counterpoint in the sound era was Errol Flynn's dashing Custer in the 1941 Warner Bros. epic *They Died with Their Boots On*. That film proved to be a huge box-office success.

Artists were also quick to embrace Custer. The *Illustrated Police News* had the distinction of publishing the very first artistic rendering of Custer's Last Stand as the cover art for the July 13, 1876, issue. William M. Cary's *The Death Struggle of General Custer* graced the *New York Daily Graphic* for July 19, and its portrayal of the long-haired, saber-wielding Custer set the standard for literally thousands of "last stand" images to follow, on canvas and as lithographs, chromos, engravings, posters, etchings, cartoons, and book and magazine illustrations. The most famous—and influential—of these was F. Otto Becker's 1896 lithograph based on an oil painting by Cassilly Adams and used by the Anheuser-Busch Company as a beer advertisement. Over 150,000 framed copies of *Custer's Last Fight* were distributed by the brewing company, and it quickly became a standard element of the decor in saloons across America for over half a century. Countless bar patrons studied the nuances of the garish painting over the decades that followed its appearance. So identified did it become with the last stand that several movie companies used it as part of their ad campaigns. Thus did Custer—long hair streaming in the western wind, resplendent in golden buckskins, standing alone and wielding his saber with all his men fallen around him as the Indian hordes charge—enter the dreamscape of the American mind. The last stand became an iconographic image to rival Paul Revere's midnight ride, Washington crossing the Delaware, the fall of Alamo, or the raising of the flag at Iwo Jima.

Custer's dead troopers had yet to receive a proper burial before entertainer William F. Cody had a new play—*The Red Right Hand; or Buffalo Bill's First Scalp for Custer*—enthralling eastern audiences. Cody had left the eastern stage to scout for his old regiment, the Fifth Cavalry, in the Great Sioux War in the summer of 1876. At Warbonnet Creek (often called Hat Creek), Nebraska, on July 17, 1876, an advance party of Cheyennes on their way north to join Sitting Bull clashed with a detachment of scouts led by Cody. Buffalo Bill brought down the only casualty in the skirmish, a Cheyenne warrior named Yellow Hair (usually incorrectly called Yellow Hand), and promptly lifted the fellow's topknot and warbonnet, proclaiming the trophies as "the first scalp for Custer."[2] The soldiers then chased the Cheyennes back to Red Cloud Agency. Sandoz always disputed this incident. She claimed that her sources, both Indian and soldier, described Yellow Hair as riding up and down the soldier line in order to screen the fleeing women and children. A volley from twenty soldier rifles finally brought him down. Few frontier stories annoyed her as much as the "first scalp" tale. She disliked the showboating Cody almost as much as she despised Custer. Perhaps it was the long hair. In a 1944 letter to Thomas Ferril of the *Rocky Mountain Herald*, she asserted that during the campaign Cody "was along, pretty drunk much of the time, always lagging behind" and that "one of the soldiers scalped Yellow Hand and later got $5 from Buffalo Bill for the scalp."[3] She also dismissed the story in her 1961 book *Love Song to the Plains*: "Years later the Cheyenne woman Cody usually hired to make his buckskin shirts laughed at the story. She had seen the killing and their friend Buffalo Bill was not there. They would have made no beadwork for any civilian who killed Yellow Hand."[4] Sandoz was wrong of course, not only in the details of the skirmish but also in her acceptance of the story told by her Cheyenne informants over multiple white eyewitnesses who recorded the event—and who had no particular interest in promoting Cody's career. Her position may well be understandable and certainly came to be shared by others who also felt her disdain for the triumphalist narrative of western conquest in which Cody and Custer were central figures.

The bottom line was that Sandoz did not much care for these long-haired, buckskin-clad exponents of rugged individualism. She collected considerable material on Wild Bill Hickok as well but ultimately found him too unsavory a character to write about. Custer, Cody, and Hickok all seemed too much flash and too little substance to her—not at all like the sturdy, hardworking folk of western Nebraska she had known while growing up there.

Cody soon returned to the eastern footlights, where his new play proved quite the success. When he initiated his famous Wild West arena show in 1883, he continued his identification with Custer. The Last Stand was often reenacted as the climax of the show, and Sitting Bull even toured with Cody for one season. The "first scalp" episode was a regular feature of the entertainment. It further cemented Custer's heroic status as a martyr to western expansion for both American and European audiences during the show's three-decade run.

Equally important to Custer's glorious legend were the three books lovingly penned by his widow, Elizabeth Bacon Custer. She devoted her long life to perpetuating a shining image of her dead husband. Her saintly hero was immortalized in three best-selling books: *Boots and Saddles* (1885), *Tenting on the Plains* (1887), and *Following the Guidon* (1890). She also lectured extensively. Most of the soldiers who might have been critical of her husband remained silent regarding the battle as long as she lived, but she outlived them all, not passing away until April 4, 1933, four days before her ninety-first birthday. Cathryn Halverson's chapter in this anthology discusses Elizabeth Custer at length.

By the mid-twentieth century, a towering Custer myth had come to dominate the national psyche. Here was a tale that more than confirmed national exceptionalism to Americans, for it seemed yet another facet of what made the country unique. Custer was the golden sacrifice to their continental destiny—their "Empire for Liberty."[5] The irony of the conquerors being conquered was lost on them. The shining image of the gallant young soldier standing alone on that lonely Montana hilltop, his troopers fallen around him, surrounded by a fiendish foe, blinded them to the darker side of the story. The Custer mystique was international as well, being one of the few events from American history that people around the globe might easily recognize.

This was the legend that Mari Sandoz set out to dismantle when writing *The Battle of the Little Bighorn* in Hanson Baldwin's Great Battles of History series for the J. B. Lippincott Company. She was facing a last stand of her own at the time, as she battled terminal cancer all through the torturous writing of the book (she signed each copy of a limited edition for James Carr's Books from her hospital deathbed—her signature as bold as ever on each of the 249 books in the short press run). Her courage and tenacity in completing the book as she fought her own last battle are awe inspiring—as discussed in Elaine Marie Nelson's excellent chapter in this volume.

A few writers had made attempts to reimagine Custer before Sandoz did, most notably Frederic Van de Water in *Glory-Hunter* (1934). The book proved a modest success, and the author's interpretation of Custer as an incompetent soldier who led better men to their deaths at Little Bighorn in his headlong pursuit of fame became a favorite of novelists such as Harry Sinclair Drago, Ernest Haycox, Clay Fisher, and Thomas Berger. Historians, however, still tended to treat Custer with considerable sympathy, as in W. A. Graham's *The Custer Myth* (1953), Edgar I. Stewart's *Custer's Luck* (1955), and Jay Monaghan's *Custer* (1959).

Sandoz forcefully dissented from their viewpoint in *Cheyenne Autumn* (1953). While she often criticized the "romantic fictions" that so often paraded as western history, she was herself an unabashed romantic of the first order.[6] This comes across clearly in every paragraph of her elegant prose. It is on particular display in *The Battle of the Little Bighorn* through her lyrical descriptions of landscape, discussed here in the chapters contributed by Cheryl Wells and Leisl Carr Childers.

Her romantic view of Indian source material, as well as her casual acceptance of Native testimony as gospel over other sources, proves particularly problematic in her Little Bighorn book. Her most controversial, and influential, point of interpretation in the book is her contention that Custer attacked the Indians early at Little Bighorn before other supporting troop columns could arrive and that he did so in the hope of securing for himself the 1876 Democratic presidential nomination. This is a main thesis of the book, and she elaborates on it in some detail. Her sole source for this is a 1912 interview with Arikara scout Red Star, which appeared in Orin G. Libby's 1920 edited volume, *The Arikara Narrative of the Campaign against the Hostile Dakotas, June, 1876*, published in the North Dakota Historical Collection series.

Red Star, who was eighteen at the time of the battle, told Libby that he had heard that Custer had told scout Bobtail Bull, who was killed in the battle, that if he won a victory, "even though it was against only five tents of Dakotas, it would make him president, the Great Father."[7] Red Star also claimed that one time, when Custer was eating with the scouts, he declared through the interpreter Fred Gerard (Sandoz misspells his name Girard, as other writers have also done) that after his troops defeated the Sioux, "I will go back to Washington, and on my trip to Washington I shall take my brother here, Bloody Knife, with me. I shall remain in Washington and be the Great Father."[8] Bloody Knife was killed at Little Bighorn while the interpreter, Gerard, never mentioned this incident, despite giving detailed testimony at the Reno Court of Inquiry.

In her book Sandoz embellished Red Star's tale with considerable detail: "It was an excellent time to defeat the warring Sioux, and today [June 25] the best time of all, with the Democratic Convention opening the day after tomorrow, and James Gordon Bennett of the New York *Herald* or his lieutenant surely prepared to stampede the convention for his friend, General George Armstrong Custer. . . . Victory now would leave two days and three nights to get the news to the telegraph office and to the Convention at St. Louis."[9] She has Custer preparing to send scouts off in different directions with the news of his victory dispatched to various telegraph offices (none of which could possibly have been reached in time even if this fantasy plan had been real). Sandoz ends her book with a recapitulation of Custer's presidential plans: "Custer was well aware that the nation gave the presidency to such men as Washington, Taylor, and Grant because they won her wars. . . . Now the sense of destiny that often appears in youths intolerant of discipline and restraint was upon him, a sort of desperate destiny. . . . Custer was very well aware that no one voted against a national hero."[10]

Her argument was presented with such clarity, style, and conviction that it was widely accepted. David H. Miller promptly repeated the story in his popular 1967 book *Custer's Fall*, and it was a major plot point of Arthur Penn's 1970 film *Little Big Man* (which became the second highest-grossing movie of that year). By the 1970s the tale of Custer's presidential ambitions had become commonplace. Custer, ever the symbol of the Indian Wars, now became the villain of that story. The noted historian Alvin M. Josephy Jr., writing for *Life* magazine in 1971, labeled Custer a crazed glory hunter and described his battlefield monument in Montana as "a sore from America's past that has not healed."[11] Sandoz's book had a decisive influence in this dramatic shift in Custer's reputation.

Her tale of Custer's 1876 presidential ambitions is of course preposterous. While it provided dramatic motivation for the Custer character in her book, the story reflected a total lack of understanding of Gilded Age politics. Custer's name was never mentioned in the press as a potential candidate. He was, in fact, barely old enough to run for president even if any important Democratic politicos had even remotely considered him, which they did not. The only soldier discussed during the lead-up to the Democratic National Convention in St. Louis was the hero of Gettysburg, General Winfield Scott Hancock (he was passed over in 1876 but was nominated in 1880, only to lose to James Garfield). The 1876 Democratic Party delegates nominated Samuel J. Tilden of New York on the first ballot, and the next day Thomas Hendricks of Indiana was nominated as his running mate. Custer was never mentioned by anyone at any time, even as a dark horse candidate. News of Custer's death at Little Bighorn did not reach St. Louis until July 5, a week after the convention had ended.

Custer's assault on the great village along the banks of the Little Bighorn was indeed a day premature, but not because he had 1876 presidential ambitions. He had planned to rest his troops and attack on June 26, but when news reached him that his column had been spotted by Sioux scouts, he decided to advance at once. (The supporting column under General Alfred Terry actually arrived a day late, on June 27.) Custer, like all the military officers in the field that summer, was obsessed with the idea that the Indians would escape. He was of course anxious for his regiment to win a victory, which might well win him a promotion. Martial glory, the driving force of his entire career, was his goal, not any political fantasies. Might Custer have run for president one day in the future on the record of his Civil War and frontier exploits? Of course—anything was possible in a future world he would not live to see.

Despite the reality of the national political situation in 1876, the Sandoz tale of Custer's presidential ambitions proved catnip to Custer's many critics. The story soon became a standard trope of the new Custer myth. Aspects of the evolving Custer image are discussed in the chapters by Kent Blansett and Taylor Hensel in this collection.

On another Custer controversy, Sandoz was almost certainly correct. In *Cheyenne Autumn* she had written that Custer had a sexual relationship with the Cheyenne captive Monahsetah after the 1868 Battle of the Washita River and that a child came of this union. Despite the fact that Monahsetah was featured prominently in Custer's *My Life on the*

Plains and in Elizabeth Custer's *Following the Guidon* as an attractive and able intermediary between the soldiers and the Cheyennes during the campaign, Custer partisans were quick to denounce Sandoz over what they considered slander. This was all quite reminiscent of the firestorm faced by the historian Fawn Brodie over her revelations about the Thomas Jefferson–Sally Hemings relationship. Like Brodie, Sandoz would be vindicated. Since the 1953 publication of *Cheyenne Autumn*, considerable new evidence has come to light on Custer's affair with Monahsetah (most notably in Cheyenne oral tradition used by Sandoz and in the stories related by the always reliable scout Ben Clark as well as the less reliable Captain Frederick Benteen). Sandoz has since been supported by Custer scholars such as Robert Utley, Jerome Greene, Louise Barnett, myself, and T. J. Stiles, all of whom accept the Monahsetah story as true.

Long before tackling her Little Bighorn book, Sandoz had considered writing a biography of Custer. Several friends and colleagues urged her to do so. She ultimately demurred, feeling that important materials in the archives that she had used in the 1930s when writing *Crazy Horse* had since been purposefully purged or "lost" by the National Archives to protect Custer's reputation, while other papers were closely guarded by private collectors. "Your suggestion that I write a book on Custer is a genuinely flattering one, but I must beg off," she wrote to John Frame in the spring of 1955. "The subject," she continued, "has been so marked, pawed over, and warmed over that I'm not interested in it. It is true that most of the books are merely rewrites of the sensational and sentimental newspaper accounts of the times, when the public had been led to believe that the Indians were blood-thirsty savages, without mentioning Custer was on land where, by treaty, no white man had the right to go, and that the charge of blood-thirstiness was certainly more applicable to Custer than to Crazy Horse, Sitting Bull, or the other leaders on Little Big Horn."[12] She had also wearied of the constant attacks on her books by Custer partisans. "The hipped Custerites have little use for me," she told Donald Danker in 1957. "For them one must swallow the legend whole."[13]

Despite her hesitancy in tackling a Custer biography, she finally relented to Hanson Baldwin's repeated pleas that she tell the story of the Little Bighorn battle in his military series for Lippincott. He had first approached her to write for his series in May 1960, but feeling overcommitted she had reluctantly declined. Baldwin, a Pulitzer Prize–winning war correspondent, noted book author, and military editor for the *New York Times*, persisted. He wooed her with the opportunity to finally tell the Indian side of the story, as well as with an open-ended contract and an extended deadline. Her busy schedule and serious health issues delayed the completion of the book even further; she was tardy by over a year in sending in her final manuscript. After three years of off-and-on research and writing, she finally submitted the manuscript in August 1965. By then she was desperately ill with the bone cancer that would take her life on March 10, 1966.

At the conclusion of *They Died with Their Boots On*, the highly romanticized 1941 Warner Bros. Custer epic—that Sandoz surely must have disliked—General Phil Sheridan assures Libbie Custer that "your soldier won his last battle, after all."[14]

Mari Sandoz, whose final work was *The Battle of the Little Bighorn*, most certainly won her last battle after all as well.

Sandoz Studies, Volume 2 originated with the October 2016 annual Mari Sandoz Society Conference held at the Mari Sandoz High Plains Heritage Center at Chadron State College in Chadron, Nebraska. As early as 1971 the college began work to establish a Sandoz study center focused not only on the author's remarkable literary career but also the heritage of western Nebraska. However, it was not until 2002 that fundraising efforts culminated in the opening of the present center. Housed in the historic 1929 college library, the center houses a gallery dedicated to Sandoz's life and career as well as high plains paleontology and ranching. In the six-thousand-volume library are Sandoz manuscripts, recordings, and many of her personal possessions. Gardens surrounding the center celebrate Sandhills botany, while a statue of Sandoz by the noted sculptor George Lundeen welcomes visitors to the center.

The 2016 conference began with the annual Pilster Great Plains Lecture, which I delivered: "Sandoz, Custer, and the Indian Wars." This was followed by a two-day symposium in which several of the contributors to this volume spoke. The editors also solicited essays from scholars in an effort to present the wide diversity of critical approaches to the study of Mari Sandoz and her writing.

The historical approach to Sandoz studies is presented in Elaine Nelson's deeply insightful and ultimately poignant account of the actual writing of *The Battle of the Little Bighorn*. Nelson, executive director of the Western History Association, brings Sandoz to life in "Draft by Draft" with the compelling story of the long, painful journey that marked the creation of her final book. It is an inspiring story of remarkable endurance and final triumph amid looming tragedy.

Independent scholar Cheryl Wells invites us to immerse ourselves in the sensory world Sandoz so masterfully re-creates in her Little Bighorn book. Wells illuminates the careful way Sandoz re-creates the sensory chaos of the heat, dust, and smoke of the battlefield. Wells also discusses how Sandoz, as she did in all her books, invokes the harsh beauty of the western landscape. Grand vistas, the sweet smell of sage, the acrid dust of the prairie trail—these are the sights and sounds and smells that Sandoz used to bring the past to vivid life in her writing. There is a rhythm to this language that is critical to the success of her prose. It allows the reader, as Wells makes clear, to feel a part of the action and to be captured by the romance of the western frontier. "Although the truth remains elusive," Wells concludes, "sensory analysis offers a connection to the disparate places in Sandoz's life as well as a novel and creative way of thinking about *The Battle of the Little Bighorn*."

Cathryn Halverson, of Södertörn University in Sweden, deconstructs the creation of the Custer myth in her chapter on Sandoz and Elizabeth Custer. Halverson approaches the two women from a literary perspective. This is a fresh approach to Elizabeth Custer, and Halverson's chapter proves particularly insightful. Halverson also candidly admits that the Sandoz book "straddles the line of history and fiction." The stark contrasts between the writings of the two authors are particularly evident in their depiction of Custer: "Mari Sandoz's *The Battle of the Little Bighorn* reads as both a continuation and a rebuttal of Elizabeth Bacon Custer's portrait of Armstrong, razing the legend that she had done so much to fix in the national imagination."

Taylor G. Hensel of the University of Wyoming focuses on how Sandoz recentered our perspective of the story of the battle by telling it from the Native point of view and thus "portrayed it less as a tragic American defeat and more as a triumphant and inevitable Native victory." The Sandoz perspective on the "Winning of the West" had certainly been on display in her earlier works—most notably *Crazy Horse* (1942) and *Cheyenne Autumn* (1953)—but Hensel sees a culmination of sorts in *The Battle of the Little Bighorn*: "Through her interactions with the Lakota, she understood it as a violent and aggressive action, a complicated and often horrifically brutal colonization of an already inhabited land upon which people had been living with relative success for over a millennium." Hensel notes how Custer is less the major protagonist in the book but rather "more of a fulcrum around which the entirety of the text revolves." Hensel insightfully notes how Sandoz's Custer is much like Herman Melville's Ahab in *Moby Dick*: "Like Ahab, Custer knows what lies ahead of him. . . . Sandoz's Custer is an eagle, trapped, yes, but trapped by *himself*, not the circumstances or the physical environment surrounding him." It is this remarkable interpretive device of the protagonist doomed by his own hubris that gives such literary power to the book.

Custer and his last battle as symbol and metaphor are the subject of Kent Blansett's chapter, "Writing against Empire: Mari Sandoz and the Fog of War." Blansett, who teaches at the University of Kansas, positions Sandoz's *The Battle of the Little Bighorn* within the context of American military involvement in Vietnam and the simultaneous rise of both the antiwar movement and the Red Power movement. He casts Sandoz's final volume as "one of the most significant antiwar and Indigenous rights books of the mid-twentieth century." The Custer myth of heroic sacrifice was transformed, Blansett contends, into a new "Indigenous Custer myth" that "eventually served as a critical battleground for the ideological foundations that define the Red Power movement." Music, art, literature, and the initiation of academic programs in Native American studies are all topics Blansett uses to illuminate this radical alteration of the Custer myth.

In the final contribution to this collection, Leisl Carr Childers of Colorado State University presents a fascinating overview of the landscape at today's Little Bighorn Battlefield National Monument and the "disjunction of the historic and current environment" that poses a problem for those seeking to interpret the battle within its physical context. Mari Sandoz's use of landscape, as Cheryl Wells emphasizes in her chapter, is central to the literary construction of her book. Carr Childers complements this theme with a careful comparison of what the field looked like in 1876 as opposed to its appearance when Sandoz visited late in the 1940s and to the much altered environment of today. The clumps of bunchgrass and bundles of sagebrush have given way to lush grassland punctuated by only occasional sagebrush as a result of a massive fire in 1983. The battlefield that Sandoz visited in the 1940s and 1960s was closer to the original landscape environment of 1876. The environmental transformation of the battlefield since 1876 is subtle but significant, and this alteration was something that Sandoz understood. Carr Childers notes how this sensitivity allows Sandoz's book, "with its rich environmental descriptions, [to provide] a profound look at the place for those visitors generations removed from the historic fight."

Here then, in the second volume of Sandoz Studies, is a rich selection of writings that highlight the diverse approaches—literary, historical, environmental, sensory, Native—used to interpret Mari Sandoz's final book. All are intended to give the modern reader a fresh and engaging perspective on this literary masterpiece.

NOTES

1. Undated 1926 newspaper advertisement for *The Flaming Frontier*, Paul A. Hutton Collection, Albuquerque NM.

2. Paul L. Hedren, *First Scalp for Custer: The Skirmish at Warbonnet Creek, Nebraska, July 17, 1876* (1980; Lincoln: University of Nebraska Press, 1987), 68; William F. Cody, *The Life of Hon. William F. Cody Known as Buffalo Bill: The Famous Frontier Scout and Guide* (Hartford CT: Frank E. Bliss, 1879), 342–47.
3. Mari Sandoz to Thomas Ferril, April 23, 1944, in Helen Winter Stauffer, ed., *Letters of Mari Sandoz* (Lincoln: University of Nebraska Press, 1992), 213.
4. Mari Sandoz, *Love Song to the Plains* (New York: Harper & Brothers, 1961), 200.
5. Thomas Jefferson quoted in Gordon S. Wood, *Empire of Liberty: A History of the Early Republic, 1789–1815* (New York: Oxford University Press, 2009), 357.
6. Mari Sandoz to Editorial Office, Westerners Brand Book, New York Posse, August 22, 1962, in Stauffer, *Letters of Mari Sandoz*, 396.
7. Orin G. Libby, *The Arikara Narrative of the Campaign against the Hostile Dakotas, June, 1876* (Bismarck: North Dakota Historical Society, 1920), 58–59, cited in Paul Andrew Hutton, ed., *The Custer Reader* (Lincoln: University of Nebraska Press, 1992), 236n3.
8. Libby, *Arikara Narrative*, cited in Hutton, *Custer Reader*, 236n3.
9. Mari Sandoz, *The Battle of the Little Bighorn* (1966; Lincoln: Bison Books, an imprint of the University of Nebraska Press, 1978), 54, 55.
10. Sandoz, *Battle of the Little Bighorn*, 182.
11. Alvin M. Josephy Jr., "The Custer Myth," *Life*, July 2, 1971, 55.
12. Mari Sandoz to John Frame, April 16, 1955, in Stauffer, *Letters of Mari Sandoz*, 275.
13. Mari Sandoz to Donald Danker, May 25, 1957, in Stauffer, *Letters of Mari Sandoz*, 297.
14. Raoul Walsh, dir., *They Died with Their Boots On*, starring Errol Flynn and Olivia de Havilland (Los Angeles: Warner Bros. Pictures, 1941).

SANDOZ STUDIES, VOLUME 2

1

Draft by Draft

The Battle of Sandoz and Her Bighorn Manuscript

ELAINE MARIE NELSON

From behind the trailing smoke, blown aside now and then, he could see an immense moving mass starting up the low breaks to the prairie on the west, the left side of the river, apparently heading toward the mountains. One after another the men forgot all danger and gathered in close groups on the ridges to watch under their palms, shielding their eyes against the late sun. Even the officers forgot the danger from skulking snipers left behind and passed the field glasses around. Although the movement was miles away, it looked like one of the vast buffalo herds that once marched those prairies; but they were all gone and besides this was not so dark. It was the great camp of the Indians in a solid, moving flow of riders and family travois with their lodges and belongings, the poles stirring up dust that drifted slowly away, curiously golden in the evening sun.
—Mari Sandoz, *The Battle of the Little Bighorn*

On February 11, 1966, Mary Ann Pifer, age twenty-seven, penned a letter from her home in Boulder, Colorado, destined for New York City. "Dear Aunt Mari," she began. "I do want to thank you for the copy of *Old Jules Country*," a compilation of Sandoz's nonfiction writing published in 1965. "I get an immense pleasure from reading passages from books I've read before. . . . I also find that I appreciate your work so much more now that I have an idea of how much 'sweat' went into it."[1]

Fifty years later, in the fall of 2016, Mary Ann Pifer Anderson reflected on those years. As the niece of prolific Nebraska writer Mari Sandoz (1896–1966), Anderson acknowledges that her aunt Mari's writing career made an impact on her many fans and readers. It shaped Anderson's own personal and professional life as well. She saw that "women actually could have a fulfilling career, which at the time, not many women did, especially in the arts." Anderson wrote, "Literature, like history, was a huge part of my maturing." As a young woman in the 1960s, Anderson changed her attitude "toward many things" as she learned "that not everything was as I had thought." She concluded, "Obviously, books such as *Crazy Horse* and *Cheyenne Autumn* played a role in that."[2]

Writing is hard, and all writers pick their own poison to get to the heart of their work and see it through to its final form. Mari Sandoz published dozens of award-winning books, articles, and essays in her lifetime. But she struggled to meet her own personal standards for meticulous research and writing of fiction and nonfiction titles that focused on the history of the Great Plains. American novelist, teacher, and nonfiction writer Anne Lamott muses over the work of writing as the careful, agonizing process that authors and historians often endure when they sit down to compose a sentence, a paragraph, a chapter, and finally a book. In her 1994 book of essays, *Bird by Bird*, Lamott declares that "good writing is about telling the truth." There is anxiety in the "hugeness of the task ahead," but it is best to just take things one step at a time.[3]

Sandoz did just this. She pored through her research notes, chapters, and scrutinized every page and passage. She developed a distrust and disdain for copy editors, which resulted in heated debates with her publishers. Sandoz was a skilled writer, but her manuscripts did not take shape in her first or even second versions. Instead they evolved—draft by draft—into stories with a verve for authentic language and an authoritative grasp of the history of the people, places, and events in the Great Plains.

Perhaps no manuscript was more difficult for Sandoz to write than her final book, *The Battle of the Little Bighorn*, published posthumously in 1966. In the spring of 1965 Mary Ann Anderson moved to New York to assist her aunt Mari with the completion of the manuscript. The famous writer was fighting her second cancer diagnosis at the time. During these weeks that she spent with her aunt, Anderson witnessed firsthand that writing was a complex process, especially while she watched Sandoz endure painful periods of treatment and recovery. As the illness consumed Sandoz in her final months of life, she clung to her business-as-usual methods for completing her last book, which required energy, determination, and a lot of revisions. Anderson was responsible for typing these revisions over and over for several weeks until they met her aunt's approval. This experience is ingrained in Anderson's mind, as she humorously noted about her own written memories, "I don't think [Aunt Mari] would have approved of a sentence of this length."[4] Ironically, while many believe Sandoz's Little Bighorn manuscript is her finest work, it also receives the least attention from literary scholars and historians. Very few publications examine the years, months, and days that Sandoz spent researching and writing drafts for *The Battle of the Little Bighorn* while also fighting aggressive bone cancer that destroyed her health. This chapter traces aspects of Sandoz's life and work in New York City and offers a glimpse of the battles she won and lost to complete her final story.

GREAT PLAINS INTERPRETER

Mari Sandoz is one of Nebraska's homegrown literary giants. Her work spanned three decades and made tremendous contributions to the history of the American West, Great Plains studies, and Native American and Indigenous peoples. From a young age Sandoz was inspired by the history that surrounded her. She was born in 1896 on a homestead near the rolling hills of the Niobrara River valley in Nebraska to immigrant parents. From a young age she endured physical abuse and was made to perform laborious farm work by her father. He transferred his agitation and obsession with settling and taming the dry, uncooperative land of northwestern Nebraska to his succession of wives and his six children. The isolation, seclusion, and hardships of prairie life provoked Mari to seek an appreciation for the land that enveloped her existence. Although restricted from traveling far from home, she immersed herself in the culture of the country that paraded through her family's land. The Sandoz homestead sat on an old river crossing of what became a well-traveled path of trappers, hunters, soldiers, miners, traders, and Native American nations. She listened attentively to their stories and observed their relationships to the land. When Mari was a teenager, the Sandoz family moved southward into the Sandhills, a region of Nebraska quite different from the Niobrara River valley. Mari Sandoz was "sometimes frightened by, sometimes attracted to the Sandhills." It is treeless, flat, and dry. But she fell in love with this land and the people connected to it, despite the historical conflict layered throughout its past. This region, and this conflict, inspired most of her research and writing.[5]

Sandoz was relentless in her convictions as a historian. She was a critical thinker about the American past, and she had strong literary aspirations. She was fervently devoted to providing her readers with an "authentic" view of the past. Sandoz scrutinized every detail of her writing, as she wished to publish work that accurately reflected her true Sandhills roots. For her, this meant that she portrayed the peoples, places, and events of Nebraska and the Great Plains using the voices and oral testimonies of people marginalized from historical records, primarily women and Native Americans but also ranchers and farmers. At the time, her reliance on oral interviews was unconventional in the history profession. But, seeking to create her own unique "interpretive approach" to writing history, Sandoz was determined to verify her broad array of sources (which included photographs, records from the National Archives, newspapers, genealogy materials, and documents found in private collections, libraries, and historical societies) to "correct the biases and to eliminate the omission that characterized traditional Western histories."[6]

Several scholars view her books, essays, and letters as proof of her unquestionable dedication to telling the stories of individuals through the voices of Native Americans, women, laborers, and farmers, as well as

1. Mari Sandoz, circa 1957. Image 0080-02914, Mari Sandoz Collection, Archives and Special Collections, University of Nebraska–Lincoln Libraries.

to detailing the interests of the military and every level of the government. The topics and the people transformed by conflict contributed to Sandoz's worldview, which challenged the celebratory overtones of America's western expansion and colonization that, at the time, were so evident in U.S. historical scholarship. This approach to historical writing connects Sandoz's work to a group of white women intellectuals who published landmark fiction and nonfiction works on culture, nature, ethnohistory, and social forces that transformed the American West in the nineteenth century.[7] She, along with Caroline Bancroft, Angie Debo, Dorothy Johnson, and others, produced dozens of books that received widespread acclaim from the public. As her work attempted to tell the story of the American West "from the margins of the historical establishment," she often received extra scrutiny. Editors, politicians, and academics questioned Sandoz's research methods and writing techniques, hoping to damage her integrity as an expert on the western past. "Historians were repulsed by her use of invented dialogue" and discredited her work as lacking proper citations for evidence. Regardless, Sandoz's career flourished with the general public outside the shadows of the male-dominated academy, and numerous scholars, historians, and graduate students revered her nonfiction works as paramount in the field.[8]

2. Mari Sandoz at a book signing in 1959 at a public library in Lincoln, Nebraska. Image 2003.001.00091, Caroline Sandoz Pifer Collection, Mari Sandoz High Plains Heritage Center. Courtesy of the Mari Sandoz Society.

WESTERN WRITING FROM THE EAST

The conflict that played such a significant role in shaping Sandoz's nonfiction works often represented a West-versus-East narrative. In her view, the wealth and influence of the eastern United States exploited the vulnerability of western lands and people. Yet Sandoz realized that if she wanted a writing career, she would be forced to succumb to the powerful publishing houses in the East and relocate to its hub. Despite her permanent move to New York City in the 1940s, she continued her role as a strident defender of Great Plains languages, lifeways, cultures, and identities. She fervently insisted that the city would never replace her Nebraska home. In fact, she publicly claimed that she hated New York. In a letter to the editor of the *Lincoln Journal Star* in 1960, she wrote to quickly correct a Denver newspaper that had quoted her "as saying I  hate eastern Nebraska." She swiftly stated her "affection for eastern Nebraska" and clarified her position: "It's the east and New York that I hate." Sandoz continued, arguing that "the provincialism of the east and New York would not matter at all if they did not control so much of the creative work of the nation, particularly the writing." She concluded, "Unfortunately the town has grown monstrous on the blood of the nation, with the . . . contempt of the parasite for the host."[9] Her niece Mary Ann Anderson also recalled her aunt's hatred

3. Mari Sandoz, circa 1939, with her research notes and index cards in her apartment at the Shurtleff Arms, Lincoln, Nebraska. Image 2003.001.00069, Caroline Sandoz Pifer Collection, Mari Sandoz High Plains Heritage Center. Courtesy of the Mari Sandoz Society.

of New York City, especially while she lived with her for a short time in the spring of 1965: "One thing New York City taught me was that I didn't want to live there," Anderson wrote, probably, she mused, "for the same reason Aunt Mari kept a file entitled 'Why I Hate New York'; we [both] needed wide open spaces."[10]

In reality, Sandoz did well in New York City and flourished in a scene that supported writing and the arts. She lived in Greenwich Village, first on Barrow Street and later on Hudson Street. She thought her 23 Barrow Street fourth-floor apartment looked "like a deserted love nest," with images of red roses stretching across the paneled walls. Sandoz asked for a fresh coat of paint and then hung a "Sioux painting" and "a wall-sized map" she had worked on "for twenty years recording the movements of the Plains Indians as fast as I could verify their camps and trails." She also hung her cowboy hat on the wall, "a reminder, in moments of anger and disgust with the east, that there was another country and another people." She enjoyed the close-knit community among the tenants, but fifteen years later a new syndicate bought the building and raised her rent. This, combined with her desire for more storage and security, prompted her to move.[11]

When Sandoz relocated to a nearby apartment at 422 Hudson Street, she had tall, west-facing windows that filled her work space with light. Multiple closets stored her research, and she even had access to additional storage in the building's basement. The walls displayed a few pieces of art, posters, and her large map of Native trails and camps. Books, memorabilia, typewriters, and awards filled her tables and shelves. One colleague who visited her there observed that the room was filled with an "air of mid-America directness."[12] A reporter for the *New York Times* commented that "large and small filing cabinets overflowed into the kitchens and closets."[13] There were many endearing qualities of New York City that Sandoz enjoyed. She took breaks to explore it with newfound friends by taking walks, visiting museums and galleries, and going to cafés. But for the most part, when she was in New York she was writing. It was in the Village that she buried herself in her work, writing draft after draft of her most famous books

4. Mari Sandoz (*right*) with Sylvester Vigilante and a friend at the New York Strawberry Festival, where Sandoz gave a talk in 1957. Sylvester Vigilante was the chief librarian in the American Reading Room of the New York Public Library for fifty years. Image 2003.001.00458, Caroline Sandoz Pifer Collection, Mari Sandoz High Plains Heritage Center. Courtesy of the Mari Sandoz Society.

about the American West: *Cheyenne Autumn* (1953), *The Buffalo Hunters* (1954), *The Cattlemen* (1958), *These Were the Sioux* (1961), *Miss Morrissa* (1955), *Son of a Gamblin' Man* (1960), *Love Song to the Plains* (1961), and *The Beaver Men* (1964). Her writing paid the bills and supported her travels. Each year she looked forward to swapping the city for the Sandhills with an escape to the West for book signings, speaking engagements, and research trips.[14]

Sandoz's internal conflict with the East did not undermine her ability to write about her love for Nebraska and the West. She was truly an expert on that part of the country, a fact she was quick to affirm. Beginning in the 1930s, Sandoz built upon her reputation as a "western" writer. Her audience appreciated her honest tone

and style, which was full of both grit and grace. She understood the region and people she wrote about on a deeply intimate level, and her insistence on this knowledge drew contentious debates with the historical establishment and publishers. No one could deny that Sandoz was born into and grew up in the world of the West that became the topic of her books. But academic historians disliked the "novelistic" prose that had made her work so popular with large audiences. Publishers and editors often questioned her language and word choice, which Sandoz took as a personal attack on her knowledge of living in the West. These engagements forced her to fervently defend the Great Plains as a place with distinct phrases and expressions. In one complaint to her publisher Sandoz wrote, "You seem to want *drought* [instead of *drouth*]. . . . West of the Missouri it is a plain affectation, see [the] *Dictionary of American English* for the difference in the word, regionally. I'll receive a dozen letters on this change alone, with the charge that I am 'selling out.'" She concluded that "everybody" from the plains "realizes that I know better than to use *drought*."[15]

5. Mari Sandoz in her apartment on Barrow Street in New York, 1956. In view behind her are rows of filed and boxed letters for research, books piled on shelves, and *The Writer*, a portrait painting of Mari Sandoz by Nebraska artist, neighbor, and friend Louise Austin. Sandoz's sister Caroline wrote that "Mari liked it for the hands. She felt the long sensitive fingers could be those of a surgeon" (Caroline Sandoz Pifer, *Making of an Author: Mari Sandoz Book III, 1931–1932* [Gordon NE: Mari Sandoz Corporation, 1984], illustration between pages 90 and 91). Image 2003.001.00138, Caroline Sandoz Pifer Collection, Mari Sandoz High Plains Heritage Center. Courtesy of the Mari Sandoz Society.

6. A portrait of Mari Sandoz in her apartment at 422 Hudson Street in New York City, circa 1960. Image RG1274-0012, Nebraska State Historical Society.

This recognition and respect made Sandoz even more determined to deliver her version of authentic western stories that included "voices previously unheard by chroniclers of the West." It also prompted her to write a book for the series Regions of America, published by Harper and Brothers to depict America's "natural regions, their history, development and character." The book—her "love song" to her home state of Nebraska—was published as *Love Song to the Plains* in 1961. Like most of her books, it received widespread praise as "a lyric salute to the earth and sky and people who made the Great Plains," despite the conflict that often engulfed their lives.[16]

SANDOZ'S WRITING AS A LABOR OF LOVE

Sandoz solidified her place as a regional historian for the West and Great Plains early in her career. She was therefore honored to receive

writing requests from beyond this niche. Hanson Baldwin—longtime military writer for the *New York Times* and recipient of the Pulitzer Prize—contacted Sandoz in May 1960 with a proposal from the publisher J. B. Lippincott. "Would you be interested in authoring a book . . . on the Battle of the Little Big Horn, and its implications to the ultimate winning of the west?" he wrote. "No one could deal with this subject . . . better than you." The book, he informed her, would be included in Lippincott's Major Battles in History series. A month later Sandoz replied, declining his offer and citing her tight publication schedule. "I am immediately pleased to be asked to do this. . . . I tried to work the book into my schedule. The problems proved too great." Yet in the same letter, she launched into detailed paragraphs that reaffirmed her intimate familiarity with the topic, in which she mentioned the "mass of stuff in the [Adjutant General's Office] Records over on Virginia Avenue [in Washington DC]" that she had accessed in the 1930s. As if to further spark Baldwin's interest, she claimed this "stuff" had "never been touched upon in any account that I've seen." She concluded, "Anyway, I wish you great and good success." Baldwin responded that he was "greatly disappointed" by her decision. "It is so evident your heart is keyed to our project, and your knowledge of sources is so obviously vast," he wrote, that he wished to persuade her to "reverse" her position on the matter.[17]

An editor-writer courtship between Baldwin and Sandoz ensued. Baldwin's complimentary persistence and reputation made an impact

7. Mari Sandoz in her apartment on Barrow Street, during her proofreading of *The Cattlemen* in February 1958. Barrow Street was her New York City home for fifteen years before she moved to 422 Hudson Street in May 1958. Image 2001.002.00304, James F. Carr Collection, Mari Sandoz High Plains Heritage Center. Courtesy of the Mari Sandoz Society.

on Sandoz. And so did her bank account. In a letter to her longtime literary agent, Mary Squire Abbot, Sandoz stated that over the duration of twenty-nine months she had earned only $600 for new writing. This is "not enough to cover my apartment rent here, let alone anything for . . . my living," she wrote. So, she continued, "with the situation as it is, I've decided that I better commit myself to the book on the Little Big Horn for Lippincott. That will make a good seller . . . even if the publisher muffs it." Plus, she had already told Abbot, "I have special information and special approaches" on the topic. She warned Baldwin that he "could not expect to get the Custer fight book for six, seven years" but that "I shall be happy to write the book on the Little Big Horn . . . when I can squeeze it in." Baldwin replied triumphantly: "I am delighted . . . without a doubt . . . you are the author for us." Abbot, who worked at the McIntosh and Otis agency, arranged for Sandoz to receive $250 upon signing the contract, $1,000 when work began, and $750 upon completion of the manuscript. These were consequential sums at the time, an amount well over $15,000 if issued in 2018.[18]

Baldwin and Sandoz's conversational correspondence lasted until fall 1960, at which time Sandoz found herself deeply invested in completing her "Nebraska" manuscript. Later titled *Love Song to the Plains* and released by Harper and Brothers in 1961, it would be one of the most revered books of Sandoz's writing career. Each chapter in *Love Song* unfolds as one lyrical story after the next. The language Sandoz used in the book gave it a meaning and an aura that could be genuinely reflected only through the eyes of someone from the plains, an insider who grew up there. She later admitted that writing *Love Song* was "sheer self-indulgence. . . . For years I had wanted to measure the larger events and personages of the Plains with the rueful yardstick of the region and consider how they must have appeared in their time, both to the general public and to the presumably informed." Finally, she reflected, "I got to Love Song."[19]

There is no doubt that Sandoz was passionate about the material. But she confronted the same struggles with beginning the writing process as she did with most of her books. To write *Love Song*, Sandoz recalled, "at last I had to settle down to the drudgery of the writing. . . . I tore into a sustained rough draft, which I always write in long-hand and as rapidly as possible." She admitted, "I write the worst first draft of any author." After typing her work, she sorted hundreds of sheets that needed to be "painfully revised." And then, draft by draft, Sandoz churned out one page at a time, to create chapters upon chapters for her books, "clean copies made for more revision, over and over, a process every bit as ridiculous as the most absurd little stories I had discovered and was adding, like raisins dropped into a son-of-a-gun-in-a-sack of pudding to steam in some chuckwagon kettle." One can imagine her smiling with confidence and certainty in this recollection of writing *Love Song*, as well as her other popular titles: "That's how I came to write the book. It was fun, work too, but fun."[20]

Writing a book *can* be fun. But writers also lament how the draft-by-draft process is one of personal torture that takes unexpected turns. What Sandoz did not fully anticipate with *Love Song* (or with any of her other books) was how combative she would have to become in her back-and-forth dialogue with copy editors and publishers. Marion S. "Buz" Wyeth Jr., a prolific Harper and Brothers editor whose projects included *Old Yeller*, was Sandoz's editor for *Love Song*. Although he praised her early drafts, Sandoz remained wary of his enthusiasm: "Your kind words on LOVE SONG are welcome but I have a feeling that I had better be protecting my jugular."[21] She reported similar sentiments to her friend and colleague Bruce Nicoll, director of the University of Nebraska Press: "Reports on Love Song . . . are enthusiastic from . . . Harpers . . . but I'm reserving my enthusiasm . . . if they want any serious changes I'll be gone so fast they'll not even find any dust." Accustomed to Sandoz's conflicts with eastern publishers, Nicoll responded to her, "I often wonder why you don't tell those characters in New York to go fly a kite."[22]

Early in her career Sandoz earned a reputation in the publishing world as an independent, strong-willed author who expected to have unusually heavy involvement on the production of her books—from the text and copyediting to the maps and illustrations. Most publishers she worked with were from and resided in "the East" (New York City) and did not have a tight grasp on the history of the plains or the American West. She often complained that copy editors frequently tried to change her vocabulary, alter her research, and rearrange history according to *their* ideas of the language she should use to describe western people, places, and events. Sandoz vehemently responded to these actions when they emerged in her drafts of *Love Song*: "Do not insert either nouns or verbs in material unfamiliar to you. The author may have a very good reason for avoiding certain words. . . . *Spouse* instead of *wife* of the trader is a real howler and would get me laughed out of the countenance anywhere outside of a publishing house. On the Plains *Spouse* is a word of ridicule for women of the east." With careers in the publishing business, Sandoz's editors had one goal: to sell books. But Sandoz was confident in her talents as a writer and her ability to have a broad appeal to readers across the country. She did not believe she needed to betray the history and authenticity of the Great Plains for the bottom line.[23]

She did not let her copy editors in 1961 get away with altering her words. Her exchanges with them were curt, irritable, and explosive: "*Slay* is a word for Shakespeare, not for the wilderness. . . . You question *plew*. This is a perfectly good Webster word meaning beaver hide." Also, she wrote, "by changing 'But the lack of boundaries encouraged the old French . . .' to 'The general ignoring of boundaries' is an appalling misstatement on your part. This was long before the Louisiana Purchase. What boundaries could there be to be ignored?" Sandoz aggressively argued that these editorial modifications changed the book's context and undermined her integrity as an expert on the Great Plains and American West. In the same heated exchange, she wrote, "Never change dates in a manuscript, query but do not change. The change might be overlooked by the author and his reputation be ruined by the error," and concluded in bold letters, "But enough of this. I will not go through this whole book on the original trying to correct all of your errors. . . . I don't care to have weeks of my time wasted trying to restore the accuracy of my work."[24]

Sandoz eventually won most of her battles with copy editors. Buz Wyeth ran interference between the Harper and Brothers copy editors, and Sandoz and took over all communication regarding her manuscript. Wyeth placated Sandoz more than editors normally did with authors at that time. He wrote frequent letters to request input and permission from her on every decision regarding *Love Song*. He even wrote to fervently apologize for a mistake he made on the galley proofs.[25] Ultimately, *Love Song to the Plains* was an exceptionally popular book. Sandoz biographer Helen Winter Stauffer has observed that it "stands out among [her] works because of its literary merit. . . . The land itself is the thread upon which the narrative is spun."[26]

THE CASE OF THE MISSING FILES

After she published *Love Song to the Plains* in 1961, Mari Sandoz worked toward the completion of *Storycatcher* (1963) and *The Beaver Men* (1964). On and off throughout these years she was also deeply immersed in her book on the Little Bighorn. When she initially agreed to write the book, Sandoz referenced her large index card file and told Baldwin, the series editor, that she had already completed most of the research and interviews on the subject. "All of the material is cross-indexed by individual and activity, etc., and makes a solid section in the 350,000 card index to my notes," she wrote. Sandoz promised to gather Little Bighorn research into one file while in progress on other manuscripts,

8. Mari Sandoz, circa 1961, likely during a book tour for *Love Song to the Plains*. Image 0080-01728, Mari Sandoz Collection, Archives and Special Collections, University of Nebraska–Lincoln Libraries.

asserting that "a book seems to ripen in the back of my mind as the file grows."[27]

As the summer of 1964 passed, Sandoz liberated old research notes to focus solely on the Little Bighorn. She again recalled a gap in her files from 1937 to 1938 (the "mass of stuff" she had previously mentioned to Baldwin). That was the year she had visited Washington DC, to study the Adjutant General's Office (AGO) records held in the Department of the Interior's storage facility known as "Haley's Garage" on Virginia Avenue.[28] Sandoz mentioned these files several times in her letters to other authors, such as Custer biographer Jay Monaghan, who inquired about her Custer research in 1957. She replied to him, "Much of the personal material on Custer and other individuals that I ran into in the piles and bales of records from the dismantled frontier posts gathered over on Virginia Avenue, Washington, was classified when it was moved into the National Archives in 1940 or there abouts." (Congress created the National Archives as an agency in 1934, and a new National Archives building opened in 1937.) Even though Sandoz possessed detailed references to these files (with dates, locations, and document numbers recorded), she wrote, "I've not been able to get another look at much of this. . . . I was told, as others were 'No such material can be located.'" But, she told Monaghan, she hoped that the "Moss Subcommittee is bringing out what happened to this material and much that I'm certain I never saw. Material that none of us know anything about."[29]

Sandoz's "Moss Subcommittee" comment to Monaghan references the work of thirteen-term representative John E. Moss (D-CA), who, beginning in 1955, served as chair of the Government Information Subcommittee with the charge to investigate government agencies suspected of withholding documentation from "those who are entitled to received it." Those entitled included journalists, television broadcasters, reporters, and "trained and qualified research experts" like Sandoz and other historians and writers. Writing in 1957 to Monaghan, Sandoz was hopeful that the "Moss investigations" would declassify important historical documents for future research and prove the existence of files that corresponded to her research notes from 1937 to 1938. She admitted, "I got what was important to me: Custer's relationship to the Cheyennes, etc. and the relationships of several other men to the western scene through their personal life." But Sandoz undoubtedly desired vindication for her claims that these materials existed: "Time after time I've been left looking like a liar."[30]

More than twenty-five years after her late 1930s trip to Washington DC, Sandoz needed the missing materials for her Little Bighorn manuscript. She wrote to an archivist in the "Army and Air Corps Branch" of the National Archives and demanded she have access to the records from Camp Carlin, also known as the "Cheyenne Depot," a supply station in Wyoming. More specifically, she cited three topics pertinent to her discussion of events leading up to the 1876 battle: the ammunition records for Lieutenant William W. Cooke's expeditions in 1876, the delays of supply deliveries to starving Sioux populations on reservations, and the medical records of James Butler "Wild Bill" Hickok (in which a recent diagnosis of glaucoma or trachoma supposedly prevented him from scouting for General George Crook). Sandoz concluded, "I plan to come to the Archives in about two weeks. By that time I expect word from you that the requested materials [are] now available." Signed "Impatiently," her letter received a response indicating that the materials were found in the "Quarter Master files."[31]

In August 1964 Sandoz wrote to Stewart "Sandy" Richardson, her editor at Lippincott, ecstatic about the news: "At last, after many years of insistence, I managed to get the War Records Department National Archives to admit that the files from which I took notes in 1937–38 exist and that I can take another, more comprehensive look into the material on the Custer battle, now that I am writing a book on the subject." But when Sandoz arrived, she learned that certain records in the AGO files were *still* missing. She predicted that, in their move to the new National Archives building (which took place in the years after the facility opened in 1937), many of the loose papers were "bowdlerized" during the microfilming process.[32] A year later, she believed her suspicions were confirmed when she was forwarded a letter from a colleague regarding a research inquiry for the same missing files. The chief archivist replied that records examiners in the late 1930s "surveyed the non-current records of the Federal Government then in the custody of the various government agencies." They discovered records in several basement and garage storage facilities (such as "Haley's Garage") and worked to relocate the "large quantities of the older records that were adjudged to have permanent research value." Subsequently, the archivist wrote, "It is probable . . . that many other records of merely temporary administrative usefulness that were maintained in such agency storage facilities were later disposed of with Congressional authority." Frustrated, Sandoz gave up and accepted that the files were no longer available. Despite this setback in her research, she had no choice but to move forward with the Little Bighorn manuscript.[33]

Sandoz faced serious challenges that extended beyond the Little Bighorn book. She received discouraging news of a second diagnosis of cancer and underwent surgery for it in January 1964 (her first cancer diagnosis was in 1961). Only slowly did she recuperate from the pain and discomfort that accompanied her surgery and illness. Less than a year later she underwent a mastectomy and learned that she had bone cancer. She took the news of her health in stride and tried to continue her work on the Little Bighorn book, this time with more urgency. She turned away requests to read the work of aspiring writers, a task she had previously prioritized. "Just now I can't take the time to look at anything except the Little Big Horn. . . . It is already a year late," she wrote.[34]

However, that same month she agreed to yet another project—to write the introduction to a book on the ledger art of Lakota artist and historian Amos Bad Heart Bull. The manuscript included hundreds of illustrations of Bad Heart Bull's unique depictions of late nineteenth-century events that impacted his people. He had drawn several pieces on Native-white conflict, including the Battle of the Little Bighorn from Bad Heart Bull's perspective of having observed the fight. The images were accompanied by the edited writings of Helen Blish, a

9. ABOVE: Mari Sandoz in the office of her New York apartment on Hudson Street, circa 1965, while writing *The Battle of the Little Bighorn*. Image 2001.002.00322-2, James F. Carr Collection, Mari Sandoz High Plains Heritage Center. Courtesy of the Mari Sandoz Society.

10. RIGHT: Stacks of Sandoz's books, cabinets of note cards, and drawers of research files likely stored in a closet or the basement of her apartment building, circa 1965. Image 2003.001.00356, Caroline Sandoz Pifer Collection, Mari Sandoz High Plains Heritage Center. Courtesy of the Mari Sandoz Society.

dear friend of Sandoz from their days of attending the University of Nebraska in the 1920s. Aware of her impending deadlines and her discouraging prognosis, Sandoz viewed this as a "labor of love." She wrote, "If I'm alive I'll be happy to write the introduction for the book." However, she firmly advised, "I still have all of January committed to The Battle of the Little Big Horn."[35]

Sandoz's plan to tackle the manuscript head-on was foiled by the cancer that continued to attack her body. In February 1965 she was back in the hospital and "ordered to drop all activities." For the next several weeks Sandoz halted her correspondence except for the standard replies her sister, Caroline Sandoz Pifer, issued during a brief New York City visit. After returning to Nebraska, Pifer received phone calls on March 10 from Mary Towner, her sister's landlady, and Jim Carr, a close publishing friend. She recalled, "Both called urgently for someone to come. Mari had been taken to the hospital hemorrhaging seriously." Caroline Pifer flew to New York with her daughter Mary Ann and received news from Sandoz's doctor that her sister would not be alive in six months. Pifer was both shocked and amused in disbelief: "From the way [Mari] held her visitors on the phone, groomed her hair and fussed over my provincial appearance, I could not think the end was near."[36]

Ten days later Caroline Pifer returned home. But she decided that her daughter Mary Ann would stay in New York to keep a close eye on her aunt. She later wrote that "Mari did not care if anyone looked after her. It was the writing and research materials that were important." Mary Ann Pifer "soon found herself typing, retyping and retyping the first chapter of the Bighorn book."[37]

WORKING FOR AUNT MARI

Approached in 2016, Mary Ann Pifer Anderson, then seventy-seven years old, claimed she did not have much to say about the time she worked for her aunt Mari in New York City. "I'm sorry to have to disappoint you but there is not a whole lot to tell of that period," she wrote, as she turned down my request for an oral interview. Anderson said she would "try to answer" questions about her time in New York in written form. Like her aunt, she wrote, "I too like to revise." Her written answers provide considerable insight into the extended Sandoz family and the time when Mari Sandoz experienced an intense period of writing and recovery.[38]

Mary Ann Pifer was born in 1939 in the hospital in Alliance, Nebraska. "I went home to my parents' ranch in Sheridan County where I grew up. My sister and I rode horseback to a rural school for eight years, often being the only pupils. One year, school was in the bunkhouse at the ranch and my mother was the teacher," she wrote. Anderson recalled, "I didn't like that so much and likely she didn't either." Young Mary Ann's mother was Caroline Sandoz Pifer, who was born in 1910 and the youngest of six Sandoz children. Pifer had, it was remembered, "a kind of spiritual need to carry on Mari's legacy" and keep her work alive after her sister died. She did this by delivering talks on her work, donating her family's papers, photographs, and records, and contributing to the establishment of the Mari Sandoz High Plains Center in Chadron, Nebraska.[39]

According to Anderson, Mari and Caroline were as close as could be expected in the Sandoz family: "The nature of the relationship between my mother and Aunt Mari is a tough question. Old Jules's outbursts aside, these were not emotionally expressive people; I don't think the word love was in anyone's vocabulary. But they were fiercely loyal, stuck together like glue in times of adversity." She also observed how her aunt's career influenced her mother: "I think her siblings were proud of her and her accomplishments, in particular I suppose, *Old Jules* since it was in a way, their story as well, and because it established her as a successful author."[40]

Anderson "vaguely" remembered when, "in the mid-forties, Aunt Mari asked my parents to drive her to the Pine Ridge Reservation (which they did) to interview Oglala Sioux who had known or had information handed down to them about Crazy Horse. There was unease in the area; Indians were not treated well in the local towns and whites were understandably not welcome visitors to the reserva-

11. Cultural historian Eleanor Hinman (*pictured*) and Mari Sandoz's camp on White Clay Creek during one of Sandoz's trips to Pine Ridge Reservation to conduct oral interviews: "Our camp on White Clay Creek. Eleanor Hinman ready for the day." Image 2003.001.00248, Caroline Sandoz Pifer Collection, Mari Sandoz High Plains Heritage Center. Courtesy of the Mari Sandoz Society.

tion. Because of her childhood experiences with Native Americans, Aunt Mari was able to gain their confidence and speak with them."[41]

Gathering oral histories was central to Sandoz's research methods. Most historians writing in the mid-1900s did not consider Native voices and oral testimonies valid sources for interpreting historical events. But these unheard voices laid the groundwork for many of Sandoz's articles and books. Although she received criticism for her reliance on oral histories, she also received high praise for her approach to researching and writing about the historical conflicts that shaped Native Americans. Some of this praise came from Native people. In 1965 a Cheyenne man named Charles Eagle Plume wrote to Sandoz after he heard that she had taken ill. He wanted to send her his "most sincere wishes" for her recovery: "I consider you one of America's greatest writers and have been proud to hold in my memories a few hours that

I had the rare privilege of having with you . . . after a program I had given at a lodge" in Evergreen, Colorado. Eagle Plume continued, "Many things you said that evening have been an inspiration to me for these many years. These and your writings have played a great part in my life. Thank you."[42]

Another example hails from one of the most recognizable names in Indian Country. In his introduction to the 2004 reprinting of *Crazy Horse*, Vine Deloria Jr. admitted that he had first read this Sandoz title "as a young man . . . [and] due to my hasty read it did not impress itself upon me." But later in life he came to hold great appreciation for *Crazy Horse* and Sandoz's work in general. Just before his death in 2005, he wrote, "In summing up Mari Sandoz's portrait of the strange man of the Oglalas we find that her description is the most accurate of all. . . . I doubt if anyone else could tell the life of Crazy Horse as well as Sandoz does. She must have known many Sioux people during her formative years." Contemporary Lakota writer and scholar Joseph Marshall III publishes extensively and is revered as an expert on Lakota history and the life of Crazy Horse. In his book *In the Footsteps of Crazy Horse*, Marshall writes at the top of his bibliography, "As always my primary source is the Lakota oral tradition. . . . I also consulted the following sources," and Sandoz's *Crazy Horse* is on Marshall's short list of six books.[43]

As a child and young adult, Anderson did not have much of a relationship with her aunt. "Aunt Mari's visits to the Sandhills were infrequent. I saw photographs of her on dust covers of her books," she noted, "and thought she must be quite glamorous and I was in awe. Having been instructed that children were meant to be seen and not heard, there was not a lot of interaction." But, she continued, "of course I was impressed by her poise and self-confidence." Even though Anderson grew up in a well-known family with strong-willed relatives, she admitted that she took this country life somewhat for granted. "In my youth I was anxious to shed the persona of a 'country hick' and was never vocal about my background. Later on," she commented, "I realized it was my advantage to have been raised in the unique atmosphere of the Sandhills." After she attended high school—a boarding school sponsored by the University of Nebraska in the town of Curtis—she took a trip to Europe and then attended and graduated from the University of Colorado at Boulder.[44]

After graduation Mary Ann was out on her own for a few years. She was twenty-six years old when, in March 1965, she received a request from her mother to accompany her to New York City and visit her aunt Mari in the hospital. Mary Ann's mother, she remembered, "always went [to New York] and would not have thought of doing otherwise" if Aunt Mari was sick. But Caroline Pifer could not stay in the city permanently with her sister. After visiting for ten days, the Sandoz women agreed on a plan: Caroline Pifer would return home and Mary Ann would stay, with the understanding that she was to look after her Aunt Mari's health. "It's unclear," Anderson wrote, "if Aunt Mari asked for help or the family realized she needed some as she was hospitalized." Mary Ann wrote, "I'm also unclear whether I volunteered or was conscripted but I was the only one even remotely available, not having the responsibilities other family members had. I was single, adventurous, and my boss was willing to give me a month off." Knowing her aunt's sentiments, she concluded, "I am sure she did not ask for me."[45]

Indeed, it is likely that Anderson volunteered with her mother's encouragement. The *New York Times* printed a story focused on the need to rezone Sandoz's building to allow "someone standing by for emergencies" related to both health and work. "A niece wanted to do this . . . 'to look after her,'" wrote award-winning journalist Edith Evans Asbury. Sandoz's sister Caroline and Nebraska governor Frank Morrison placed considerable pressure on New York City buildings commissioners, urging them to rezone Sandoz's Greenwich Village apartment so that Mary Ann could take up residence there. They complied and rezoned an office room on the upper-level of her apartment building into a residence.[46] Sandoz accepted that her illness forced her to be "a desk writer, like everybody else," but refused the idea that she required a nurse. What she really needed was assistance with her Little Bighorn manuscript.[47]

Draft by Draft

For a "Nebraska hayseed," Anderson recalled, "New York City was daunting. Even though I had been to Europe, graduated from college, and been out on my own . . . the city was an enigma!" It was "a world apart from any city I was familiar with." Her main comparison at the time was Denver, which was, in her words, "still a cow-town where people were friendly, helpful, and in no hurry." In New York she was alone: "I didn't leave the apartment after dark and what little time I had to myself I spent in art galleries and museums, and once, a matinee at the Metropolitan Opera (which was a total thrill)."[48]

With the Little Bighorn manuscript entering the phase of Sandoz's demanding revisions, Anderson kept very busy working for her aunt almost around the clock. "Aunt Mari was hospitalized almost the entire time," she recalled. "Our conversation consisted mostly of day-to-day operations, things she wanted me to do with the mail, phone messages, and most importantly, the typing," the most vital part of her job. Anderson moved between the apartment and the hospital daily, taking "her mail to her at the hospital," and her aunt "would have revisions for me to type up that evening and return to her the

12. This photograph, published in the *New York Times* on May 8, 1965, shows Mari Sandoz by the mantel in her apartment on Hudson Street less than a week after her niece Mary Ann Anderson left New York after a month in residence. Behind Sandoz is a portrait she called *Oilcloth Bag*, which was painted by her friend Leonard Thiessen, a Nebraska artist. It was one of the only pieces of art she ever purchased. Image 2010.011.00077, Caroline Sandoz Pifer Collection, Mari Sandoz High Plains Heritage Center. Courtesy of the Mari Sandoz Society.

next day." Anderson remembered, "Since she was doing the revisions from her hospital bed, they were done in long hand—and brown ink, of course—probably the same way she had always done it." Sandoz carefully proofread all of her manuscript drafts and was notorious for using her oft-preferred brown ink to slice and dice each page with editorial corrections.[49]

Anderson emphasized, "I didn't know her well, only from her rare visits to the Sandhills." That was why "most of our conversation concerned the manuscript. She was totally focused on completing the book while she was able." Anderson wrote, "Obviously, she knew she didn't have much time left and all her energy was focused on getting the book off. . . . The research was completed, [but] . . . she was fine-tuning. And she was meticulous about that aspect! Even revisions got revised. . . . It is doubtful that the illness changed her revision process other than add urgency. This is not a fact, but I'm quite certain it was as meticulous as it had been with her other books."[50]

Anderson's assistance was more crucial to her aunt during this time than she realized. Her work on basic administrative tasks helped Sandoz conserve her energy, time, and the mental focus required for the completion of the Little Bighorn book. Sandoz always prided herself on answering every single letter she received (from fans, curious hobbyists, Nebraska locals, graduate students, writers, activists, politicians, librarians, friends, and family). But cancer forced her to halt most correspondence to one single statement: "I am having . . . my niece, who is taking care of my preliminary note work, send you the following, (it goes to everybody): I am sorry that you had to hear of my illness. I am told . . . that there can be no positive answer for some time. Either I come out feet foremost, or I come out for some interval, return for more treatment, etc." Besides, she wrote, even though "there is no known cure," things could be much worse: there is "no cause for grief—some people are struck by drunken drivers." With her correspondence under control through her niece's assistance, Sandoz turned her attention fully toward the Little Bighorn manuscript. In a letter to her friend Caroline Bancroft, Sandoz admitted her niece was essential to these arduous tasks: "Mary Ann . . . is helping keep a sort of even keel around here," she wrote. Furthermore, she wrote to Bancroft, "with her typing, perhaps I can get the final draft of the Custer book into manuscript. We'll see."[51]

When the news of Sandoz's cancer reached the public, letters of support poured in from around the country. Fans, friends, and colleagues who learned of her disease expressed their sincere wishes for her quick recovery. Mrs. Arnold Gesterfield wrote, "I find myself admiring most your fighting spirit, your refusal to be doomed . . . and your determination to continue to work and live as long as you are able. . . . I hope that the pain which I know you must have is bearable and I hope that you have time and strength to do some of the things you want to do." Kathleen Nagle wrote, "The whole world owes much to the little girl who sat in the woodbox and listened to the stories told by her father and his visitors. You will leave a wonderful legacy to all of us." Etta Shipp, one of Sandoz's old schoolmates, sent her a memory from their childhood in the Sandhills: "You came one morning bearing a cardboard placard edged in hand-drawn forgetmenots. In the center was the printed letters G.B.Q. After looking at it Mrs. Lathrap said, 'This is very nice, Marie, but what does it mean?' [You replied,] 'The letters mean "Get Busy Quick" . . . so that we don't waste our time.'" Shipp concluded, "In view of your prolific writings and research I would say that you have wasted very little time."[52]

After one month in residence, Mary Ann Anderson left New York. Her close contact with Sandoz changed her views of Great Plains history, and she realized the impact her aunt Mari had had on her own mother's life and devotion to storytelling. Anderson recalled how "Aunt Mari's arduous struggle to survive and succeed wasn't lost on us. . . . Her career certainly encouraged my mother to put her own stories on paper." After her aunt Mari passed away, Anderson's mother "devoted her next 40 years to perpetuating her sister's works and creating her own, both of which gave her satisfaction and pleasure." Ron Hull, a close friend of the Sandoz sisters and an influential force behind the establishment of Nebraska Educational Television (NET) and the Nebraska Public Broadcasting System, remembered, "They were both deeply tied to the land, trappers, Native Americans, and keeping the history of the Plains alive."[53]

THE PAIN OF WRITING AND THE WORK OF LIVING

Alone again, Mari Sandoz aimed to "Get Busy Quick." On May 25 she wrote that the Little Bighorn book was "finished through the next to the last draft and if I can get three weeks or so of comfortable time I'll get it completed." In June she noted that she had made progress by polishing chapters but still needed more time. It took much longer than three weeks to complete the manuscript—it took all summer. Throughout her life Sandoz acknowledged that writing never came "easy" to her and that it was a "tedious, laborious process." Even though her "style was every bit as important to her as the subject matter," she always struggled with the work of meeting her own rigidly high expectations. She worked from file cards, draft by draft, using "often ten or more reams of paper for a book."[54]

Sandoz sent chapters to series editor Hanson Baldwin and to Lippincott editor Sandy Richardson, who provided her with encouraging feedback. Baldwin was ecstatic, proclaiming that the manuscript "reads like a dream." To Sandoz, he wrote, "You write with a verve, authenticity, and sheer readability which carries the reader along at a gallop. The story is very familiar to me and I knew what was going to happen next, but the way you told it I couldn't put the manuscript down!" Richardson wrote, "To say that I was absorbed, excited, impressed, edified, and pleased is an understatement. It is a wonderful book, so rich in the sights, sounds, and smells of the country that I not only felt I was back there, but back there at the time of the battle. . . . I was completely in your hands throughout the book."[55]

After she finished the Little Bighorn manuscript chapters and sent them to the publisher, Sandoz turned her attention to work on maps for the book. Although it would be a difficult task, she insisted on including a detailed map of the complexities of the Indian camp. It was a map she had sketched and revised over several years of research; it showed "the location of the great council lodge with its eighteen foot poles—where most of the major chiefs were when Reno attacked." It was a "conference lodge" that leaders such as Gall and Crazy Horse "were so anxious to protect. . . . None of these conference lodges was ever captured by an enemy." Like most writing feats, Sandoz was confident she had the experience and research to create a map of the lodges, which had never been included in previous books published about the battle. In addition to collecting oral histories from Native people at the battle, Sandoz "picked up a lot of cartridges, buttons, etc. . . . and mapped out what seemed the movements then," when she camped on the ridge of the battlefield in 1930.[56] But Sandoz's health made her worry that she was living on borrowed time and would not be able to complete the maps. She formed a backup plan should this happen: "If I should not be able to make them, due to my health, I'll leave the information for the cartographer." Not two weeks later she reported she had "trouble standing for any lengthy period but I can work sitting for some hours." She later admitted it was difficult to work on the maps because her "hands got painful."[57]

Sandoz completed the maps but experienced "six weeks of trouble" with her hands. She wrote to her agent, Mary Abbot, apologizing for the delay: "I'm sorry this took so long but my hands have been pretty bad. I had to give up making tea because I dropped the teakettle with boiling water." Yet Sandoz persisted. Her painful hands diminished her physical strength but did not destroy her avid spirit to defend her work to editors. She told Richardson she would need to see the copyedited manuscript. "Even if there are no serious queries, please let me see [it] before it goes to the printer," she wrote. She repeated this to Carolyn Blakemore, an associate at Lippincott who prepped Sandoz's Little Bighorn book for publication: "If there is to be any extensive copyediting before this goes to the printer, may I see the manuscript again? I don't want to pay for having a lot of changes returned to my version." Sandoz also requested to see the final version of her intricate battlefield map, the culmination of years of research. "Please let me see the final draft before it goes to print," she wrote.

"I've had one cartographer put Bismarck into Minnesota, and I hope to avoid such errors in the future."[58]

As the weeks of the fall season passed, Sandoz grew more fatigued from fighting her cancer. At one point she seemed unlikely to engage in strained editorial exchanges on the Little Bighorn manuscript, appearing to concede to any changes they made. "We'll work it out," she told Abbot, "whatever they want."[59] But when she received the publisher's proofs of her maps, she discovered changes that had been made without her consent. So, despite experiencing complete "immobilization" of her left hand after it was placed in a sling and admission of being in a "fuzzy state" from sedation, Sandoz gained the strength to carefully review the proofs for mistakes.[60] She reverted to the proper names for tribes and landmarks: "About the spelling of Indian names and words: That has been decided by the American Bureau of Ethnology. . . . Shoshoni, Shoshonis for the tribe. Shoshone, Shoshones for the river, the canyon, etc. . . . It is tipi, not tepee, which is the name for the white man version, the boys' backyard version."[61] She also corrected "Medicine Tail Cr. and N. Medicine Tail Cr., instead of Trail, as the map now indicates."[62] Although knowing it would be an exhausting task, Sandoz asked to see every single version of the maps prior to printing, because she was "not convinced that the cartographer understood their importance."[63] Finally, when it came to the index for the manuscript, Sandoz was notably frustrated: "I shall make one more attempt to get at least a couple of rudiments of indexing across to [your staff], although why I should expect that the third time might succeed where twice made no impact at all I don't know. . . . I have made this as elementary as possible. I should expect a good seventh grader to follow it intelligently." Blakemore reassured her and replied, "Everyone understands that no changes are to be made, other than those you have specifically approved."[64] Finally, on February 11, 1966, she wrote to Blakemore, "Here are the proofs of THE LITTLE BIGHORN. . . . I need to see the index with the page proofs. I'll hurry that as fast as my eyes permit." Blakemore responded, "Thank you . . . I'll send the index down to you" as soon as possible.[65]

THE END?

In the weeks during which she waited for the page proofs and index on the Little Bighorn manuscript, Sandoz filled her time with friends and outings as much as her health allowed. In late February she met with David Lowe, the associate editor of *American Heritage* magazine. The two had traveled in the same circle of friends and colleagues and spoken on the phone, but they had never met in person. Hearing she was seriously ill, Lowe arranged for a meeting. He remembered walking to her Hudson Street apartment and thinking it an appropriate home for a western writer, "for Hudson Street is about as far west as you can go in New York without falling into the river." She welcomed Lowe into her apartment and "in a matter of minutes we were discussing our mutual experiences in the Midwest like two natives of a foreign land who unexpectedly meet in a strange country." Throughout the evening, which lasted several hours, they talked about art, literature, politics, war, and the environment. She expressed strong frustration about the Vietnam War and the nation's environmental policies. Sandoz also spoke about her father and childhood on a Nebraska homestead and showed Lowe a "row of metal filing cases" that "represented years of research" for her manuscript on the Battle of the Little Bighorn. "She drew my attention to them with the pride of a farmer showing his bursting barns in autumn," he remembered. Lowe almost forgot that she was battling cancer until, toward the end of the evening, "she got up, excused herself and hurried into the bathroom. . . . I knew that she had gone to take something to kill the terrible pain, the pain which would grow worse and worse, until at last it would kill itself."[66]

"I'm so glad you came," Sandoz told Lowe. Before leaving, he looked back over her apartment to take in "the memorabilia of a great historian" and imagined the land outside her windows, thinking, "Stretching to the west—New York, Ohio, Indiana, Illinois, Iowa, to her own Nebraska . . . how lucky any region was to have had such a wise, such a capable, interpreter."[67]

While she waited for the final page proofs and index, Sandoz received a letter from Mary Ann. The two rarely, if ever, corresponded. Writing from Boulder, her niece began the letter with "Dear Aunt Mari: If our mental telepathy has been working, you'll know that I've been thinking of you even though I haven't written." She thanked her aunt for sending her a copy of *Old Jules Country* and expressed the pleasure she had felt when reading it. Mary Ann continued the letter with a personal note: "I suppose Mom has told you that I'm getting married, which, I realize, probably seems like a poor idea for anyone from our family." She continued, "But perhaps, as Uncle Jule[s] says, everyone ought to try it once. I never supposed that I would ever care to get married, but then, I never found anyone before whose company I enjoyed as much either (or maybe that enjoyed mine!)." She ended the letter on an emotional tone, "Hope you are taking care of yourself," and signed it "Love, Mary Ann." The sentimental closure signaled a close relationship with her aunt, especially considering Anderson's earlier reflection that in the Sandoz family, "I don't think the word love was in anyone's vocabulary."[68]

Sandoz immediately replied: "Dear Mary Ann: Best wishes for a fine, long and happy married life. Don't let the example of your grandfather's four attempts chill your outlook. The only miracle is that mother managed to outlast him." Rather than end the letter with a discussion of her manuscript, research, or writing projects (as she often did in correspondence), she offered her young niece a piece of sage advice: "—don't expect perfection. Life is a series of compromises, in and out of its various partnerships as you know. Make the most of richness the two of you can bring to each other. Affectionately, Aunt Mari." This was one of the last letters she ever wrote.[69]

Several days later, Sandoz relapsed. Mary Ann's mother received phone calls urging her to immediately board a plane to New York. As Caroline Pifer's plane circled the city for hours in a fog bank before it landed, Sandoz was rushed to the hospital and placed under sedation to ease her pain and discomfort. "I never saw my sister again when I thought she was really clear in her mind," Caroline remembered. She was at her side when Mari Sandoz died of bone cancer on March 10, 1966.[70]

13. Mari Sandoz, circa 1965 or 1966, in her Hudson Street apartment with the Levi Strauss Golden Saddleman Award, which she received from the Western Writers of America in 1964 for *The Story Catcher*. It was called the Saddleman Award from 1961 to 1990, during the period when it was sponsored by Levi Strauss & Company, but the name was changed in 1991 to the Owen Wister Award for Lifetime Achievement in Western Writing. Images 2003.001.00368 and 2003.001.00371, Caroline Sandoz Pifer Collection, Mari Sandoz High Plains Heritage Center. Courtesy of the Mari Sandoz Society.

SANDOZ'S BATTLE IN PRINT

The Battle of the Little Bighorn, Sandoz's last major work, was published posthumously in June 1966. Sandoz biographer Helen Winter Stauffer noted that many Sandoz fans "consider this her finest book, the apogee of both her historical and literary career." The book earned accolades from writers, historians, and Sandoz fans. Renowned scholar Alvin Josephy wrote that the book was "a perfect mating of subject and author . . . and it is probably the best account of the battle ever written." There may not have been any "surprises" in Sandoz's version of the battle, but by "selecting, fitting, and drawing together" an intricate timeline of events, she wove together the disparate strands of a story that previous works on the battle ignored because they were not central to the American mythic hero embodied by Lieutenant Colonel George Armstrong Custer. Sandoz's passages provide stunning verbal visuals of a violent battle that engulf the reader's imagination: "It was true that troopers were riding over the little hill that was all in bloom, the recumbent loco weed like a painted robe under the feet—white, pale pink and lavender, rose, vivid magenta, and deepest purple." She also captures the graphic scenery of the encounter: Reno's men, Sandoz wrote, "flattened down low in their shallow holes and trenches and behind dead horses, the buzzing gases in the heat bloating the bellies up high until hit by bullets. Any that struck bone released not only a terrible stench but blew the rotting flesh over the men hid behind them." Josephy concluded his review by stating that Sandoz's book offers "writing that takes us there."[71]

But the book's focus on the intricate moving parts of the battle caused much controversy. Some fans of "Custeriana" viewed it as "anti-Custer" and scorned Sandoz's "arrogance, impetuosity, and conceit" in focusing on Benteen and Reno instead of Custer. Custer enthusiasts protested her interpretation that Custer's careless pursuit of highly skilled Lakota and Cheyenne warriors was motivated by presidential aspirations. To this day Custer scholars do not forgive Sandoz for spinning "fabulous tapestries" and outright "fictional contrivance" to conclude her interpretation of the battle.[72]

But these same scholars still cite Sandoz's *The Battle of the Little Bighorn*, along with her earlier book *Crazy Horse*, when discussing other aspects of the military engagement. They accept most of her rendition of the battle itself, which also forces them to accept that—despite their protestations—Sandoz's interpretation of Custer's actions "cannot be disproved." Josephy makes a similar argument in defending the merits of Sandoz's final book: "No one will ever know for sure why Custer did what he did." Many historians trusted Sandoz's reputation. Rudolph Umland concluded that "no writer was ever a more meticulous researcher. . . . I'll wager my chips on her." Regardless of any controversy, the manuscript presented "some of her finest writing. . . . It is undoubtedly the most exciting, the most detailed the most accurate account of Custer's and Reno's mauling by the Sioux." Stauffer acknowledged that while Sandoz's *The Battle of the Little Bighorn* "disturbed some historians," others "believed that it fit her message" of trying to provoke readers. "The louder the controversy," Stauffer wrote, "the better she would have liked it; good literature was supposed to arouse, aggravate, stimulate."[73]

Mary Ann Anderson observed Sandoz's determination to provoke her readers in the weeks that she labored over her aunt's revisions, typing and retyping the drafts of her last book. Anderson experienced firsthand the fact that for Sandoz, "being a serious western writer meant doing battle." Even though her body lost its fight with cancer, Sandoz was triumphant in her spirited efforts to go to battle and, draft by draft, complete her final story.[74]

NOTES

An earlier version of this chapter originally appeared in *Great Plains Quarterly* 39, no. 2 (Spring 2019): 131–58. The author wishes to thank Mary Ann Pifer Anderson, Jamison Wyatt, Courtney Kouba, Charles Rankin, Paul Hutton, the Mari Sandoz Society, anonymous reviewers, and the late Susan J. Rosowski and John Wunder for offering ideas, reflection, and assistance with earlier research on Sandoz and on earlier versions of this work. A special acknowledgment goes to Olga Josephine Freeouf Hoffman, whose love of reading, education, and Nebraska was inspired by the works of Mari Sandoz.

Epigraph: From the J. B. Lippincott edition (1966), 196–97.

1. Mary Ann Pifer to Mari Sandoz, February 11, 1966, Folder 20, Box 39, Series 4: Correspondence, Mari Sandoz Collection (MS080), Archives and Special Collections, University of Nebraska–Lincoln Libraries (hereafter cited as Sandoz Collection, UNL).
2. Mary Ann Pifer Anderson, email to author, September 28, 2016.
3. Anne Lamott, *Bird by Bird: Some Instructions on Writing and Life* (New York: Pantheon Books, 1994), 3, 19.
4. Anderson email, September 28, 2016.
5. Helen Winter Stauffer, *Mari Sandoz: Story Catcher of the Plains* (Lincoln: University of Nebraska Press, 1982), 31–32 (quote, 32); Barbara Rippey and John R. Wunder, "Mari Sandoz: Nebraska Sandhills Author, a Centennial Recognition," *Great Plains Quarterly* 16, no. 4 (Winter 1996): 5.
6. Julie Des Jardins, *Women and the Historical Enterprise in America: Gender, Race, and the Politics of Memory, 1880–1945* (Chapel Hill: University of North Carolina Press, 2003), 13–14; Mary Dixon, "*Crazy Horse: The Strange Man of the Oglalas* by Mari Sandoz: Historiography, a Philosophy for Reconstruction," *Great Plains Quarterly* 27, no. 4 (Winter 2007): 39–43 (quote, 40).
7. Betsy Downey, "'She does not write like a historian': Mari Sandoz and the Old and New Western History," *Great Plains Quarterly* 16, no. 4 (Winter 1996): 11–12; Kurt E. Kinbacher, "Contested Events and Conflicting Meanings: Mari Sandoz and the Sappa Creek Cheyenne Massacre of 1875," *Great Plains Quarterly* 36, no. 3 (Fall 2016): 309–10; Rippey and Wunder, "Mari Sandoz," 5–7.
8. Des Jardins, *Women and the Historical Enterprise*, 15; Dorothee E. Kocks, *Dream a Little: Land and Social Justice in Modern America* (Berkeley: University of California Press, 2000), 97. Dorothy M. Johnson's publications on Montana and the West include "The Man Who Shot Liberty Valance" (1953), *The Hanging Tree* (1957), and *Some Went West* (1965); Caroline Bancroft wrote about Colorado and the American West in *Silver Queen: The Fabulous Story of Baby Doe Tabor* (1950), *Historic Central City* (1951), and *Colorado's Lost Gold Mines and Buried Treasure* (1961); Angie Debo published hundreds of articles and thirteen books about Oklahoma, Native Americans, and the American West, including *The Rise and Fall of the Choctaw Republic* (1934), *And Still the Waters Run: The Betrayal of the Five Civilized Tribes* (1940), and *Geronimo: The Man, His Time, His Place* (1976). See also Patricia Loughlin,

Hidden Treasures of the American West: Muriel H. Wright, Angie Debo, and Alice Marriott (Albuquerque: University of New Mexico Press, 2005); and John M. Rhea, *A Field of Their Own: Women and American Indian History, 1830–1941* (Norman: University of Oklahoma Press, 2016), for examinations of the ways that white women intellectuals writing in the twentieth century shaped cultural views about the West.

9. Mari Sandoz to Editorial Offices at *Lincoln Journal Star*, May 25, 1960, Sandoz Collection, UNL.
10. Mary Ann Anderson, email to author, September 29, 2016.
11. Mari Sandoz, "Outpost in New York," *Prairie Schooner* 37, no. 2 (Summer 1963): 98–99; see also "Outpost in New York," *Lincoln Journal Star*, June 23, 1963; Stauffer, *Mari Sandoz: Story Catcher*, 216–17. Stauffer also mentions that a building fire in 1956 convinced Sandoz she should move to a brick building for fear that her research files could be destroyed.
12. David Lowe, "A Meeting with Mari Sandoz," *Prairie Schooner* 42, no. 1 (Spring 1968): 23.
13. *New York Times*, May 8, 1965.
14. Caroline Sandoz Pifer, *Making of an Author: Mari Sandoz Book III, 1931–1932* (Gordon NE: Mari Sandoz Corporation, 1984), illustration gallery between pages 90 and 91.
15. Des Jardins, *Women and the Historical Enterprise*, 14–15; Mari Sandoz to Buz Wyeth, April 14, 1961, Sandoz Collection, UNL.
16. Des Jardins, *Women and the Historical Enterprise*, 17; Mari Sandoz, *Love Song to the Plains* (New York: Harper and Brothers, 1961), n.p.; *Muscatine Journal and News-Tribune*, November 17, 1961.
17. Hanson Baldwin to Mari Sandoz, May 26, 1960; Mari Sandoz to Hanson Baldwin, June 13, 1960 (in this letter Sandoz referred to the "AGO Records"); Hanson Baldwin to Mari Sandoz, June 16, 1960, all in Sandoz Collection, UNL.
18. Mari Sandoz to Mary Abbot, August 23, 1960; Mari Sandoz to Mary Abbot, June 20, 1960; Mari Sandoz to Hanson Baldwin, August 23, 1960; Hanson Baldwin to Mari Sandoz, n.d., 1960; Mary Abbot to Mari Sandoz, October 3, 1960, all in Sandoz Collection, UNL. Her twenty-nine months' worth of new writing ($600) would have equaled a little over $5,000 in 2018.
19. Mari Sandoz, "Portraying the Plains: An Article," n.d., Sandoz Collection, UNL.
20. Sandoz, "Portraying the Plains."

21. Buz Wyeth to Mark Sandoz, n.d. [February 1961]; Mari Sandoz to Buz Wyeth, April 14, 1961, Sandoz Collection, UNL. Wyeth's editing career included positions at Doubleday, Macmillan, and Harper and Brothers, and the authors whose works he edited included Ursula Le Guin, Roger Kahn, Fred Gipson, George Plimpton, and Richard McKenna. He was in his early thirties when he worked with Sandoz. "Marion S. Wyeth, Jr.," *Princeton Alumni Weekly*, February 8, 2012; *New York Times*, October 28, 2011.
22. Mari Sandoz to Bruce Nicoll, February 18, 1961; Bruce Nicoll to Mari Sandoz, March 3, 1961, both in Sandoz Collection, UNL. Nicoll served as the University of Nebraska Press director from 1958 to 1973 and is largely credited with having a significant impact on the expansion of the press list in the field of western history.
23. Mari Sandoz to unnamed copy editor, n.d. [February 1961], Sandoz Collection, UNL.
24. Mari Sandoz to unnamed copy editor, n.d. [February 1961].
25. Buz Wyeth to Mari Sandoz, June 16, 1961, Sandoz Collection, UNL.
26. Stauffer, *Mari Sandoz: Story Catcher*, 237.
27. Mari Sandoz to Hanson Baldwin, June 14, 1960, Sandoz Collection, UNL.
28. Jane F. Smith to Mrs. William A. Neiswanger [aka Lilian Hughes Neiswanger], August 2, 1965, Sandoz Collection, UNL. Smith, an archivist at the National Archives, refers to "Haley's Garage" as the storage facility for the War Department and Department of the Interior that Sandoz had visited in the 1930s.
29. Mari Sandoz to Jay Monaghan, December 16, 1957, in Helen Winter Stauffer, ed., *Letters of Mari Sandoz* (Lincoln: University of Nebraska Press, 1992), 299–300. Monaghan wrote numerous books on the American West, including *Custer: The Life of General George Armstrong Custer* (Boston: Little, Brown, 1959), one of the first comprehensive biographies of Custer.
30. U.S. Congress House Committee on Government Operations, Special Subcommittee on Government Information, *Availability of Information from Federal Departments and Agencies: Hearings before a Subcommittee of the Committee on Government Operations, House of Representatives, Eighty-fourth Congress, First Session* (Washington DC: U.S. Government Printing Office, 1955), 2; Sandoz to Monaghan, December 16, 1957, in Stauffer, *Letters of Mari Sandoz*, 300. As indicated in the congressional hearings cited above, the Moss investigations aimed to create an "informed public" that supported the ideals of a "democratic government" (2). Representative Moss's work

over twelve years resulted in the Freedom of Information Act, a law that went into effect in 1967.
31. Mari Sandoz to Victor Gondos Jr., July 25, 1964, in Stauffer, *Letters of Mari Sandoz*, 432–33. The reply about the Quarter Master Files is also from Stauffer, *Letters of Mari Sandoz*, 432–33.
32. Mari Sandoz to Stewart Richardson, August 16, 1964, Sandoz Collection, UNL; Stauffer, *Mari Sandoz: Story Catcher*, 248.
33. Stauffer, *Mari Sandoz: Story Catcher*, 248; Smith to Neiswanger, August 2, 1965, Sandoz Collection, UNL. In her letter, Jane Smith, chief archivist of the Social and Economic Branch of the National Archives, explained in more detail the separation of the agency records and said that there were not ever any "Bureau of Indian Affairs" records stored in "Haley's Garage" on Virginia Avenue in Washington and that this facility only stored "large quantities of War Department records." It is likely, Smith wrote, "that these records—some of which probably related to the Indian Wars and other aspects of Indian affairs—were the materials that Mari Sandoz remembers having seen about 1937–8. . . . Any permanently valuable War Department records that were stored in Haley's Garage were probably accessioned somewhat later by the National Archives." She recommended to Neiswanger that she contact Victor Gondos, the chief archivist of the Army and Navy Branch of the National Archives. Sandoz had already contacted him the previous year about the missing records, and he was unable to produce them during her trip to the archives in 1964.
34. Stauffer, *Mari Sandoz: Story Catcher*, 252; Mari Sandoz to Richard B. Williams, December 1, 1964, in Stauffer, *Letters of Mari Sandoz*, 442. Sandoz had a mastectomy in October 1964; see Caroline Sandoz Pifer, *Making of an Author, Book I* (Gordon NE: Gordon Journal, 1972), 7.
35. Mari Sandoz to Bruce Nicoll, December 28, 1964, in Stauffer, *Letters of Mari Sandoz*, 445. For years, Sandoz encouraged Blish to publish her work on Bad Heart Bull's art, but she only printed her findings in a three-volume report to the Carnegie Institution in 1934. After Blish died in 1941, Sandoz urged several publishers to take on the task of publishing the project and the pictures of the images (the originals of which were buried with Bad Heart Bull's sister in 1947). Finally, in 1960, the University of Nebraska Press committed to the project. It was published, with Sandoz's introduction, in 1966 after her death. Amos Bad Heart Bull, *A Pictographic History of the Oglala Sioux*, ed. Helen Blish (Lincoln: University of Nebraska Press, 1966).

36. Unknown to unknown, February 11, 1965, Sandoz Collection, UNL; Pifer, *Making of an Author, Book I*, 7.
37. Pifer, *Making of an Author, Book I*, 7.
38. Sarah Pollack, email to author, March 16, 2016; author email to Mary Ann Anderson, July 19, 2016; Mary Ann Anderson, email to author, July 20, 2016. I sent a letter to Anderson on March 16, 2016, and sent a follow-up email message on July 19, 2016. Anderson replied to the email on July 20, 2016.
39. *Scottsbluff Star Herald*, March 14, 2012.
40. Mary Ann Anderson, email to author, September 29, 2016. Jules Sandoz was the patriarch of the Sandoz family. He had a rough temperament and was extremely physically and emotionally abusive to his wife and children. He was the central character in Mari Sandoz's *Old Jules*. Although she wrote and circulated numerous pieces before it was published in 1935, *Old Jules* is the title that earned nationwide attention and catapulted Sandoz into a successful writing career.
41. Anderson email, September 29, 2016.
42. Charles Eagle Plume to Mari Sandoz, August 21, 1965, Sandoz Collection, UNL.
43. Vine Deloria Jr., introduction to Mari Sandoz, *Crazy Horse: The Strange Man of the Oglalas* (1942; Lincoln: University of Nebraska Press, 2008), v, xiv; Joseph Marshall III, *In the Footsteps of Crazy Horse* (New York: Amulet Books, 2015), n.p.
44. Anderson email, September 29, 2016.
45. Anderson email, September 29, 2016.
46. *Omaha World-Herald*, May 10, 1965, Sandoz Collection, UNL.
47. *New York Times*, May 8, 1965.
48. Anderson email, September 29, 2016.
49. Anderson email, September 29, 2016. Sandoz's biographer also commented on the writer's use of brown ink for revisions and research. See Stauffer, *Letters of Mari Sandoz*, viii, and Stauffer, *Mari Sandoz: Story Catcher*, 145.
50. Anderson email, September 29, 2016.
51. Mari Sandoz to Charles Aronson, April 7, 1965; Mari Sandoz to Ruth Hooper, April 15, 1965; Mari Sandoz to Caroline Bancroft, April 20, 1965, all in Sandoz Collection, UNL.
52. Mrs. Arnold Gesterfield to Mari Sandoz, February 3, 1966; Kathleen Nagle to Mari Sandoz, August 23, 1965; Etta Shipp to Mari Sandoz, September 27, 1965, all in Sandoz Collection, UNL.

53. Anderson email, September 29, 2016; Hull quoted in *Scottsbluff Star Herald*, March 14, 2012.
54. Mari Sandoz to Grant Bohzien, May 25, 1965, Sandoz Collection, UNL; Stauffer, *Letters of Mari Sandoz*, xxv–xxvi.
55. Hanson Baldwin to Mari Sandoz, June 19, 1965; Stewart "Sandy" Richardson to Mari Sandoz, September 7, 1965, both in Sandoz Collection, UNL.
56. Mari Sandoz to Hanson W. Baldwin, June 26, 1965, in Stauffer, *Letters of Mari Sandoz*, 456.
57. Mari Sandoz to Mary Abbot, August 1, 1965; Mari Sandoz to American Museum of Natural History Librarian [name unknown], August 11, 1965; Mari Sandoz to Mary Abbot, September 30, 1965, all in Sandoz Collection, UNL.
58. Mari Sandoz to Stewart Richardson, August 1, 1965; Mari Sandoz to Carolyn Blakemore, October 4, 1965; Mari Sandoz to Stewart Richardson, October 10, 1965; Mari Sandoz to Mary Abbot, October 13, 1965, all in Sandoz Collection, UNL. The map errors occurred during the publication of *The Buffalo Hunters*; see Stauffer, *Letters of Mari Sandoz*, xxx.
59. Mari Sandoz to Mary Abbot, October 13, 1965, Sandoz Collection, UNL.
60. Mari Sandoz to Carolyn Blakemore, November 17, 1965; Mari Sandoz to Dan Walden, November 18, 1965; Mari Sandoz to Dan Walden, November 19, 1965, all in Sandoz Collection, UNL.
61. Mari Sandoz to Carolyn Blakemore, October 22, 1965, Sandoz Collection, UNL.
62. Mari Sandoz to Dan Walden, November 10, 1965, Sandoz Collection, UNL.
63. Mari Sandoz to Carolyn Blakemore, November 7, 1965, Sandoz Collection, UNL.
64. Mari Sandoz to Jim [no last name], November 11, 1965; Carolyn Blakemore to Mari Sandoz, November 19, 1965, both in Sandoz Collection, UNL.
65. Mari Sandoz to Carolyn Blakemore, February 11, 1966; Carolyn Blakemore to Mari Sandoz, February 11, 1966, both in Sandoz Collection, UNL.
66. Lowe, "Meeting with Mari Sandoz," 26.
67. Lowe, "Meeting with Mari Sandoz," 26.
68. Mary Ann Pifer to Mari Sandoz, February 11, 1966, Sandoz Collection, UNL.
69. Mari Sandoz to Mary Ann Pifer, February 17, 1966, Sandoz Collection, UNL. Anderson did not comment on her aunt's death in her written reflections, but she did confirm that she has been married for over fifty years and her

husband was a history major. The two, Anderson wrote, have been "learning history" together for over half a century. Anderson email, September 29, 2016.

70. Pifer, *Making of an Author, Book I*, 8; *Fresno Bee*, March 11, 1966; *New York Times*, March 11, 1966. Newspapers throughout the country covered Sandoz's death.

71. Stauffer, *Mari Sandoz: Story Catcher*, 260; Alvin M. Josephy Jr., "Soldiers and Indians," *New York Times*, July 3, 1966; Kathleen Walton, "Mari Sandoz: An Initial Critical Appraisal" (PhD diss., University of Delaware, 1970), 244–45; Mari Sandoz, *The Battle of the Little Bighorn* (Philadelphia: J. B. Lippincott, 1966), 116, 152.

72. Jack Burrows, review of *The Battle of the Little Bighorn*, by Mari Sandoz, *Arizona and the West* 9, no. 1 (Spring 1967): 65–67; Paul Andrew Hutton, ed., *The Custer Reader* (1992; Norman: University of Oklahoma Press, 2004), 236–37; Brian Dippie, "Jack Crabb and the Sole Survivors of Custer's Last Stand," in Hutton, *Custer Reader*, 474.

73. Robert M. Utley, *Cavalier in Buckskin* (Norman: University of Oklahoma Press, 2001), 129; Josephy, "Soldiers and Indians"; Rudolph Umland, "Just Take Her Word for Some of It," *Kansas City Times*, July 8, 1966; Stauffer, *Mari Sandoz: Story Catcher*, 261. Five years after Sandoz's book was published, Josephy publicly shamed the Little Bighorn Battlefield gift shop for not offering it for sale. See *Billings Gazette*, July 6, 1971; and Stauffer, *Mari Sandoz: Story Catcher*, 261.

74. Stauffer, *Letters of Mari Sandoz*, xxvii.

2

Mari Sandoz, Sensory Conjuror, and *The Battle of the Little Bighorn*

CHERYL A. WELLS

The men flattened down low in their shallow holes and trenches and behind dead horses, the buzzing gases in the heat bloating the bellies up high until hit by bullets. Any that struck bone released not only a terrible stench but blew the rotting flesh over the men hid behind them. Even less fortunate were the troopers lying beside corpses swarming with flies, those dead since yesterday bloating like the horses, with maggots beginning to work in the blackened mouths and eyeballs, the sight even more horrible than the stench. . . . The occasional spatter of rain running over the grass was only a tantalization, the smell of water driving the horses to wilder plunging. Even so, the dust was never laid, gritty and burning in the dry mouths of the able as well as the burning and delirious wounded. The men were forbidden the comfort, and the drying effect, of a smoke or a cud of tobacco.
—Mari Sandoz, *The Battle of the Little Bighorn*

Admittedly "ungracious," critic Jack Burrows's review screamed out his "wish that Mari Sandoz [had] eschewed" the writing of her 1966 posthumously published book, *The Battle of the Little Bighorn*. It offered "no fresh insights, no new theories." Burrows chided the author for the work's "narrowness of scope" and cast shadowy aspersions of plagiarism.[1] Douglas Keller joined Burrows in his chorus of condemnation, finding the work the "all time worst . . . riddled with factual errors and apocryphal statements, . . . biased," and the vilest type of history generated from this type of "popular literature."[2]

Fulsome praise accompanied these sharp criticisms. Sandoz had passionate defenders. "It is probably the best account of the battle ever written," cooed historian Alvin M. Josephy Jr., a sentiment fervently echoed by writer Rudolph Umland, who applauded the work as "undoubtedly the most exciting, the most detailed, the most accurate account of Custer's and Reno's mauling by the Sioux."[3] Most reviewers of Sandoz's *The Battle of the Little Bighorn* vacillated between these two extremes, yet an astonishing number of her reviewers inadvertently—certainly unconsciously and without meaningful reflection—acknowledged the sensory worlds embedded in Sandoz's work.

Sandoz's editor at J. B. Lippincott Company, Stewart "Sandy" Richardson, first remarked on the sensory aspects of the work: "To say that I was absorbed, excited, impressed, edified, and pleased is an understatement. It is a wonderful book, so rich in the sights, sounds, and smells of the country that I not only felt I was back there, but back there at the time of battle."[4] For Umland, Sandoz's "words race[d] along at times like raindrops making light running sounds over the dry earth of the prairies she knew so well."[5] Upon reading the book, reviewer Robert D. Price "smell[ed] the powder smoke," felt "the dusty heat," heard "the war-whoops of the massed Sioux and Cheyennes."[6] She made "flowers bloom," for critic Robert Palmer, "along forgotten trails" and made "the sun shine hot, and winds blow." She "conjure[d] the sounds of ninety years ago and sen[t] them ringing through the pages of a book."[7] Military historian Barton M. Hayward enthusiastically declared that "Miss Sandoz . . . created a work so convincing that one is almost able to taste the dust and hear the whine of bullets."[8] She wrote in a style, mused one unnamed critic, "that sings like one of those Seventh Cavalry bugles."[9] Even the crusty critic Burrows recognized that "Sandoz assaults the reader's sensibilities with endless circling horses, churning hooves, smoke, dust, gunfire, and screeching Indians."[10] Bill Brooks put it bluntly in his review for the *Indianapolis Star:* Sandoz "reproduc[ed] the smells, the sights, the sounds of dusty, hot, exhilarating and savage fighting."[11]

But did she really? Notorious for consciously forgoing citations and for boldly "embroider[ing] fiction onto the facts," Sandoz's methods make it virtually impossible, without her guidance, to untangle the strands of her imagination from historical facts.[12] Sandoz plausibly drew from the pleasing multisensory worlds of her youth and the harsh multisensory worlds culled from her experiences in New York City to create her version of the Battle of the Little Bighorn.

Witness her multisensory description:

> The men flattened down low in their shallow holes and trenches and behind dead horses, the buzzing gases in the heat bloating the bellies up high until hit by bullets. Any that struck bone released not only a terrible stench but blew the rotting flesh over the men hid behind them. Even less fortunate were the troops lying beside corpses swarming with flies, those dead since yesterday bloating like the horses, with maggots beginning to work in the blackened mouths and eyeballs, the sight even more horrible than the stench. . . . The occasional spatter of rain water running over the grass was only a tantalization, the smell of water driving the horses to wilder plunging. Even so, the dust was never laid, gritty and burning in the dry mouths of the able as well as the burning and delirious wounded.[13]

To paraphrase sensory historian Mark M. Smith, such a passage begs several questions: Whose nose is smelling the stench? Whose dry tongue is tasting the grit and flinching at the burning? Whose ears prick to the buzzing of gases and the swarming of flies? Whose skin experienced the textures of this world? Whose eyes axiomatically declare vision's dominance over smell's authority?[14] These are important questions. Senses changed over time. A focus on the senses is, per Laura Davis, "a biased human act, an act that is committed and interpreted differently depending on who is doing the sensing and when, as well as what historical and cultural beliefs that person may hold."[15] As Smith points out, to perhaps answer these questions, historians must "read conventional sources," in this case Sandoz's *The Battle of the Little Bighorn*, "with, ironically, an eye to nonvisual evidence."[16]

Contemporaries of Sandoz and several Sandoz scholars have offered tantalizing but hazy clues to these answers. Sandoz, declares LaVerne Harrell Clark, "never ceased to look and listen with discernment at all the sights and sounds of her frontier-flavored homeland." As a result, "Mari Sandoz was able to catch the heartbeat of her Nebraska birthplace and render it with a perception and skill unique to American letters."[17] Her writings, muses Helen Winter Stauffer, "reveal her determination to tell her message in her own way, in her voice, the authentic voice of her region—sometimes raspy, scratchy, raucous, sometimes softly, lyrical, but also unmistakably western and Sandoz."[18] Her longtime friend Bernard DeVoto as well as her editors repeatedly commented that "accents and rhythms" in her writings rang acoustically strange and alien in their eastern ears.[19] Sandoz, however, did not "give a good God damn" about these critiques.[20] Through her purposeful cadence, she strove "to capture the aura" of the Sandhills.[21] Indeed, as Stauffer notes, "no matter how sedulously writers try to keep the personal element out of their work, their quality as human beings, their integrity, their passions and their vision of the world cannot be effaced from the printed page."[22] This was precisely the advice Sandoz offered writers seeking her guidance. In a 1956 letter to writer Charley O'Kieffe, Sandoz counseled that his words should "let the reader see and hear, feel, and smell it all."[23] A 1965 letter to budding author E. T. Worley issued similar advice. "Your kind of life," wrote Sandoz, "can never happen again and you owe it to society and yourself, to put it down. Write it as frankly and openly as possible. Give the reader everything you can, so he *must see* and smell and hear and feel and sense as it happens."[24] Sandoz followed this guiding principle and indulged, as scholar Dorothee E. Kocks has written, in "the very personal experience of the senses."[25]

Sandoz's writings are "fervently devoted to providing . . . readers with an 'authentic'" view of the past and not only a view but smells, sounds, tactilities, and tastes. Sandoz "scrutinized every detail of her writing, as she wished to publish work that accurately reflected her true Sandhills roots."[26] Yet authenticity is not the truth. It is manufactured.[27] Sandoz, as scholar Helen Stauffer points out, often used "imaginative fill in[s]" in her writing.[28] Plausibly, this was the case with *The Battle of the Little Bighorn*. Her sensory impressions, memories, and imaginations rather than those of the participants fill the book's pages.

Sandoz transferred her sensory understandings of her past and those of her present (as she was writing) onto the events and people of the 1876 battle. The application of sensory history to Sandoz's *The Battle of the Little Bighorn* offers a fresh approach to the work. It is entirely possible that Sandoz conjured the sensory worlds apparent in her writings from the outside, from her experiences, perspectives, and imagination, rather than from those of the participants. As Andrew Rotter rightly argues in his *Empires of the Senses: Bodily Encounters in Imperial India and the Philippines*, "All human relationships . . . are shaped by the five senses: how we understand others, even more how we feel about them and thus how we act toward them, have a good deal to do with how we apprehend them through every sense."[29] This absolutely applies to Sandoz's writing. It is not only her vision of the world that permeates the pages of *The Battle of the Little Bighorn* but her way of smelling, of tasting, of touching, and of hearing that combined to create the sensory worlds that appear in the book. Writing in the midst of a grueling, unwinnable fight against cancer and mindful of her imminent death, she placed her sensory memories of growing up in the Sandhills region, as well as the sensory alienation she felt working and living in New York City, onto the pages of *The Battle of the Little Bighorn*.

Sandoz's passionate and ongoing love affair with the West generally, and the Sandhills specifically, was as legendary as her venomous hatred of the haughty East and its snooty epicenter, New York City. She viewed the East as a hungry leech sucking on the West, exploiting "the vulnerability of western lands and people."[30] In her view, "without the wealth drained from the rest of the country," she wrote, "New York [City] would be little more than a sleepy fishing village revived for two weeks every spring by the shad run in the Hudson." "Unfortunately," she continued, New York City "has grown monstrous on the blood of the nation, with the contempt of the parasite for the host."[31] This eastern parasitic elitism highlighted for Sandoz the contrast between easterners who viewed westerners as quaint, seemingly frozen in the nineteenth century, and the free and "superior people" of the West.[32] The East's failure "to conceive of the Sandhills and the frontier as a real place" incited and fed her contempt.[33] She increasingly felt that easterners remained intentionally uninterested and purposely indifferent "to the area she valued—the Sandhill region of the Great Plains."[34] Her eastern editors confirmed and reinforced her views by peppering her manuscripts with, in her opinion, odd criticisms of her writing as articulated on eastern tongues informed by eastern ears. She flat out and repeatedly refused to deodorize her work to suit eastern senses.[35] She pointedly accused "eastern publishers of crass provincialism and bland disinterest in anything that happened in the vast middle of the country." She bluntly stated on more than one occasion, "It's the east and New York [City] that I hate," and she allegedly kept a file of related jottings, with an eye to writing a book that explored all the reasons she hated New York City.[36]

Moving to New York City, the publishing center of the country, did little to soothe her hatred. It instead reinvigorated her loathing while simultaneously deepening her love for the unique sights, sounds, smells, tastes, and textures of home. New York City was "in all ways, the opposite of her native land."[37] New York City shocked her senses. Sandoz made clear to all who listened that she "consider[ed] the Sandhills of Nebraska [her] home" and that although she might be in New York City, she was most certainly "not of it."[38] A 1956 letter to writer Jesse Stuart revealed that Sandoz "counte[d] the time spent in New York [City] as just so much lost from life."[39]

Sandoz openly admitted that when in New York City, she often "tried to pretend that [she] was in the West."[40] This alienation from the West and her attempts to re-create a western oasis in her apartments made her more determined to recall it through sensory description.

In short, she could write the West because she missed it and could, for brief moments, pretend to be in it. Her final apartment boasted "tall west-facing windows that filled her work space with" western light.[41] The apartment, located on Hudson Street in Greenwich Village, was geographically as "far west as you go in New York [City] without falling in the river."[42] Editor David Lowe, who visited Sandoz shortly before her death, "could not help but look . . . out [her apartment] windows and think of the land stretching to the west—New York, Ohio, Indiana, Illinois, Iowa, to her own Nebraska."[43] Sandoz likely did as well. Within the confines of her apartment, she purposely created visual reminders of her home—cultural touchstones, so to speak. If she could not view her home physically, she could do so virtually. One of the first things she hung on the walls of her soon-to-be "typical[ly] dirty New York" City "hole" of an apartment was her cowboy hat.[44] "It had been a cheap one," recounted Sandoz, "and now it was old and burn-stained from the time it helped save me and my horse from a prairie fire years ago." Also, "in moments of anger and disgust with the east," the shabby hat served as "a reminder . . . there was another country and another people."[45] Under the hat, she "tacked . . . a combination of bullet molds, and reloading tools that [her] father had used in his gun repair," and to complement this collection she hung a

> canvas copy of one picture from the sacred Crazy Horse tipi. It is an allegorical painting of the fight to save the Black Hills, which are a tree-sprigged mound in the center of the picture. On one side is He Dog on his black war horse, on the other Crazy Horse on his golden spotted horse, the calf-skin cape of the war floating from his shoulders. The two men bear the sacred lances of the Oglalas, and above, just over the Black Hills is the symbol of the buffalo, the buffalo skull, the symbol of the dead buffalo, the vanished buffalo.[46]

She added her own hand-drawn wall-size map. The map represented the culmination of "twenty years recording the movements of the

Plains Indians" and no doubt conjured up memories and images of her beloved West.⁴⁷ A "detailed map of the Custer battlefield" soon joined the other features on the walls.⁴⁸

Sandoz's visual collection of western Americana continued to grow. As she was unable to return to Nebraska for the holidays in 1964, her sister sent her a powerful memento of home. That December, a large box of "soapweed seed pod stalks, sprays of prairie rose hips and buckbrush berries, sulphur plant, wild flax pods, blue joint, trembling grass, etc." arrived at her apartment, and Sandoz "made up a rather handsome Christmas spray for [her] door." The sight and perhaps lingering nostalgic whiffs of home ushered in a wave of "homesick[- ness] for the hills."⁴⁹ Inside her apartment, she continued to battle her crippling wistfulness for home via decoration. "Small western items," western books, research papers, a buffalo sculpture, "Indian objects, and the plaques and statuettes which represented a dozen literary awards" cluttered the surfaces of her apartment.⁵⁰ A painting, titled *The Oilcloth Bag*, completed her western theme. As the only piece of art Sandoz owned that had been painted by her dear friend Leonard Thiessen, the work depicted "a loaf of bread, . . . [an] oilcloth bag, and the daily paper." The Nebraska-born artist's work offered Sandoz a visual reminder of "the soundness of the people . . . the common folk of the world, the people who not only did the daily work of the world but from whom have always risen those who create the things of permanence, the beautiful, the noble, the wise." In short, it served as an ocular nod to the people who populated her beloved Sandhills. Living in New York City, she seemed to have felt that a revolution was in progress "against all these things." She took comfort in this painting, in this symbol "before [her] eyes."⁵¹

Sandoz often said that when "she was in New York [City] she could write about the hills because she was lonely for them."⁵² While her apartment decor pleased her eye, she could not keep her senses from rebelling against foreign and alien sights, sounds, tastes, textures, and smells, which undoubtedly contributed to her progressing illness and increasing malaise. When overwhelmed by these alien sensory worlds and the accompanying paralyzing gushes of homesickness, Sandoz, daughter of the prairie, abandoned her apartment for Washington Square, where she could find "a little sense of space" in the bustling claustrophobia of New York City and gaze at "a little open sky to ease [her] homesickness for the Plains."[53] While New York City fed her growing personal inferiority complex, it also stoked a superiority complex regarding her native part of the country. Sandoz resisted New York City altering her sensory culture. She pushed back by seeking and writing the sensorium of her Sandhills. Sandoz lived and wrote *The Battle of the Little Bighorn* in and between these two rival and antithetical sensory worlds: the physical sensory worlds of New York City and the remembered sensory worlds of the Sandhills.

Sandoz's father, Jules, "had nothing against dirt." She shared his view. As a "small girl . . . [she] love[d] to walk barefoot in the dust or mud."[54] The sensation on her skin represented a deep connection to the land and to her home, yet when she moved to New York City, these same textures experienced through her skin took on a different meaning and a different feeling. Almost immediately, the grime, grit, dust, and dirt of the city greeted her and clung to her. The landlord of her first New York City dwelling "stood in the middle of the floor . . . his shoe soles deep in dust." The entire apartment "was full of dust, several years of New York soot and dust."[55] Writing to her dear friend Melvin Van den Bark in April 1958, she wished that he could have seen her new apartment before the "fine and gleaming" place became "the typical dirty New York hole."[56] The dirt and grit from the street blew in the windows, infiltrated her apartment, and covered her belongings (the very visual symbols of her Sandhills home) and herself in a layer of grime that betrayed her fond memories of dirt's texture.

Sensory conflicts in the forms of harsh accents, raucous languages, and unpleasant city sounds assaulted her ears. In one notable instance of such an assault, Sandoz attended a cocktail party at publisher Blanche W. Knopf's home, where most guests spoke in French or Spanish.[57] While there, she met the journalist, writer, and activist Agnes Smedley. Agnes arrived in "one of those dollar chenille turban things wound around her head." She made no attempt to be a New York City lady. She reminded Sandoz of a "blousy ranch woman from western Nebraska and as genuine and unpretentious." Unlike the other guests, Smedley and Sandoz spoke "their bold and bawdy frontier lingo. It was priceless," Sandoz recounted, for it "saved me from ever having to go to another one of those things so long as I live. New Yorkers aren't very subtle and when Agnes and I get together they seem to see that I'm not their kind." For Sandoz, speaking French and Spanish seemed to reflect a judgment and pretension those women placed on her inferior accented English, while Smedley's cadence and diction reminded her of home.[58] The languages of her youth, the Swiss-German of her mother, the "profane and bawdy tongue" of her father, the Sioux dialects of visiting Indians, and eventually her own English created an authentic and wholesome symphony that played in her memory. At New York City cocktail parties, her ears heard condescension in the indecipherable French and Spanish chatter.[59]

Sandoz initially enjoyed the acoustic diversity, the mingling Italian, Slavic, and German that floated up from the streets of New York City and into her ears. The pleasant gossip of visiting and the sound of children "playing noisily in the narrow street below" comforted Sandoz, as the sounds reminded her of home.[60] New York City rapidly changed. The chitchat became less melodious. Jarring and unruly noises, including the distressing sounds of bullets, assaulted her senses. "One bullet," she recounted, "hit a hard surface and with the ricocheting whine that [she] knew very well . . . struck the window above [her] . . . sending a chip of glass down upon [her] head." The sound of bullets admittedly took her "back [to] . . . the cattleman-settler troubles of her childhood."[61] This unpleasant sensory reminder stands in general contrast to how Sandoz characterized the soundscape of her childhood. The "panting of horses," "galloping and bucking of calves," "the snap and crackle of the tough roots as they were cut" out of the ground, the howling and screeching of the winter wind, "the sharp howl of a coyote," "black birds chattering," the roar of prairie fires, "the whistling curlew on a knoll, the yellow breasted meadow lark singing his morning song," and the joyous music of the phonograph; these were the sounds of her beloved home that whispered in her ears, even perhaps in the midst of the harsh cacophony of urban life's assault on them.[62]

Her taste buds also yearned for the flavors of prairie life, and her olfactory senses missed the scents of home. Notoriously stench-ridden in the nineteenth century, New York City had somewhat tamed its olfactory terrain.[63] Yet the aroma of rotting garbage wafted up from the streets, and the pungent, reeking fumes of raw waste burning on Staten Island floated over the city into the noses of its residents. Although Sandoz made little mention of the insalubrious air and noxious odors of New York City in her writings, the fetid fragrances no doubt reached and, based on how she described her other sensory reactions, likely disturbed her nose. She did write of the scents of the Sandhills and the joy with which her nose welcomed them. She especially noted the pleasant, smoky smells of the family kitchen as she silently listened to her father and his visitors.[64] As a child, Sandoz often dropped "down in the feathery green of the asparagus." The "sharp, dusty smell," she wrote, "comes back to me."[65] She often wished to deeply inhale the sweet, magical fragrances of the first pink prairie roses of the season.[66] The pleasing smells of the Sandhills lingered, even decades later, in her nostrils.

Her tongue had its own set of gustatorial cravings tied to the nostalgic memory of her Sandhills youth.[67] While she often dined at a small restaurant in Greenwich Village, the culinary delights of her youth remained with her. She wrote of her love for her mother's "wonderful sausage," for the "good sweet lard in the cellar in crocks," and the delicious "pork tenderloin with the animal heat and sweetness still in it."[68] The *Central New Jersey News* explicitly tied her tongue to her home. In her obituary, the *News* printed that "Mari Sandoz, daughter of the prairies . . . got used to buying her food in a supermarket, but she remembered the taste of wild geese she had shot down on the wing in days gone by."[69] People understood the importance of the Sandhills to Sandoz. She struggled with the juxtapositions of her worlds—the glorious sensory worlds of her home state and the alien sensory worlds of her life in New York City. In this context, she wrote *The Battle of the Little Bighorn*.

The contours of the battle are familiar. In an attempt to drive the Plains Indians from the West, Lieutenant Colonel George Armstrong Custer and the Seventh Cavalry Regiment of the U.S. Army engaged with an Indigenous coalition of Lakotas, Northern Cheyennes, and Arapahos under the leadership of Sitting Bull. Overwhelmed by the unexpectedly large numbers of Indians and plagued by miscommunication and poor decision-making, the doomed Seventh Cavalry troops led by Custer fell in battle with Indian forces. Custer emerged as a posthumous hero while the defeat spurred increasingly aggressive American attempts at Indian removal. "Never one to pull a punch," Sandoz uncompromisingly characterized Custer as a "deaf and brooding" narcissist.[70] Her descriptions presented a man who scarified his men in an attempt to emerge as a war hero in order to secure the Democratic nomination for president.[71] Sandoz, wrote reviewer Paul H. Hass, "comes down on [Custer] like a band of war-crazed Sioux."[72] The resulting backlash against Sandoz's depiction of Custer resulted in some critics panning the book and in the book being "banned from Park service stores at the Little Big Horn."[73]

Dissecting the battle and the character of Custer is not the intent here; the intent here is to investigate the sensory worlds of Sandoz's work. Because her work lacks solid, traceable documentation, it is impossible to know for certain who, for example, tasted what at the Battle of the Little Bighorn. Sensory war history can and has been written.[74] Sensory histories of the West likewise constitute a burgeoning field. Scholars Quincy D. Newell and Sarah Keyes have investigated colonizing soundscapes in the West.[75] Keyes's work is of particular importance in its application to Sandoz. According to Keyes, overland settlers believed that "their sounds [had] . . . the power to subdue the savage wilds and help transform the West into American territory." Natural sounds were thus not the desired American sounds of progress and modernity, and this is precisely what Sandoz rebelled against.[76]

Aspects of the sensory worlds of Sandoz's youth and aspects of the lived reality of Sandoz's New York City sensory worlds found their way into *The Battle of the Little Bighorn*.

In Sandoz's buildup to the battle, Custer and his men consumed and produced the pleasant nostalgic scents and sounds of Sandoz's Sandhills home. While impossible to know how Custer and his men understood or interpreted what they smelled, heard, and produced or whether they smelled, heard, and produced the things Sandoz suggested, Sandoz certainly understood these scents and sounds as part of the smellscape and soundscape of her home, and to her they were important enough to include.

The sweet fragrance, which so often greeted her nose, of "wild roses still a pink cascade in late-blooming patches," now Custer and his men inhaled.[77] Their ears, like hers, took in the blackbirds that "sang in the rushes," "the stir of insects," "the far howl of the coyotes," "the deeper howl of the prairie wolves," "the early croak of the frogs," and the "sound of arrow hawks falling upon their prey."[78] Music enlivened the air just as it had in the Sandoz home. While the Sandoz family joyfully danced to musical stylings emanating from their phonograph records, the air for Custer and his men became filled with a "chorus of trumpets" that emitted the "shining" sound of "Boots and Saddles," which sounded "golden against the wind."[79] On the march, the trumpets often "came up to send their call to the wind and to glisten as they were lowered."[80] The glorious morale-raising, perhaps victory-ensuring melodies of the trumpets made up only one part of the soundscape Custer and his men produced on their march. The rustling of the wind whipped Custer's personal flag against the sky, the "rhythmic thud of shod hoofs, the creak of leather, the jingle of bit and thump of slung carbines," and "the nose-clearing snorts of the stomping horses" echoed across the landscape.[81] Perhaps aware of the alien cacophony he and his men were producing, which could act as an alert to the Indians, Custer attempted to produce quiet. He eventually banned his scouts from shooting their pistols "except at the enemy," limited the trumpets' blare to once daily at 5:00 p.m., and forbade morning reveille.[82] Apparently he was unsuccessful in his sound-dampening effort, as his Indian scouts moved away from camp to escape the noise of the troops.

Indians, like the Seventh Cavalry, produced and consumed scent and sound. On June 22, 1876, while camped at Rosebud, Custer's men failed to even listen "for Sioux war whoops."[83] Custer's Indian scouts, "Bloody Knife, the Ree-Sioux, and Half Yellow Face," conversely sat on a "little rise to catch any night breeze that might carry a remote sound to their ears, and away from the sour smell of the sweaty white men."[84] Here Indians' ears and noses are sharp and alert while white ears and nostrils are closed and careless. The stink of the white man required geographic distancing. In the nineteenth and twentieth centuries, it was usually the noses of white people that used smell as indicator of race.[85] Sandoz offers a different take: Indian noses discerned race. Indian noses smelled the stench of whites. But did they or are they smelling through Sandoz's nose, the nose of a white woman, which finds the stench of white men offensive?

Sounds, like scents, are open to interpretation. The rebel yell, for example, sent shivers up the spines of more than one Yankee and invoked terror, but in Confederate ears it rang as a tribute to the cause and a rally to battle. White and Indian ears, according to Sandoz, heard and understood sound differently. Her lifelong sympathy toward the injustices faced by American Indians may offer an explanation. Sandoz aligned herself with the Indians. As she was familiar with both the soothing sounds and the dangerous sounds of her environment, it follows that the Indians would be as well. It also follows that the invading army remained oblivious to the nuanced sounds and noises of the West. On June 22, 1876, no Indian war whoops sounded in white ears, according to Sandoz, perhaps because Indians didn't produce them, or white ears didn't receive them, or Sandoz didn't create them. Sandoz also described Indian war whoops, made at various times before the conclusion of the battle. Sandoz's ears heard them as the sound of white exploitation and the justified sound of defense against white intrusion. She pointedly explains that "since Custer's report of 'gold at the grass roots,' two years earlier, miners ran like ants over the rocks and burrowed into the earth of the Hills, many so near that, with the wind right, the loud whoop of a gold strike around Deadwood Gulch could be heard at the Butte of the Crouching Bear."[86] Given Sandoz's explicit criticisms of the East's extracting the riches of the West for its own benefit, the whoops here ring of abuse and injustice. Reading the account this way, the use of Indian war whoops can be heard, through Sandoz's experiences, as symbolic of the violation of Indigenous peoples and as a coordinated rallying call for justice.

Sandoz's Indians whooped, but the white ears of Sandoz's Seventh Cavalry did not receive or understand the sounds until it was too late. Her prose details Indians emitting war whoops at various times before engaging Custer's men.[87] Whites should have been able to hear the forthcoming assault, as "sound carried easily against the perceptible wind." Yet, despite repeated warnings that the Indians outnumbered Custer and his men, Custer's ears remained "closed . . . to the warnings of his scouts."[88] Sandoz palpably makes these distinctions between Indian and white ways of hearing. While Indians, she argued, "could feel the cadence of" the Seventh Cavalry hooves simply by listening with their "fingertips, laid to the bare earth," or by putting "a naked ear to the ground to detect faraway sounds of" hoofbeats, Custer's men remained deaf. Even in the midst of the fight, they failed to hear and understand Indian sounds.[89] Certainly, Sandoz points out, they heard the noise around them, but "with hands cupped to ears" they heard "no sound . . . nothing . . . except the faint whooping from the village" below them.[90] These faint whoops excited but did not alert the troops to the impending assault because their ears failed to understand the meaning. Indians produced sounds that white ears didn't consume. On the signal of "the high, thin call" of Lakota warrior "Gall's war flute . . . the Indians rose together with a great whooping" and "with whoops and battle songs, the leaders headed the thousands" toward the surprised Seventh Cavalry.[91]

Taste and touch featured in the sensory worlds of *The Battle of the Little Bighorn* yet, like smell and sound, remained embedded rather

Mari Sandoz, Sensory Conjuror

than reflected on and explored. Although invisible to the eye, alkali dust coated tongues, entered noses, and irritated the skin of man and beast alike.[92] The dust and dirt burned and grated, as New York City dirt and grit had, rather than comforted and soothed, as the dirt and dust of Sandoz's childhood had. The eye may not have seen the dust, but the eye felt the dust. Custer's "dust-reddened eyes" burned, and Commander of the Scouts Charles Albert Varnum returned after "seventy hours of dusty scouting . . . with blurred and bloodshot" eyes.[93] Occasionally, smell trumped vision. At night, when the eye failed "in the darkness," and when the wind dissipated, the abrasive alkaline dust disturbed white nostrils. Even with "a bandanna drawn up over" them, white noses flared with displeasure as the gritty dust unpleasantly penetrated nostrils and disturbed smellscapes.[94] Many men, including "young Boston Custer and Autie Reed[,] tried to ease . . . the sting of the alkali." Weary veteran soldiers "sprawled on the ground snoring the dust from their nostrils." Other men and horses tried to soothe the irritation by rolling or throwing themselves in water. The water, unbeknown to man or horse, "was so alkaline" that the animals "snorted and threw themselves back from the [stinking] water." Coffee made from such water was undrinkable.[95] Men and beast became increasingly thirsty. Horse tongues became "so parched that the oats they tried to eat fell dry from their muzzles."[96] "Several light sprinkles" alleviated no thirst. Raindrops danced and made "light running sounds over the dry earth, like timid mice. But there was not enough to wet one parched tongue."[97] These "occasional spatter[s] of rain . . . [and] the smell of water" drove the horses wild as the dust lay, "gritty and burning," in their mouths. That same sound and scent tortured the mouths of the able-bodied men, "as well as the burning and delirious wounded."[98] Doctors struggled to "keep the men comfortable in spite of dust and alkali and buffalo gnats, swarming and tiny as cycling dust particles, biting the eyelids until they swelled half-shut, the ears until they were thick as florid saucers."[99]

As doctors labored, men fought, and the wounded suffered, the chaotic cacophony of battle raged around them, and the scent of death clung to them. "The thin line of foot soldiers wavered ... and shrank from the crack and whine of the bullets about them and the pale zing of arrows, but they steadied and began to fire."[100] An "excited and blinding roar of guns" ensued.[101] "The roar of guns and the snap and pop of the [gun] fire" deafened Major Marcus Reno's men to his orders; "his voice was lost" in the thunderous dissonance of battle.[102] Indians whooped, carbine bullets whined, and "the sound of battle grew louder and more continuous, more pronounced and insistent."[103] Soon, however, sound predicted the impending defeat of Custer and his men. The soundscape changed, but to whose ears is unknown. For Sandoz, the quieter nature of Indian combat, the zing of arrows and thumps of "spears and clubs," replaced "the roar of the soldier guns." By the end of the battle, wrote Sandoz, the guns "seemed little more ... than the popping of the winter ice going out of the Yellowstone in the spring."[104]

While the battle ended for Sandoz in a restoration of the pastoral nature of her Sandhills home, namely the hopeful sounds of winter's thaw and spring's rebirth, for the majority of the battle the alien harsh sounds, scents, textures, smells, and sights invaded her West. Sounds, smells, sights, tastes, and textures more akin to the unpleasantness and nastiness of her New York City experiences saturated her telling of the battle. Men died, their bodies bloated, and the unmistakable stench of death embraced the battlefield. The dead and the wounded huddled in "shallow holes behind dead horses, the buzzing gases in the heat bloating the bellies up high until hit by bullets. Any that struck bone released not only a terrible stench but blew the rotting flesh over" the skin of "the men hiding behind them." Some men suffered the sounds of flies swarming the corpses next to them, and the maggots invading "blackened mouths and eyeballs, the sight even more horrible than the stench."[105] Dr. Henry R. Porter "soak[ed] the stinking bandages of the wounded."[106] With temperatures spiking well "above 100 degrees," the brutal heat of June soon brought buzzing, hungry "flies, carrion beetles, and some" enthusiastic "circling vultures" hoping to peck the flesh of the dead.[107] Some bodies became so black and bloated as to be unrecognizable, their "faces like the wounds, puffed and swollen, oozing and flyblown."[108] Bodies of dead horses lay with "great bloated bellies, the gases stewing and whistling in the climbing heat of the sun, the rushing sound of maggots busily gnawing, great dark flies crawling heavily over it all."[109] Those men trying to "examine the decomposing bodies" became overcome by "the heat and stench." They began to "vomit so violently that [Captain Thomas Mower] McDougall finally had great chunks of earth and sod cut" to block the scent and sight of the dead of Company E.[110] Scattered across the battlefield, "like handfuls of pale Indian corn," several hundred naked and mutilated human bodies and thousands of pounds of dead animal flesh putrefied in the sun and exploded in the heat, releasing the sickly sweet scent of death to the heavens.[111]

These are the sensory worlds of Sandoz's battle. Sandoz plausibly drew from the pleasing multisensory worlds of her youth and the harsh multisensory worlds culled from her experiences in New York City to create her version of the Battle of the Little Bighorn. Overwhelmingly, she created a sensory world in which the obstreperousness of battle as characterized by thundering guns and Indian war whoops accompanied the gritty taste and feel of dust, the putrid aromas of death, and the munching sounds of insects as they dined on the dead, together overcoming nature's pastoral harmonies. She failed to specify whose nose smelled those odors, whose tongue tasted the bitter flavors, whose skin felt the searing pain, whose ears heard the astonishing cacophony of battle, and whose eyes witnessed the brutality of the fighting. These are important yet ultimately unanswerable questions. It is plausible that the answers lay with the author herself. Perhaps, as mentioned earlier, critic Robert Palmer correctly noted that Sandoz "conjure[d] the sounds of ninety years ago." Perhaps she also conjured the smells, tastes, textures, and sights of ninety years before she penned her account. The sensory worlds she created in *The Battle of the Little Bighorn* contain striking aspects of both the harsh, jarring, and alien sensory worlds of the New York City she inhabited when she wrote it and the soothing, welcoming, and familiar sensory worlds of the youth to which she yearned to return. Although the truth remains elusive, sensory analysis offers a connection to the disparate places in Sandoz's life as well as a novel and creative way of thinking about *The Battle of the Little Bighorn*.

NOTES

Securing research materials is challenging at the best of times. Securing research materials in the middle of a global pandemic and from another country was, in words I think Mari Sandoz would appreciate and approve of, damn difficult! I am indebted to Susan Asbury, Lisa M. Denmark, Mary T. Gross, Darren Hill, Kendra M. Gage, William J. Bauer Jr., Miles Mathews, Adrian H. Roberts, and Brenda T. Schoolfield. I thank the anonymous reviewer for the thoughtful critique, Renée Laegreid for the opportunity, and Mark M. Smith for sparking my interest in sensory history. All errors are of course mine.

Epigraph: From the University of Nebraska Press edition (1978), 191–92.

1. Jack Burrows, review of *The Battle of the Little Bighorn*, by Mari Sandoz, *Arizona and the West* 9, no. 1 (Spring 1967): 65.
2. Douglas Keller, review of *The Battle of the Little Bighorn*, by Mari Sandoz, *Journal of the Indian Wars* 2, no. 1 (2001): 14.
3. Alvin M. Josephy Jr., "Soldiers and Indians," *New York Times*, July 3, 1966; Rudolph Umland, "Just Take Her Word for Some," *Kansas City Star*, July 8, 1966. Also see Virgil A. Stanfield, "Writer Critical of Gen. Custer," *News Journal* (Mansfield OH), October 24, 1971; and Bill Shelton, "A Look at New Books," *Press Telegram* (Long Beach CA), December 9, 1971.
4. Stewart "Sandy" Richardson to Mari Sandoz, September 7, 1965, in Elaine Marie Nelson, "Draft by Draft: The Battle of Sandoz and Her Bighorn Manuscript," *Great Plains Quarterly* 39, no. 2 (Spring 2019): 150.
5. Umland, "Just Take Her Word for Some."
6. Robert D. Price, review of *The Battle of the Little Bighorn*, by Mari Sandoz, *Post-Crescent* (Appleton WI), August 21, 1966.
7. Robert Palmer, review of *The Battle of the Little Bighorn*, by Mari Sandoz, *Montana: The Magazine of Western History* 17, no. 3 (Summer 1967): 86.
8. Barton M. Hayward, review of *The Battle of the Little Bighorn*, by Mari Sandoz, *Military Review* 46 (October 1966): 110.

9. Quoted in Helen Winter Stauffer, "Mari Sandoz," *Boise State University Western Writers Series* 63 (1984): 35.
10. Burrows review, 66.
11. Bill Brooks, review of *The Battle of the Little Bighorn*, by Mari Sandoz, *Indianapolis (IN) Star*, July 17, 1966.
12. Stauffer, "Mari Sandoz," 6. On her merging of fictions and nonfictions and her lack of documentation, see LaVerne Harrell Clark, "A Dedication to the Memory of Mari Sandoz, 1896–1966," *Arizona and the West* 18, no. 4 (Winter 1976): 311; Craig Bird, "Books in Review," *Lawton (OK) Constitution and Morning Press*, November 7, 1971; Betsey Downey, "She Does Not Write Like a Historian: Mari Sandoz and the Old and New Western History," *Great Plains Quarterly* 16, no. 1 (Winter 1996): 11; Keller review, 14; John H. Monnett, *Massacre at Cheyenne Hole: Lieutenant Austin Henely and the Sappa Creek Controversy* (Niwot: University Press of Colorado, 1999), xiv; Michael F. O'Keefe, *Custer, the Seventh Cavalry, and the Little Big Horn: A Bibliography* (Norman: University of Oklahoma Press, 2012), 443; Nelson, "Draft by Draft," 134–35, 154, 155, 158; Barbara Rippey and John R. Wunder, "Mari Sandoz, Nebraska Sandhills Author: A Centennial Recognition," *Great Plains Quarterly* 16, no. 1 (Winter 1996): 5; Edgar I. Stewart, review of *The Battle of the Little Bighorn*, by Mari Sandoz, *Pacific Northwest Quarterly* 58, no. 2 (April 1967): 103; John R. Wunder, "Some Notes on Marie Sandoz," *Prairie Schooner* 80, no. 4 (Winter 2006): 41. Other western women writers of Sandoz's ilk, such as Grace Raymond Hebard and Angie Debo, likewise merged fact and fiction, to the chagrin of critics. On Hebard and fictionalizing facts, see T. A. Larson, *History of Wyoming* (Lincoln: University of Nebraska Press, 1965), 111, 639; W. Dale Nelson, *Interpreters with Lewis and Clark: The Story of Sacagawea and Toussaint Charbonneau* (Denton: University of North Texas Press, 2003), 123–25; Mike Mackey, *Inventing History in the American West: The Romance and Myths of Grace Raymond Hebard* (Casper WY: Western History Publications, 2005); and Jane Wenzel, "Dr. Grace Raymond Hebard as Western Historian" (MA thesis, University of Wyoming, Laramie, 1961). On Debo, see Julie Des Jardins, *Women and the Historical Enterprise in America: Gender, Race, and the Politics of Memory, 1880–1945* (Chapel Hill: University of North Carolina Press, 2003), 194.
13. Mari Sandoz, *The Battle of the Little Bighorn* (1966; Lincoln: University of Nebraska Press, 1978), 152.

14. Mark M. Smith, "Producing Sense, Consuming Sense, Making Sense: Perils and Prospects for Sensory History," *Journal of Social History* 40, no. 4 (Summer 2007): 843. On the state of sensory history, see Mark M. Smith, *A Sensory History Manifesto* (University Park: Pennsylvania State University Press, 2021).
15. Laura Davis, "The Smeller's (Almost Always) a Feller: A Sensory Studies Approach to Examining Gender and Sexuality across Nine Faulkner Texts," *Faulkner Journal* 28, no. 2 (Fall 2014): 54.
16. Mark M. Smith, ed., *Smell and History: A Reader* (Morgantown: West Virginia University Press, 2019), x.
17. Clark, "Dedication to the Memory of Mari Sandoz," 311.
18. Helen Winter Stauffer, ed., *Letters of Mari Sandoz* (Lincoln: University of Nebraska Press, 1992), xvi.
19. Bernard DeVoto, "A Violent, Fighting Pioneer," *Saturday Review of Literature* 13, no. 1 (November 2, 1935): 5. On Sandoz's clashes with eastern publishers over the meter, measure, and choice of her diction, see Des Jardins, *Women and the Historical Enterprise*, 14–15; Nelson, "Draft by Draft," 138, 140; Mari Sandoz to Bill Hooker, February 9, 1937, in Stauffer, *Letters of Mari Sandoz*, 115; Mari Sandoz to Alfred R. McIntyre, March 22, 1937, in Stauffer, *Letters of Mari Sandoz*, 121.
20. Mari Sandoz to Edward Weeks, September 19, 1936, in Stauffer, *Letters of Mari Sandoz*, 108.
21. Stauffer, *Letters of Mari Sandoz*, xvi, xxi.
22. Helen Winter Stauffer, *Mari Sandoz: Story Catcher of the Plains* (Lincoln: University of Nebraska Press, 1982), vii.
23. Mari Sandoz to Mr. O'Kieffe, February 13, 1956, in Stauffer, *Letters of Mari Sandoz*, 288. O'Kieffe often solicited advice on his writings from Sandoz; see Charley O'Kieffe, *Western Story: The Recollections of Charley O'Kieffe, 1994–1898* (Norman: University of Oklahoma Press, 1954).
24. Mari Sandoz to Mr. Worley, December 24, 1965, in Stauffer, *Letters of Mari Sandoz*, 500. Per Stauffer's footnote, budding Oglala Sioux author E. T. Worley sought Sandoz's advice for his manuscript on his life.
25. Dorothee E. Kocks, *Dream a Little: Land and Social Justice in Modern America* (Berkeley: University of California Press, 2000), xix.
26. Nelson, "Draft by Draft," 134. See also Helen Stauffer, "Mari Sandoz and Western Biography," in *Women, Women Writers, and the West*, ed. L. L. Lee and Merrill Lewis (Troy NY: Whitston, 1979), 57, 59.

27. On the distinction between authenticity and truth, see Philip J. Deloria, *Playing Indian* (New Haven: Yale University Press, 1998), 4; William Handley and Nathaniel Lewis, eds., *True West: Authenticity and the American West* (Lincoln: University of Nebraska Press, 2004), 2; Miles Orvell, *The Real Thing: Imitation and Authenticity in American Culture* (Chapel Hill: University of North Carolina Press, 1989), xv; Paige Raibmon, *Authentic Indians: Episodes of Encounter from the Late-Nineteenth-Century Northwest Coast* (Durham NC: Duke University Press, 2005), 3; Daniel H. Usner Jr., *Indian Work: Language and Livelihood in Native American History* (Cambridge MA: Harvard University Press, 2009), 94; and Cheryl A. Wells, "'Why[,] These Children Are Not Really Indians': Race, Time, and Indian Authenticity," *American Indian Quarterly* 39, no. 1 (Winter 2015): 1.
28. Stauffer, "Mari Sandoz and Western Biography," 61.
29. Andrew J. Rotter, *Empires of the Senses: Bodily Encounters in Imperial India and the Philippines* (New York: Oxford University Press, 2019), 1.
30. Nelson, "Draft by Draft," 135.
31. Mari Sandoz letter to the newspaper quoted in the "More or Less Personal" column, *Lincoln (NE) Journal and Star*, June 5, 1960, 6. On the parasitic nature of the East, see Nelson, "Draft by Draft," 136; and Mari Sandoz to Bill Hooker, February 9, 1937, in Stauffer, *Letters of Mari Sandoz*, 115. On westerners' ideas of the East, see Flannery Burke, "The Arrogance of the East: How Westerners Created a Region," *Western Historical Quarterly* 49, no. 4 (Winter 2018): 383–407.
32. Mari Sandoz to Tyler Buchenau, December 6, 1933, in Stauffer, *Letters of Mari Sandoz*, 64. On easterners' views of westerners, also see Stauffer, *Mari Sandoz: Story Catcher*, 101; and Mari Sandoz, "The Look of the West—1854," *Nebraska History* 35, no. 4 (December 1954): 244.
33. Stauffer, *Letters of Mari Sandoz*, xxii–xiii. See also Herb Hyde, "Books: Portrait of the Artist as a Young Woman," *Lincoln Journal Star*, August 15, 1982.
34. Stauffer, *Mari Sandoz: Story Catcher*, 61.
35. Mari Sandoz to Alfred R. McIntyre, March 22, 1937, in Stauffer, *Letters of Mari Sandoz*, 121.
36. Sandoz letter quoted in "More or Less Personal" column, *Lincoln Journal and Star*, June 5, 1960. On her never-completed book to have been titled *I Hate New York*, see John Bentley, "After Thoughts," *Lincoln Journal Star*, May 29, 1965.

37. Joe Duggan, "Sandoz's Sandhills a Big Draw," *Lincoln Journal Star,* January 6, 2002.
38. Stauffer, *Mari Sandoz: Story Catcher,* 163; Stauffer, "Mari Sandoz," 14.
39. Mari Sandoz to Jesse Stuart, March 31, 1956, in Stauffer, *Letters of Mari Sandoz,* 286. On the life of Appalachian author Jesse Stuart, see James M. Gifford and Erin R. Kazee, *Jesse Stuart: An Extraordinary Life* (Ashland KY: Jesse Stuart Foundation, 2010); and H. Edward Richardson, *Jesse: The Biography of an American Writer, Jesse Hilton Stuart* (New York: McGraw-Hill, 1984).
40. Mari Sandoz, "Outpost in New York," *Prairie Schooner* 37, no. 2 (Summer 1963): 102.
41. Nelson, "Draft by Draft," 136.
42. David Lowe, "A Meeting with Mari Sandoz," *Prairie Schooner* 42, no. 1 (Spring 1968): 22.
43. Lowe, "Meeting with Mari Sandoz," 26.
44. Mari Sandoz to Melvin Van den Bark, April 13, 1958, in Stauffer, *Letters of Mari Sandoz,* 311.
45. Sandoz, "Outpost in New York," 95.
46. Mari Sandoz to Hanson W. Baldwin, June 13, 1960, in Stauffer, *Letters of Mari Sandoz,* 358–59.
47. Sandoz, "Outpost in New York," 98.
48. Lowe, "Meeting with Mari Sandoz," 24.
49. Mari Sandoz to Bruce Nicoll, December 28, 1964, in Stauffer, *Letters of Mari Sandoz,* 445–46. See also Sandoz, "Outpost in New York," 102.
50. Lowe, "Meeting with Mari Sandoz," 23.
51. Stauffer, *Mari Sandoz: Story Catcher,* 137. On Leonard Thiessen, see William Wells, *Prairie Symphony: The Story of Charles Leonard Thiessen* (Los Angeles: Lone Wolf Editions, 2010).
52. Duggan, "Sandoz's Sandhills a Big Draw," 6.
53. Sandoz, "Outpost in New York," 103.
54. Stauffer, *Mari Sandoz: Story Catcher,* 25, 26.
55. Sandoz, "Outpost in New York," 98.
56. Mari Sandoz to Melvin Van den Bark, April 13, 1958, in Stauffer, *Letters of Mari Sandoz,* 311.
57. On Blanche W. Knopf's publishing career, see Laura Claridge, *The Lady with the Borzoi: Blanche Knopf, Literary Tastemaker Extraordinaire* (New York: Farrar, Straus & Giroux, 2016).

58. Mari Sandoz to Lynn and Rose Van Vleet, May 2, 1943, in Stauffer, *Letters of Mari Sandoz*, 197.
59. Mari Sandoz, *Sandhill Sundays and Other Recollections* (Lincoln: University of Nebraska Press, 1984), chap. 1, Kindle ed. Agnes Smedley's autobiographical *Daughters of the Earth* (New York: Feminist Press, 1973), 238–41, suggests her agreement with Sandoz's impression of New York City society.
60. Sandoz, "Outpost in New York," 102.
61. Sandoz, "Outpost in New York," 106; Sandoz, *Sandhill Sundays*, chap. 2.
62. Sandoz, *Sandhill Sundays*, introduction, chaps. 2 and 3, and chaps. 1, 2, and 6.
63. On nineteenth-century urban odors, see Melanie A. Kiechle, *Smell Detectives: An Olfactory History of Nineteenth-Century Urban America* (Seattle: University of Washington Press, 2018), 53–77.
64. Stauffer, *Mari Sandoz: Story Catcher*, 25.
65. Sandoz, *Sandhill Sundays*, chap. 6.
66. Sandoz, *Sandhill Sundays*, chap. 7.
67. On taste, memory, and identity, see Priscilla Parkhurst Ferguson, "The Sense of Taste," *American Historical Review* 116, no. 2 (April 2011): 371–84. On the gustatorial history of America, see Gerald J. Fitzgerald and Gabriella M. Petrick, "In Good Taste: Rethinking American History with Our Palates," *Journal of American History* 95, no. 2 (September 2008): 392–404.
68. Sandoz, *Sandhill Sundays*, chap. 1.
69. "Authoress Mari Sandoz Dies; Was a Chronicler of the Old West," *Central New Jersey News*, May 11, 1966. For similar sentiments, see "Historian Mari Sandoz Part of What She Wrote," *Corpus Christi (TX) Times*, March 11, 1966; "Mari Sandoz, Author, 65, Dies; Historian of Nebraska Plains," *New York Times*, March 11, 1966.
70. Victor P. Hass, "Tarnish on a Golden Image," *Chicago Tribune*, July 17, 1966; Josephy, "Soldiers and Indians." For similar statements, see Naomi Knickmeyer, "New Book Plows Old Soil, Custer," *Ada (OK) Evening News*, July 10, 1966; and Richard O. Robinette, "Author Gives Her Own Views, Lets Readers Draw Own Conclusions," *Kannapolis (NC) Daily Independent*, July 17, 1966.
71. Sandoz, *Battle of the Little Bighorn*, 181–82.
72. Paul H. Hass, review of *The Battle of the Little Bighorn*, by Mari Sandoz, *Wisconsin Magazine of History* 50, no. 3 (Spring 1967): 268.
73. Jim Burnett, "New Answer for 'Bighorn,'" *Denton (TX) Record-Chronicle*, October 31, 1971. Also see Stauffer, *Mari Sandoz: Story Catcher*, 261.

74. On the sensory history of war, see Mark M. Smith, *The Smell of Battle, the Taste of Siege: A Sensory History of the Civil War* (New York: Oxford University Press, 2015); Kiechle, *Smell Detectives*; and Evan A. Kutzler, *Living by Inches: The Smells, Sounds, Taste, and Feeling of Captivity in Civil War Prisons* (Chapel Hill: University of North Carolina Press, 2019).

75. Quincy D. Newell, *Constructing Lives at Mission San Francisco: Native Californians and Hispanic Colonists, 1776–1821* (Albuquerque: University of New Mexico Press, 2009), 28–31; Sarah Keyes, "'Like a Roaring Lion': The Overland Trail as a Sonic Conquest," *Journal of American History* 96 (2009): 19–43; and see also my own work: Wells, "'Why[,] These Children Are Not Really Indians,'" 9–14.

76. Keyes, "'Like a Roaring Lion,'" 19.

77. Sandoz, *Battle of the Little Bighorn*, 16.

78. Sandoz, *Battle of the Little Bighorn*, 16, 30, 43, 30, 43, 44.

79. Sandoz, *Battle of the Little Bighorn*, 14, 13.

80. Sandoz, *Battle of the Little Bighorn*, 15–16.

81. Sandoz, *Battle of the Little Bighorn*, 14, 16, 15, 44.

82. Sandoz, *Battle of the Little Bighorn*, 17, 21, 32.

83. Sandoz, *Battle of the Little Bighorn*, 30.

84. Sandoz, *Battle of the Little Bighorn*, 22.

85. On the sensory history of race, see Connie Y. Chiang, "The Nose Knows: The Sense of Smell in American History," *Journal of American History* 95, no. 2 (September 2008): 405–16; Constance Classen, "The Odor of the Other: Olfactory Symbolism and Cultural Categories," *Ethos* 20, no. 2 (June 1992): 133–36; Kiechle, *Smell Detectives*, 132–34; Mark Paterson, "On Sensory History and Contemporary Placemaking in the Social Sciences," *Postmedieval: A Journal of Medieval Cultural Studies* 3, no. 4 (December 2012): 455–60; Mark M. Smith, "Getting in Touch with Slavery and Freedom," *Journal of American History* 95, no. 2 (September 2008): 381–91; Mark M. Smith, *How Race Is Made: Slavery, Segregation, and the Senses* (Chapel Hill: University of North Carolina Press, 2006); Mark M. Smith, "Making 'Others' Smell," in Smith, *Smell and History*, 187–201; and Mark M. Smith, "Transcending, Othering, Detecting: Smell, Premodernity, Modernity," *Postmedieval: A Journal of Medieval Cultural Studies* 3, no. 4 (December 2012): 380–90.

86. Sandoz, *Battle of the Little Bighorn*, 39.

87. Sandoz, *Battle of the Little Bighorn*, 34, 65, 75, 88, 118, 127, 130, 132.

88. Sandoz, *Battle of the Little Bighorn*, 34.

89. Sandoz, *Battle of the Little Bighorn*, 48, 146.
90. Sandoz, *Battle of the Little Bighorn*, 88.
91. Sandoz, *Battle of the Little Bighorn*, 124, 130.
92. Sandoz, *Battle of the Little Bighorn*, 47.
93. Sandoz, *Battle of the Little Bighorn*, 59, 52.
94. Sandoz, *Battle of the Little Bighorn*, 47.
95. Sandoz, *Battle of the Little Bighorn*, 50.
96. Sandoz, *Battle of the Little Bighorn*, 55.
97. Sandoz, *Battle of the Little Bighorn*, 145.
98. Sandoz, *Battle of the Little Bighorn*, 152.
99. Sandoz, *Battle of the Little Bighorn*, 41.
100. Sandoz, *Battle of the Little Bighorn*, 75.
101. Sandoz, *Battle of the Little Bighorn*, 76.
102. Sandoz, *Battle of the Little Bighorn*, 82.
103. Sandoz, *Battle of the Little Bighorn*, 125, 93.
104. Sandoz, *Battle of the Little Bighorn*, 127.
105. Sandoz, *Battle of the Little Bighorn*, 152.
106. Sandoz, *Battle of the Little Bighorn*, 155.
107. Sandoz, *Battle of the Little Bighorn*, 152, 157.
108. Sandoz, *Battle of the Little Bighorn*, 169.
109. Sandoz, *Battle of the Little Bighorn*, 170.
110. Sandoz, *Battle of the Little Bighorn*, 169.
111. Sandoz, *Battle of the Little Bighorn*, 167. On battle and smell, see Smith, *Smell of Battle*, 66–83.

3

"Such a Jolly Family"

Mari Sandoz Rewrites Elizabeth Bacon Custer

CATHRYN HALVERSON

To the older campaigners, Custer seemed less elated this evening than usual by tracks of an enemy ahead, certainly less overflowing with assurance and self-sufficiency than on his trike against the Cheyennes at the Washita eight years ago. There seemed unease about him standing there, even flanked as he was by his brother, Captain Tom Custer and his brother-in-law, Lieutenant Calhoun, with Boston Custer and the nephew off to the side, and his favorites around him.

When the regiment was gone—all except a couple of the pack mules running down a washout—the colonel clasped the hands held out to him there on the ridge and wheeled his horse to overtake his command. Gibbon called out after him, "Now, Custer, don't be greedy. Wait for us!" Custer lifted his gauntleted hand in acknowledgement. "No!" he shouted back, "I-I won't!" his stammer very slight, the ambiguity left hanging like a puff of pipe smoke over the shoulder as he galloped off, the wind whipping the color of his standard behind him.

—Mari Sandoz, *The Battle of the Little Bighorn*

Mari Sandoz's and Elizabeth Bacon Custer's portraits of George Armstrong Custer in *The Battle of the Little Bighorn* (1966) and *Boots and Saddles, or, Life in Dakota with General Custer* (1885), respectively, are remarkably different. In accounting for their differences, this chapter accords these two books the kind of close textual analysis they rarely receive, as both have primarily attracted the attention of historians and biographers rather than literary critics.

Elizabeth Custer's outlier position in this edited volume—the second in a series created by the Mari Sandoz Society to promote Sandoz's legacy—makes it unlikely that she will come off well in this pairing. It is not so much that her memoir is the work of a grieving widow making her first foray into print, whereas Sandoz's study marks the close of this illustrious historian and novelist's lifetime of achievement. As a writer, Custer had real ability. Rather, it is that her texts must support an aggressively imperialist agenda in order to justify her husband and his career.[1]

Custer wrote and published *Boots and Saddles*, borrowing its title from the bugle call signaling the cavalry to mount, in a bid to burnish her husband's tarnished reputation, as well as to prop up her own finances. Famously, she had not only accompanied Armstrong's regiment but also ridden by his side, and as its subtitle promises, her first book chronicles her experiences with him in Dakota Territory. It opens with their 1873 journey north from Kentucky and concludes with the departure of the U.S. Army's Seventh Cavalry for its disastrous last expedition. The book was enormously well received, soon selling fifteen thousand copies.[2] Its publication coinciding with that of Mark Twain's *Adventures of Huckleberry Finn*, *Boots and Saddles* offered Americans an alternative way to map the nation's interior, conceive its recent past, and frame its racial conditions.

In quick succession, Elizabeth Custer produced two sequels recounting earlier stages of her husband's career: *Tenting on the Plains* (1887) and *Following the Guidon* (1890). Their hagiographic quality was always recognized, but nonetheless the trio served as the textual basis for the indelible "Custer legend." That means they also reinforced popular support for western expansion and the ongoing violence of the U.S. federal government against Native peoples. Indeed, *Following the Guidon* appeared the very year of the Wounded Knee Massacre at the hands of Custer's regrouped unit.

Sandoz alleged that Custer's larger than life status incited the bloodshed, that "the exaggerations, the violent partisanship . . . help[ed] push one section of the 7th Cavalry into the most barbaric conduct fourteen years later, when they mowed down women and children with Hotchkiss guns at Wounded Knee in 1890, shouting, some reported, 'There's another blast for Custer!'"[3] Seeking to expose and undo some of the damage of frontier mythologies, she advocated for Native rights and wrote studies such as *These Were the Sioux* and *Crazy Horse: The Strange Man of the Oglalas.* The sympathies of *The Battle of the Little Bighorn* do not lie with Custer. Her views of the man and his campaigns were diametrically opposed to Elizabeth Custer's, and they are also far more aligned with contemporary perspectives.

Is it possible then to write about Mari Sandoz and Elizabeth Custer together without the latter coming off as a villain? I will try, through a focus on craft. Looking first at the powerfully effective way Custer created her portrait of Armstrong and advanced her arguments about his enterprise—shown to be an astonishingly domestic and family-oriented one—I then turn to Sandoz to read *The Battle of the Little Bighorn* as a response to Elizabeth Custer's influence, insofar as she was a driving force behind the enduring Custer legend.

From here on, I will usually refer to Elizabeth Bacon Custer as "Custer" and George Armstrong Custer as "Armstrong," not only to differentiate between author and subject but also to push back against the scholarly habit of calling the former "Libbie." Scholars regularly note that during the close to six decades she survived him, respect for Custer and her sorrow suppressed criticism of her husband. It was only upon her death that the floodgates opened and the trickle of anti-Custer commentary became a river. But while Armstrong Custer and his choices have long since been minutely dissected and critiqued, Elizabeth Custer is still admired and even idealized, her worthy personal qualities noted even as the pernicious nature of her texts is ignored. That is to say, she is still handled, critically speaking, with the same gallantry once tendered her as a general's wife and widow.

Any interrogation takes place at the personal level, in the form of discussing Armstrong's infidelity and other deceptions to question whether theirs truly was a "grand and tragic romance."[4]

An additional consequence, though, is that even as Custer is given a pass with respect to her ideology, she receives short shrift as a writer. Far more ink has been spilled on showing how she got her husband's remains reinterred at West Point and forced the removal of a statue she disliked than on how her texts operate. We have countless references to her books as "brilliant pieces of propaganda" that "restored George's reputation" and "ke[pt] his image polished."[5] However, we are not shown just what made them brilliant or how the processes of restoration and polishing took place. Her accomplishment was prodigious; the tide of national opinion is not so easily turned, after all. Louis Kraft writes that the "proclamation of [Custer's] heroism continued for decades, due in large part to the steady efforts of his wife." Biographer Shirley Leckie names Custer one of the "most successful mythmakers" in the nation's history.[6] Yet in both her time and ours, she is conceived as a widow first and as an author only second. Her portraits of Armstrong are simply expressions of her love.

Amanda Healy says this much better, in her dissertation on women writers on the frontier: "This gap between academic analysis and creative conclusion is suggestive of the recourse to the Custer marriage as an explanatory device, or a device that yields an endless deferral of explanation, for her and for her writing, that continues the depoliticization of these texts that accompanied their publication."[7] Effectively separating Custer's biography from her texts, Healy takes on the author of *Boots and Saddles* with the fierce passion of a young scholar, revealing Custer's major contribution to a rhetorical strategy among women writers in the American West that she dubs "Loving Empire." By presenting her forays with Armstrong as loving, delightful family enterprise, Custer's work naturalizes and props up American imperialism. I wish I had read *Boots and Saddles* prior to completing *Playing House in the American West: Western Women's Life Narratives, 1839–1987*, as Custer's book so clearly supports the central argument of *Playing House*—that western women writers consistently recruit wayward or fantastic housekeeping in the service of arguments about their own distinction, resembling neither the women they live among nor the readers of their books. As we shall see, Custer's text is shot through with imagery of herself, Armstrong, and his men as a "jolly family," engaging in a range of domestic and leisure activities in a vast open landscape that is figured as their personal playground and expansive home.

In contrast to Sandoz, who totted up a scrapbook of rejection slips before her first book, *Old Jules*, was finally accepted for publication after winning the *Atlantic Monthly*'s 1935 nonfiction award, Custer's best-selling authorship was precipitous. Counseled by influential friends to write a book about her private life with her husband, she had a publisher in hand before she began the first volume, and none other than Mark Twain spearheaded the publication of the second. Yet, although she had not previously had evident authorial ambition, she had long been an assiduous writer. For her ninth birthday her father gave her a journal in which to record events and thoughts; Sandoz was the same age when she finally began attending school over her father's objections. The gift launched a lifetime of dedicated journal keeping and prolific correspondence. As preparation for writing *Boots and Saddles*, Custer reviewed the many letters she and Armstrong had exchanged during their months apart. "Writing of him taxes my every breath," she lamented, as it forced her to call up buried memories.[8] But it was a technical struggle, too, as she sought to "so frame a little story of his home life that anyone would be willing to read."[9]

Armstrong's first biographer, Frederick Whittaker, urged her to "talk on paper as you talk viva voce," promising that should she do so, she'd "conquer all mankind."[10] Proving him right, reviewers lauded her books for their natural, unstudied prose.[11] However, speaking to the diligent industry that produced her vaunted artlessness, *Boots and Saddles* hints that collaborative marital narratives may have predated her memoirs and that the practice of transcribing Custer tales had its roots in the literary enterprise of Armstrong himself. In a chapter titled "General Custer's Literary Work," Custer explains that he needed her by his side as he composed the "pen pictures" that eventually made up his autobiography, *My Life on the Plains*, and we learn that he was commended for writing as he talked.[12] Recounting the rumor that it was actually she who wrote the "pen pictures," she rather coyly explains that the belief stemmed from her retelling of those same stories at parties.[13] (For that matter, Whittaker, too, drew upon her oral accounts to write *A Complete Life of George A. Custer* [1876]; no wonder he knew their value.) The explanation is couched in such a way that she does not actually deny writing them, and in any case it establishes her as the producer if not the inscriber of the book's tales, shaping the events of Armstrong's life into narrative form.

Boots and Saddles is told entirely from Custer's personal vantage point. It opens with the statement, "General Custer graduated at West Point just in time to take part in the battle of Bull Run."[14] A braided summary of his Civil War career and their courtship is economically dispatched in the next five sentences, to conclude with their 1864 wedding. By paragraph two, she has accompanied Armstrong to the front in Virginia, having "begged so hard not to be left behind."[15] She then encapsulates the span of their marriage in a single line: "It was a sudden plunge into a life of vicissitude and danger, and I hardly remember the time during the twelve years that followed when I was not in fear of some immediate peril, or in dread of some danger."[16]

The next paragraph even more succinctly summarizes seven years of postings in Texas, Michigan, Kansas, and Kentucky. A closer narration of the book's titular subject then ensues—the couple's shared "Life in Dakota." Custer sustains throughout its length the twinned focus with which it opens, asking readers to view Armstrong's military activities and their married life in tandem. She references real hardship and danger: blizzards, the threat of Indian ambush and siege, and her peculiarly vulnerable position as a woman for whom the troops have agreed to choose death over enemy capture. She also effectively conveys her unrelenting anxiety about separation from her husband—her motive for accompanying him whenever she could. Yet, all this notwithstanding, the book's prevailing atmosphere is one of intimacy, play, and delight. She can make it hard to remember that she travels with an army engaged in military campaigns, even as the power and tension of the text lies in the reader's knowledge about the outcome—never narrated and only occasionally referenced—to which all this vitality is leading.

Custer portrays Armstrong as enchantingly, incorrigibly boyish, despite always referring to him as "General." His perpetual register is one of joyous high spirits, reveling in his robust health, adored wife, generous leadership, and most especially the liberty and vigor of a rugged outdoor existence. Custer insists, "A true cavalryman feels that a life in the saddle on the free open plain is his legitimate existence."[17] Midway through the book, as a complement to its frontispiece portrait, she describes his arresting looks, the iconic "golden" hair, "clear blue" eyes, "tawny" mustache, and lithe physique.[18] In reference to his horsemanship, she continues, "His body was so lightly poised and so full of swinging, undulating, motion, it almost seemed that the wind moved him as it blew over the plain. Yet every nerve was alert and like finely tempered steel, for the muscles and sinews that seemed so pliable were equal to the curbing of the most fiery animal."[19]

According to *Boots and Saddles,* Armstrong is as adept and commanding as a husband as he is as a rider. At every turn Custer shows him lifting, carrying, reassuring, and teasing her, as well as counseling her to curb her emotions and suppress her desires. Just like his equestrian feats, this perfect marital union is enacted in a vast wild landscape that—pending the elimination of any residual Native claims—is theirs for the taking. Ranging across the Great Plains, Custer frames their love affair as inseparable from the nation's bid to command the sweeping western spaces in which it unfolds.

In a private letter, she wrote of having wished to bring Armstrong "before his people in his private life—as a Son—a brother a husband."[20] In order to do so, she offered up a "little book" comprising views of "the domestic life of an army family."[21] Of interest here is the vagueness of the term "army family." Just whom does it include?

The Seventh Cavalry was renowned for its tight-knit "Custer Clan"; Armstrong served and traveled in Dakota with a remarkably large number of family members, by both blood and marriage. His brother Thomas was an officer; their younger brother Boston worked as a contractor; their sister's husband, James Calhoun, was another officer. Like Elizabeth Bacon Custer, Margaret Custer Calhoun traveled with the regiment. Armstrong's young nephew James Reed volunteered his services, and Custer recounts that when he joined them at Fort Lincoln he was accompanied by his sister, Emma. Fellow officers, moreover, included close friends with whom Armstrong had long histories. Custer enthusiasts debate whether this preponderance contributed to the debacle: the familial affection of intimates—or, in another light, the subservience of sycophants—made them unlikely to question Armstrong's decisions even as their presence bred jealousy and conflict in the unit.[22]

The extended family included an African American woman, Mary, who worked as a cook and whom Custer identified as an influential member of the household; her two sisters later joined their staff. Adding to the family group was a young woman described as "our girlfriend," a friend from Michigan whom the couple had persuaded to join them in Dakota. "After long debates with her parents," Custer explains, "we had captured a young lady"; the men purportedly viewed her as "the daughter of the regiment."[23] Their pack of forty dogs swelled their numbers, as did Armstrong's more varied menagerie, which included "mocking-birds and canaries" and a tamed mouse. Most cherished are the horses, for which the cavalrymen steal food "as a mother would for a starving child."[24]

This is already a capacious understanding of family, driven in part, we might conjecture, by Custer's self-identification as an orphan.[25] Yet she leans on the concept even harder to make "our family" encompass every individual present—not just the officers but also the enlisted men, scouts, servants, and camp followers. It is seldom clear when her invocations of "our family" refer to the inner circle of relatives and when they refer to a larger group. "We were all like one family," she insists, accounting for the slippage in her usage. "Every one was so quick to sympathize, so ready to act if trouble came."[26]

In accord with this metaphor, the text is saturated with home activities—scenes of packing, cooking, sewing, and nursing, as well as dinners, picnics, and balls. Of their residency at Fort Lincoln, she reveals, "There were about forty in our garrison circle, and as we were very harmonious we spent nearly every evening together."[27] The tenor of these scenes is not just harmonious but jocund. Sounding a consistent note of hilarity, the text references the group's "continual chaffing and innumerable practical jokes," "incessant jokes," and "inexhaustible jokes."[28] "To joke before daylight seems impossible," Custer states, "but even at breakfast peals of laughter went up."[29] The assembly were "all jolly, all good-humored, full of their jokes," "almost too tired with the laughter," "exhausted with laughter," releasing an "endless flow of laughter" and "loud cries of laughter," even "choked with laughter."[30] This portrait of excessive mirth, which quickly strains credulity, lends the text an almost hysterical quality.

"The general, bubbling over with fun," is the merriest prankster of them all.[31] However, he is also figured as a solicitous, principled, selfless father. Despite their youth, the Custers adopt paternal and maternal roles with the enlisted men, on account of the authority of the one and the singularity of the other. The men, in their turn, appear eager to accept them as such. One would never know, from reading *Boots and Saddles*, that many immigrants (with conflicting interests) composed their number and that Armstrong was dismayed about the ragtag nature of his Indian Wars troops in comparison to the professional soldiers who had served under him during the Civil War.[32]

To support the well-being of that extended family, Armstrong is routinely shown to make personal sacrifices. Custer economically portrays his selflessness with a trivial incident: passing on a precious dish of strawberries to a surprise visitor. Her disappointment still palpable, she recounts, "I was only conscious of the fact that having been denied them all these years, he had, after all, lost his only strawberry feast."[33] He gave over his salary to "entertainments" for the garrison.[34] Insisting that "our house should belong to every one" and "be open at all hours," Armstrong even maintained that the wife of the commanding officer "belonged to every one."[35] He chastised her if she indulged in gossip, and together they worried about the enlisted men's "condition"—the state of their souls.[36] According to this presentation of his character, it is inconceivable that he would have jeopardized his men in a quest for personal glory, as detractors such as Sandoz maintained.

Continuing the hyperbole, Custer shows her husband to be not only the most high-spirited but also the most domestically adroit among them, tendering countless examples. He has "a peculiar gift for starting a fire on the wildest day."[37] He nurses sick dogs, sometimes taking them into the marital bed. During the winter, he sketches, tutors children, tends the orchard, and reads to her "constantly."[38] He plays billiards not with other officers but with her, at a table installed in their house. He also applies himself to repairing their "Rogers statuettes," the mass-produced plaster figurines that by the late nineteenth century had become ubiquitous in middle-class American parlors.[39]

The other men share his domestic proclivities if not his skill, and they readily take on household duties to relieve the overburdened women. We see, for example, a soldier volunteering to nurse a sick child, and Tom Custer—"the quintessence then of every thing military and manly"—learning to use a sewing machine to make children's clothing.[40] Such tendencies are most consistently expressed in the tender care of their wives. Custer states, "I wonder if it will seem that we were foolishly petted if I reveal that our husbands buttoned our shoes, wrapped us up if we went out, warmed our clothes before the fire, poured the water for our bath out of the heavy pitcher, and studied to do innumerable little services that a maid would have done for us in the States."[41]

Implying that men who would serve as women's "willing subjects" and treat them like "such queens" must be pursuing a just cause, her affirmations are closely entwined with her denigrating remarks about Native American gender roles and home customs.[42] The one time an officer is shown mistreating his wife, the group consensus is that "nothing but a long life among the Indians, and having the treatment of the squaw before him, would cause a man to act with such brutality."[43] Deploying the widespread stereotype of Indian women as drudges, Custer insists that they are excluded from "any but the most menial services" and that an Indian wife is her husband's "faithful slave."[44] More important, in figuring them as probable rapists of female captives, she presents Native men as potent threats to the purity of white women that girds the group's family harmony.

Consistent with Custer's emphasis on men and women's relationships, the last sight of the cavalrymen is their marching out to the tune of "The Girl I Left behind Me," and her narrative concludes with the shocked new widows mourning their loss. She leaves the Little Bighorn battle itself unrepresented, along with the circumstances and events leading up to it. The foremost reason for this choice is surely that the subject was personally harrowing. However, it also aligns with her practice of speaking only from personal experience rather than imagining unseen events or entering into the consciousness of others. Custer's authority came from her presence, reporting on what she saw and felt. Her publishers appended what they termed a "very brief outline" of the battle.[45] This outline is followed by a selection of personal letters that Armstrong sent Custer during their intervals apart. The consequence is that to the last, their relationship is the focus of the book.

Poignant as Custer's memoirs may be to many readers, Sandoz's book helps us see their insidiousness by undoing many of the putatively natural assumptions upon which they rest. *The Battle of the Little Bighorn* begins at the exact point at which *Boots and Saddles* ends, with Custer's Seventh Cavalry departing for its last campaign. Covering a much briefer time span but loaded with factual detail, it is a far denser, more challenging read. The highly visual account proceeds with deliberation, closely describing the landscape and the men who move through it and cycling through their perspectives. In addition to the narrative of events, it includes a "Résumé" that expostulates on them, plus an appendix, maps, an index, and a "Selected Bibliography for the General Reader," which includes *Boots and Saddles.*

Although historians do not accept all of Sandoz's assertions and interpretations, her scholarly rigor, attention to detail, and acumen are on display throughout the text of *The Battle of the Little Bighorn.* Like many of her books, it straddles the line between history and fiction. Such generic indeterminacy can feel unsettling, and it contributes to the relatively small amount of attention that has been accorded her considerable oeuvre. Not only her novels but also her historical studies include invented dialogue, scenes, and even entire episodes to dramatize their claims. "Sandoz concentrated on producing vivid narratives and clear perspectives, even if she had to distort or 'create' the past to do it," Betsy Downey explains, arguing that Sandoz deployed an "unconventional methodology that poses difficulties both for professional historians and casual readers."[46] Moreover, even as historians take issue with the fictional qualities of her texts, their subject matter can cause literary critics to hesitate, perhaps daunted by a wealth of historical material and analysis that seems to speak for itself.

Sandoz never mentions Elizabeth Bacon Custer's books, but the opening paragraph of *The Battle of the Little Bighorn* recollects the Custer volume with an evocative rendition of the bugle call from which it takes its name: "Off below, at the bivouac of the 7th Cavalry, the trumpets sounded 'Boots and Saddles,' the call thin and fading but golden against the wind."[47] Sandoz's choice not to respond directly to Custer's various claims has its own implications, suggesting a lack of engagement with an unworthy predecessor. She undermines, moreover, any of Custer's lingering authority as a chronicler of the regiment by making her an inconsequential character in the book. "Mrs. Custer" appears only in the Résumé, first with several other women who "come out with picnic hamper and camping equipment" to say good-bye to their husbands and shortly thereafter as a deceived wife.[48] Describing one of Armstrong's last letters to his wife, Sandoz states that he outright lied in boasting that he and his men were the first non-Natives to enter the territory from which he wrote. The general "knew better," she states. "Still, it is a revealing remark from the man who could never bear to be second."[49] There is a double sting, showing both that he lied and that he lied to his wife. The letter is one of those that Custer includes in *Boots and Saddles*, edited to open with the same statement that Sandoz pointedly debunks: "We are now in a country heretofore unvisited by white men."[50]

In her earlier work *Cheyenne Autumn*, which portrays the Northern Cheyenne tribe's thwarted efforts to return to their homeland, Sandoz destroys any illusion of the Custers' perfect marriage by referencing Armstrong's sexual relationship with a Cheyenne captive, Monahsetah, and the son she believed they had together (a theory that has since been disproven). She represents the relationship as common knowledge and as managed in order to deceive Elizabeth: "When Custer's wife was coming to him, the Cheyenne girl was sent back to the Indians, where this son was born toward the autumn moon."[51] *The Battle of the Little Bighorn*, in contrast, makes no effort to impugn Armstrong's personal life, according it not a mote of attention. Rather, it seeks to demonstrate that his regiment was far from the "jolly family" headed by the solicitous fatherly figure that Custer conjures. Riddled with distrust and infighting, Sandoz's version of the Seventh Cavalry is commanded by a reckless man who relentlessly pursues his political ambitions at the expense of his men's lives. Sandoz explains that the termination of the Civil War resulted in "further intensification on the only remaining field of conflict—the rivalry for officerships in the shrinking army and the necessity to keep the Indians stirred up not only for war profits for the manufacturers and contractors but to advance the careers of the military."[52] She continues, "The Plains had become a gaming field, a hunting ground for military trophies."[53] Consequently, military commanders routinely ignored their superiors' orders so as to pursue Native foes. As examples of this "customary disobedience," Sandoz alludes to William Fetterman's disastrous choices in 1866.[54] Those decisions resulted in an ambush by Crazy Horse and his warriors that killed all the men under Fetterman's command, as well as Joseph Reynolds's 1876 attack on a Northern Cheyenne and

Oglala Lakota Sioux village. George Armstrong Custer's decision to divide his force into three smaller units is in line with these precedents, motivated by his desire not to allow others to "share in any victory."[55]

These deadly games and high-stakes trophies are very unlike the lighthearted activities on display in the liberating plains landscape of *Boots and Saddles*—gleeful outings, riotous pranks, and the harvesting of women-pleasing curios, including "skins, specimens of gold and mica, and petrified shells of iridescent colors, snake rattles, pressed flowers, and petrified wood."[56] A more important difference is that for all the pretty relics it yields, the land appears in Custer's text as both featureless and unstoried. *Boots and Saddles* replicates a widespread conception of the Great Plains as the Great American Desert, void of meaningful human activity. Almost literally a blank slate, it offers nothing to read.

In contrast, throughout Sandoz's book we see men interpreting this territory, both the white soldiers and even more so the Indian scouts, as they search out the tracks and traces of residents and travelers. Neither empty playground nor setting for fantastic domestic life, the Great Plains as rendered by Sandoz is shown to be a thickly inhabited and closely mapped landscape. She draws on both her research and her cultural empathy in describing the places where the narrated events occur, as when she shows the cavalry cresting "the sacred hill of the wild peas" to begin an attack. Adopting the perspective of the women who sounded the alarm, Sandoz recounts,

> Troopers were riding over the little hill that was all in bloom, the recumbent loco weed like a painted robe under the feet—white, pale pink and lavender, rose, vivid magenta, and deepest purple. The long row of bluecoats on sorrel horses, and gray and brown, was crushing the flowers into the gravel—flowers that had always ripened to a mat of buffalo beans for the women to gather and boil in the meat kettles. Now enemies rode there on the hill of peace, come against them in plain daylight, coming along the pretty hill that had never shielded anything larger than the ant

and the little gray jumping mouse, the horses cutting the bloom with their iron hoofs, their manure defiling the sacred place where youths went for their puberty dreams.[57]

As we have seen, *Boots and Saddles* masks the political nature of Custer's work to depict his relationship to his troops as paternal and their joint endeavor as domestic. The Seventh Cavalry is rendered an extended family and the Great Plains, its expansive home. Sandoz exposes this fiction. In her book, Armstrong appears driven by hubris, which leads to disastrous decisions and the sacrifice of his men. Her theory is that the debacle was the direct outcome of his presidential ambition. He knew that "the nation gave the presidency" to commanders who won wars.[58]

While the nature of Sandoz's claims about George Armstrong Custer is self-evident in her book, the narrative ways that she advances them are far less so. The following brief reading of the first chapter calls attention to Sandoz's literary strategies and devices. She destroys the illusion of the assembly as family by entering into the consciousness of a range of people (officers, enlisted men, and Native scouts) with differing beliefs and goals. In addition to presenting him as one actor, albeit the most influential, among many, she further displaces him by limiting access to his interiority. Whereas readers know what many other participants thought, felt, knew, wanted, or feared, our primary access to Custer's reasoning and emotion comes from these other men's insights. This choice has the effect of emptying the book of him. Sandoz renders the man oddly elusive and remote, even as she chronicles the chain of events and crushing outcome that his choices precipitated.

The epigraph to *The Battle of the Little Bighorn*, quoting the Oglala Sioux chief Low Dog, signals Sandoz's project of radically reorienting the narrative perspective: "I did not think it possible that any white men would attack us, so strong as we were." The cinematic opening chapter then dramatizes the regiment's departure from Fort Lincoln, Custer's announcement of his decision to expand the scouting expedition into an active campaign, and the uneasy night the men pass as they digest the implications. The first person to speak within the narrative is also Native, in this case an ally, predicting that their foes would be trapped between General Alfred Terry's and Custer's forces—but with his certitude undermined by the phrase "his eyes looking far away as he spoke."[59] Only then do we hear Custer, replying to infantry leader John Gibbon's only half-joking enjoinder, "Now, Custer, don't be greedy. Wait for us!" The indeterminacy of Custer's answer is magnified by the "very slight" stammer with which it is uttered: "No! . . . I-I won't!" Sandoz states that "the ambiguity" was "left hanging like a puff of pipe smoke over the shoulder as he galloped off."[60]

The scene that follows, in which he announces "his frank determination upon a personal Indian chase even as far as Nebraska," takes place in a setting familiar to readers of *Boots and Saddles*: within Custer's private tent.[61] "The men settled around the commander's bed, everyone there from Major Reno down to the greenest second lieutenant," with Custer "flanked" by his brother Tom and his brother-in-law, his other brother and nephew "to the side," and "his favorites around him."[62] He angrily confronts the officers for privately questioning his decisions and, "his stammer more evident," orders them to desist.[63] The response is "a moment of embarrassed silence among the men not of Custer's family or favor."[64] With this scene of dismay and dissent, Sandoz rends Elizabeth Custer's portrait by showing just how many stood outside his inner circle.

Throughout the succeeding narrative Sandoz keeps the focus on the perspectives of these outsiders. As readers, we are offered views of what they thought, felt, and desired. Their knowledge is cataloged, from ranking officers to enlisted men to scouts: all that General Terry "had seen," "knew," and "understood," what "every old-timer . . . knew," what "surely the Ree [Arikaras] . . . knew," what "some of the more observant noted."[65] The Indian scouts "burned to take up the chase" on sighting game—a small detail, but one that validates their emotion.[66] Sandoz also shows the diverse responses to Custer's decision. Uneasy at what they can see but their leader cannot, some men made their wills, a few desert, and the scout Bloody Knife gets drunk, "perhaps because the load of this knowledge . . . was too heavy."[67]

In accord with this emphasis, access to Custer's emotional state usually comes only through these men's interpretations: "To the older campaigners, Custer seemed less elated"; "there seemed unease about him"; and, finally, he was "apparently full of apprehension."[68] Our deepest look into his psyche comes from their intimation of this former hero's desperation: "There were some here on the Rosebud who realized that Custer must feel trapped in the confining dimensions of the scout laid out for him, as trapped as a great winged eagle forced into a cage, making wild and desperate thrusts against the confining bars."[69] One of the youngest officers concludes, "I believe General Custer is going to be killed."[70] This moody, perverse, and ultimately unknowable figure is utterly unlike Elizabeth Bacon Custer's merry boy.

The odd absence of Custer's perceiving mind from Sandoz's text accords with his inability to register the signs clearly legible to everyone else, especially the abundance of physical evidence of an unprecedented Native gathering far too large for his unit to take on. It is also in accord with his imperviousness to his companions' observations and insights, "his ears closed to the warnings."[71] In the text, different men are shown to have different situational reading abilities, and Custer is the worst reader of them all.

Mari Sandoz's *The Battle of the Little Bighorn* reads as both a continuation and a rebuttal of Elizabeth Bacon Custer's portrait of Armstrong, razing the legend that she had done so much to fix in the national imagination. Instead of a principled, self-sacrificing hero, the man Sandoz presents is one driven by personal ambition. Instead of depicting his "jolly family," Sandoz offers snapshots of those "not of Custer's family or favor" and details their competing interests. Finally, she denies the man full interiority, choosing not to grant the same access to his thoughts and emotions that she provides for a host of minor characters, whose views from within are displayed. Whereas almost every page of Custer's memoir lauds her husband, in *The Battle of the Little Bighorn* he becomes curiously unimportant. George Armstrong Custer is neither the protagonist nor the antagonist of Sandoz's book. Its text instead showcases the geographical and cultural arena where the events unfold, seeming far more attuned to the land's traits and those of its Native inhabitants than to Custer's. With this emphasis, Sandoz shows that what really matters are not the motives and character of this particular military officer—one among countless others—but the places for which the Lakota, Northern Cheyenne, Oglala, and Arapaho people fought. She thereby refutes the legacies of both Custers, Armstrong and Elizabeth alike.

NOTES

Epigraph: From the J. B. Lippincott edition (1966), 18, 16.

1. Shirley A. Leckie, *Elizabeth Bacon Custer and the Making of a Myth* (Norman: University of Oklahoma Press, 1993), xx.
2. Leckie, *Elizabeth Bacon Custer*, 242.
3. Mari Sandoz, *The Battle of the Little Bighorn* (Philadelphia: J. B. Lippincott, 1966), 178.
4. Paul Andrew Hutton, "Libbie Custer: 'A Wounded Thing Must Hide,'" HistoryNet, August 16, 2017, https://www.historynet.com/libbie-custer-wounded-thing-must-hide/.
5. "Elizabeth Clift [Bacon] Custer (1842–1933)," Mandan Historical Society, accessed March 24, 2024, http://www.mandanhistory.org/biographiesac/elizabethcuster.html; Hutton, "Libbie Custer"; Brian Dippie, *Custer's Last Stand: The Anatomy of an American Myth* (Lincoln: University of Nebraska Press, 1994), 65.
6. Louis Kraft, "George Armstrong Custer: Changing Views of an American Legend," HistoryNet, September 1, 2006, https://www.historynet.com/george-armstrong-custer-changing-views-of-an-american-legend/; Leckie, *Elizabeth Bacon Custer*, viii.
7. Amanda Healy, "Loving Empire: Intimacy and Expansion in U.S. Women's Historical Writing, 1880–1900" (PhD diss., University of Michigan, 2018), 107.
8. Quoted in Leckie, *Elizabeth Bacon Custer*, 242.
9. Quoted in Leckie, *Elizabeth Bacon Custer*, 235.

10. Quoted in Leckie, *Elizabeth Bacon Custer*, 231.
11. Healy, "Loving Empire," 98–99.
12. Elizabeth Bacon Custer, *Boots and Saddles, or, Life in Dakota with General Custer* (New York: Harper & Brothers, 1885), 150.
13. Custer, *Boots and Saddles*, 153.
14. Custer, *Boots and Saddles*, 9.
15. Custer, *Boots and Saddles*, 10.
16. Custer, *Boots and Saddles*, 10.
17. Custer, *Boots and Saddles*, 11.
18. Custer, *Boots and Saddles*, 107–8.
19. Custer, *Boots and Saddles*, 108.
20. Quoted in Leckie, *Elizabeth Bacon Custer*, 231.
21. Custer, *Boots and Saddles*, 5.
22. "Nepotism in the Custer Clan: Battle Consequences," Little Bighorn History Alliance, online discussion, March 13–17, 2006, https://lbha.proboards.com/thread/511/nepotism-custer-clan-battle-consequences.
23. Custer, *Boots and Saddles*, 95, 118.
24. Custer, *Boots and Saddles*, 130.
25. Custer, *Boots and Saddles*, 122.
26. Custer, *Boots and Saddles*, 125.
27. Custer, *Boots and Saddles*, 139.
28. Custer, *Boots and Saddles*, 221, 233, 141.
29. Custer, *Boots and Saddles*, 38.
30. Custer, *Boots and Saddles*, 276, 12, 53, 244, 84, 52.
31. Custer, *Boots and Saddles*, 119.
32. Kraft, "George Armstrong Custer."
33. Custer, *Boots and Saddles*, 173.
34. Custer, *Boots and Saddles*, 128.
35. Custer, *Boots and Saddles*, 174, 144, 139.
36. Custer, *Boots and Saddles*, 248.
37. Custer, *Boots and Saddles*, 41.
38. Custer, *Boots and Saddles*, 145.
39. Custer, *Boots and Saddles*, 177.
40. Custer, *Boots and Saddles*, 125.
41. Custer, *Boots and Saddles*, 126.
42. Custer, *Boots and Saddles*, 130.
43. Custer, *Boots and Saddles*, 127.

44. Custer, *Boots and Saddles*, 236.
45. Custer, *Boots and Saddles*, 269.
46. Betsy Downey, "'She Does Not Write Like a Historian': Mari Sandoz and the Old and New Western History," *Great Plains Quarterly* 16, no. 1 (Winter 1996): 11.
47. Sandoz, *Battle of the Little Bighorn*, 13.
48. Sandoz, *Battle of the Little Bighorn*, 179.
49. Sandoz, *Battle of the Little Bighorn*, 179.
50. Custer, *Boots and Saddles*, 309; Sandoz, *Battle of the Little Bighorn*, 308.
51. Mari Sandoz, *Cheyenne Autumn* (1953; Lincoln: University of Nebraska Press, 2005), 21.
52. Sandoz, *Battle of the Little Bighorn*, 174.
53. Sandoz, *Battle of the Little Bighorn*, 174.
54. Sandoz, *Battle of the Little Bighorn*, 175.
55. Sandoz, *Battle of the Little Bighorn*, 176.
56. Custer, *Boots and Saddles*, 193.
57. Sandoz, *Battle of the Little Bighorn*, 116.
58. Sandoz, *Battle of the Little Bighorn*, 182.
59. Sandoz, *Battle of the Little Bighorn*, 7, 16.
60. Sandoz, *Battle of the Little Bighorn*, 16.
61. Sandoz, *Battle of the Little Bighorn*, 21.
62. Sandoz, *Battle of the Little Bighorn*, 18.
63. Sandoz, *Battle of the Little Bighorn*, 19.
64. Sandoz, *Battle of the Little Bighorn*, 20.
65. Sandoz, *Battle of the Little Bighorn*, 24, 33.
66. Sandoz, *Battle of the Little Bighorn*, 17.
67. Sandoz, *Battle of the Little Bighorn*, 31.
68. Sandoz, *Battle of the Little Bighorn*, 19, 25.
69. Sandoz, *Battle of the Little Bighorn*, 21–22.
70. Sandoz, *Battle of the Little Bighorn*, 22.
71. Sandoz, *Battle of the Little Bighorn*, 34.

4

Recentering Custer

Mari Sandoz and the Battle of the Little Bighorn

TAYLOR G. HENSEL

Once more the men before him moved in uneasiness, puzzled, particularly those who understood the accumulated desperation of the last few months and realized that the coming glories of this centennial summer, this 100th celebration of the Declaration of Independence, promised no shining place in the nation's finest show for George Armstrong Custer. The image of the adored young hero of 1862 and 1868 was now, in 1876, so tarnished that Custer could be ordered to go smell out Indians for the success of Terry and even Gibbon. There were some here on the Rosebud who realized that Custer must feel trapped in the confining dimensions of the scout laid out for him, . . . as trapped as a great winged eagle forced into a cage, making wild and desperate thrusts against the confining bars, breaking plumage, talons, and beak.
—Mari Sandoz, *The Battle of the Little Bighorn*

In 1970 the film *Little Big Man* arrived in theaters around the country. Based upon author Thomas Berger's 1964 novel of the same name and directed by Arthur Penn, the film features as the protagonist a white man, raised by the Cheyenne Nation, who stumbles into and rides along with the Seventh Cavalry during their last hurrah almost by accident. *Little Big Man*, released at the height of the Vietnam War, suggests in many ways that Custer's behavior in the film as well as the film's depiction of historical incidents such as the Washita Massacre have more to do with the U.S. military's interventionism in Southeast Asia than they do with actual western history.[1]

The film and its source material are both wildly entertaining and iconoclastic, and what they lack in historical accuracy they make up for in purpose, that purpose being to present a far different image of Custer, westward expansion, American Indians, and Manifest Destiny than had previously been depicted. However, while *Little Big Man*, both in its cinematic and in its literary form, is often credited as the first mainstream work of art to tackle these themes and concepts from a more critical perspective, it is far from the first. Nebraska historian Mari Sandoz, daughter of a high plains pioneer and friend of many aging Indigenous participants in the Little Bighorn, chose to approach the events of June 25–26, 1876, from a far different perspective. In 1966 Sandoz published her book *The Battle of the Little Bighorn*, a slim yet important volume that, when coupled with Berger's 1964 novel, reframed Custer within the context of westward expansion. By viewing the events of the Little Bighorn campaign through a more critical lens and attempting to tell the story of the battle from the perspective of Indigenous combatants, Sandoz presented a military account of the "Last Stand" that portrayed it less as a tragic American defeat and more as a triumphant and inevitable Native victory.

Sandoz was uniquely equipped to tell this story. Born in 1896 along the Niobrara River in western Nebraska, she was the daughter of Jules Sandoz, a northern plains pioneer who served as the subject of Sandoz's first book, *Old Jules*, published in 1935. *Old Jules* was a very different kind of western history book than those that had been published in the early twentieth century. Most biographies of frontier personalities favored picturesque, heavily romanticized figures like Billy the Kid, Wyatt Earp, and indeed, George Armstrong Custer. However, Sandoz took her own experiences as well as firsthand accounts of people who had known her father and crafted a richly detailed and brutal story about an often unlikable man who was just as rough-hewn and unforgiving as the land he helped colonize. Woven into Sandoz's biography of her father, with whom she had a very complicated relationship, are stories of the cowboys, fur trappers, cattlemen, and the Indigenous peoples of the northern plains. *Old Jules* was very well received by the western history community, laying the groundwork for Sandoz's career while foreshadowing the type of historian Sandoz would become: a meticulous researcher concerned with narrative voice, the preservation of oral history, and authenticity in her writing.

As a historian of Euro-American descent, Sandoz deserves praise for the uncommonly nuanced and sympathetic way in which she wrote about the Native community, specifically those tribes living on the northern plains during her childhood. Rather than portray members of the Lakota and Cheyenne nations as ignorant savages, as was the norm within the grand white-centric narrative of westward expansion, Sandoz depicted them as the kind, thoughtful, and soft-spoken people she had known growing up on the Sandoz homestead, not far from the Pine Ridge Reservation in South Dakota. By giving credence and legitimacy to the oral traditions of Indigenous peoples, Sandoz's books acted as a counterbalance to the traditional, colonization-trumpeting narrative that so dominated scholarship about the American West in the early to mid-twentieth century.

Sandoz's ability to write about Native men and women with dimensionality and pathos was noticed by the Indigenous community itself. In his introduction to the third edition of her classic biography *Crazy Horse: The Strange Man of the Oglalas,* Lakota historian and activist Vine Deloria Jr., one of the key influencers of the American Indian Movement during the 1960s and 1970s, praises Sandoz's portrayal of his people. According to Deloria, "I doubt if anyone else could tell the life of Crazy Horse as well as Sandoz does. She must have known many Sioux people during her formative years, and memories of those people must have come flooding back when she began writing. How else can we explain nuances that only a few would know and understand?"[2]

Deloria accurately acknowledges that Sandoz knew "many Sioux people" during her childhood. These early interactions formed her ability to write about the northern plains Indigenous peoples as her career progressed. In her preface to *Crazy Horse*, Sandoz reflects upon a powerful interaction with a Brule Lakota elder. According to Sandoz, there was "an old man among them [who] noticed me sneak up to listen. Reaching out, he took my hand and walked beside me to the top of the ridge above our house. There he shaded his whitish, fading eyes and looked slowly all up and down the river valley and the bluffs and ridges along our side, making a few low Sioux words, annoyed words, his grandson told me, over the white man's way of changing the face of the earth."[3] Her recollection illustrates an experience that formed Sandoz's unique understanding of westward expansion. To Sandoz, Manifest Destiny was not a bold and exciting tale of hardy and stalwart pioneers conquering an unforgiving wilderness and its backward peoples. Through her interactions with the Lakotas, she understood it as a violent and aggressive action, a complicated and often horrifically brutal colonization of an already inhabited land upon which people had been living with relative success for over a millennium.

In 1930, while researching *Crazy Horse* with fellow cultural historian Eleanor Hinman in 1930, Sandoz interviewed Lakota elders Red Feather, Little Killer, Short Bull, and "particularly He Dog, [Crazy Horse's] lifelong brother-friend." Sandoz's ability to connect with the Lakota community is evidenced by He Dog's apparent fondness for her. The last time she saw He Dog, Sandoz writes, "was in a thundershower in 1931. It delighted the blind old man to pretend that I had brought the rain. 'You will see me again in the dry time, my granddaughter?' he asked. 'Your step is good for the ears of an old man.'"[4] Such a plain statement of affection naturally moved Sandoz, and her own deep compassion for Native peoples is on vivid display in her writing.

The Lakota community's positive regard for Sandoz's writing continues to this day. It is not a coincidence that *Crazy Horse* is the only biography penned by a non-Indigenous writer recommended as further reading by Lakota historian Joseph M. Marshall III in his own book about the warrior.[5] First published in 1942, Sandoz's *Crazy Horse* hit bookstores at a time when it was highly unusual to see an account of the American West told from the Indigenous perspective, albeit one filtered through the narrative voice of a white historian. Nevertheless, the most unique aspect of *Crazy Horse* was that this was not the story of just *any* Lakota warrior; it was the life story of the man many readers familiar with the American West held responsible for the death of George Armstrong Custer.

"General George Armstrong Custer! His name reverberates like the clang of a sword!" writes Evan S. Connell in his 1984 book *Son of the Morning Star: Custer and the Little Bighorn*.[6] With this ringing rhetoric Connell taps into the mystique of the "Boy General"; the very sound of the name conjures images of guidons flapping in the summer breeze of a Montana afternoon, of sabers rattling and cavalrymen charging, of last stands and glorious tragedy. For decades leading up to the cultural shift of the 1960s, George Armstrong Custer was not a particularly controversial figure at all, at least to the broader American public. That "the General," as he was frequently referred to both in his own lifetime and after, was a tragic hero undone by the incompetency of his fellow commanding officers and the impossible odds stacked against him was common knowledge. According to scholar Michael A. Elliott, Custer's defeat was key to his remembrance as a tragic hero. As Elliott writes in his 2007 book *Custerology: The Enduring Legacy of the Indian Wars and George Armstrong Custer*, "the General" emerged from the Little Bighorn as "a martyr of the long march of civilization toward its ultimate dominion over the earth. If Custer had led his Seventh Cavalry to victory in Montana, he would now be as well remembered as his contemporaries Nelson Miles, George Crook, John Gibbon— hardly household names. Instead, the soldiers of Custer's Seventh Cavalry were treated as descendants of the Spartans at Thermopylae and of the Texans at the Alamo."[7] Here Elliott correctly illustrates how Custer, to paraphrase Larry McMurtry, "won by losing."[8] From the moment that his naked corpse was found lying on a ridge in Montana Territory known forever after as Last Stand Hill, Custer was a heroic icon who symbolized the type of sacrifices Euro-Americans would have to make in their push to civilize the wild frontier.

One year before the publication of *Crazy Horse*, Warner Bros. released *They Died with Their Boots On*. Directed by Raoul Walsh, the film reveled in a heavily fictionalized account of Custer's life leading up to and including the Little Bighorn battle. Walsh's film features silver screen legend Errol Flynn as Custer, who is portrayed as a dashing and heroic if somewhat reckless cavalier whose skill on the battlefield commands unshakable loyalty from both his men and his beautiful wife, Elizabeth, played by Olivia de Havilland. Depicting Custer as highly sympathetic to the Indigenous peoples he helped dispossess, the film shows him testifying on their behalf before the Supreme Court, arguing that the only reason the Sioux Nation, led by Crazy Horse (Anthony Quinn) feels compelled to go to war is because they have been manipulated by corrupt politicians who faked the Black Hills gold rush to steal Lakota land. Custer then dies a victim of circumstances out of his control, fighting to the last until Crazy Horse leads the final charge. While it is perhaps too optimistic to believe that audiences did not believe that this was the *actual* way events played out, the film's portrayal of Custer is inarguably indicative of what 1940s filmgoers believed Custer to be: flawed, yes, but ultimately a hero who died because he truly believed in what he was fighting for: Manifest Destiny, somehow coupled with the rights of Indigenous peoples.[9]

Such adoration for a man now justifiably associated with the atrocities of colonization was the norm until the civil rights era. Attitudes toward Custer began to change during the 1960s as the civil rights movement expanded. In 1964, ironically the same year that *Little Big Man* was published and two years before Sandoz released *The Battle of the Little Bighorn*, popular country music artist Johnny Cash released *Bitter Tears*, a concept album cowritten with Peter La Farge, telling iconoclastic stories of the American West from the Indigenous perspective. "Custer," a song penned by La Farge, paints a supremely unflattering portrait of George Armstrong, depicting him as a violent and tyrannical bully, an Indian hater who promoted and actively participated in the genocide of Native peoples. The song provides a stinging critique of Custer, with lyrics that taunt the general who "don't ride well anymore."[10] And Cash's insistence on being part Cherokee, coupled with La Farge's claim to be descended from Narragansett people, both unproven, illustrates changing attitudes toward western historical icons as white persons increasingly began to self-identify as Native Americans.

In 1970 Dee Brown published *Bury My Heart at Wounded Knee: An Indian History of the American West,* the same year that the film adaptation of *Little Big Man* arrived in theaters. This scholarly book and popular film broadened recognition that the Battle of the Little Bighorn, or the Battle of the Greasy Grass, as it has always been known to the Indigenous participants, was not a heroic tragedy on the level of Thermopylae, the Alamo, or Wake Island. Instead, it was a glorious victory in which dispossessed Native men, women, and children won the day, while Custer and the Seventh Cavalry essentially got what was coming to them. Leading the vanguard, however, in this new, more Indigenous-centric way of thinking about the battle itself, and Custer in particular, was Mari Sandoz's 1966 book, *The Battle of the Little Bighorn.*

Sandoz sets the tone of her book with an epigraph featuring the words of the Oglala Lakota chief Low Dog. The epigraph reads as follows: "I heard the alarm, but I did not believe it. I thought it was a false alarm. I did not think it possible that any white men would attack us, so strong as we were." According to Sandoz, Low Dog gave this statement in an interview with the *Leavenworth Weekly Times* on August 18, 1881, just over five years after the battle.[11] The significance of this authorial choice cannot be overstated. Prior to Sandoz's book, any text describing the battle would have emphasized the Euro-American point of view. However, by choosing to begin her narrative with the words of an Indigenous participant, Sandoz sends a signal to the reader that while Custer is assuredly the central character of the book, he is less of a protagonist and more of a fulcrum around which the entirety of the text revolves. The true point of view, the people with whom Sandoz wants her audience to identify, are not the cavalrymen riding hell-bent for leather toward the Native encampment but the Lakota, Cheyenne, and Arapaho men waiting for them on the riverbank.

Sandoz begins by introducing her audience to the diverse cast of characters who will dominate the first three-quarters of the book: the men of the Seventh Cavalry, including not just Custer, his brothers Tom and Boston, and their nephew Autie Reed but also six Indigenous scouts of the Crow Nation and Custer's "favorite scout" Bloody Knife, a tracker who had been with Custer since the Yellowstone Expedition of 1873.[12] Bloody Knife in particular is a fascinating character in the study of the Little Bighorn and the events leading up to it. Nearly fifty years old at the time of the battle, Bloody Knife was the son of an Arikara mother and a Hunkpapa Lakota father. Growing up, Bloody Knife's Lakota peers bullied him due to his Arikara heritage. When still a young boy, his mother took him to live with her people; when he returned years later to reconnect with his Lakota relatives, they rejected him. These events caused Bloody Knife to bear a lifelong resentment toward his father's people, a resentment that culminated in him hiring out his talents as a tracker and guide to the U.S. military.[13] Sandoz makes a point of describing Bloody Knife as wearing "white-man shirt and pants," showing the reader that while the scout is Indigenous, he has taken up the trappings of the white people while also leading them against his father's tribe.[14] Sandoz's intention is not to villainize Bloody Knife, yet there is a distinctly anticolonial tone that dominates the book. By characterizing Bloody Knife as a man willing to take on so many trappings of white identity, she suggests that colonization eradicated key aspects of Indigenous identity when the Native individuals chose to work within the system established by white colonizers.

Sandoz also quickly gets to the heart of how she will be portraying George Armstrong Custer himself. Throughout the book, Custer is depicted as an unrepentant egotist, a blindly ambitious, hyperactive megalomaniac who believes that a victory on the Little Bighorn will lead to a presidential nomination from the Democratic Party in the upcoming election. He is open about his goal of claiming all of the glory for himself and thus overshadowing even his higher-ranking fellow officers, such as Colonel John Gibbon. As Custer prepares to lead the Seventh Cavalry away from the banks of the Yellowstone, Sandoz writes, "The colonel clasped the hands held out to him there on the ridge and wheeled his horse to overtake his command. Gibbon called out after him, 'Now Custer, don't be greedy. Wait for us!' Custer lifted his gauntleted hand in acknowledgement. 'No!' he shouted back. 'I-I won't!' his stammer very slight, the ambiguity left hanging like a puff of pipe smoke over the shoulder as he galloped off, the wind whipping the color of his standard behind him."[15] The imagery employed here paints a picture of a man far more concerned with the thought of potential glory than the professional soldier's sense of honor and duty. Previous portrayals of Custer had emphasized the tragic and unavoidable nature of his death, as if, like Leonidas and the three hundred Spartans, they were fated to die on the field of battle that day. At the very least, circumstances outside of Custer's control resulted in his defeat.

In one of the first narrative essays written about the battle, Edward S. Godfrey suggested that three distinct factors lay behind Custer's defeat: "First. The overpowering numbers of the enemy and their unexpected cohesion. Second. Reno's panic route from the valley. Third. The defective extraction of the empty cartridge shells from the carbines."[16] Regarding the possibility that Custer's fate was also sealed when he divided his command, Godfrey concedes that this is possible, but "on the other hand, the whole command might have been wiped out."[17] Ultimately, Godfrey lays the blame primarily on Major Marcus Reno. Godfrey writes, "My studies of the battle of the Little Big Horn leave me in little doubt that had Reno made his charge as ordered, or made a bold front even, the Hostiles would have been so engaged in the bottom that Custer's approach from the Northeast would have been such a surprise as to cause the stampede of the village and would have broken the morale of the warriors."[18] Godfrey, it should be pointed out, was a West Point graduate and Seventh Cavalry veteran, having survived the events of June 25, 1876, only because he had ridden with Major Reno's command rather than Custer's men. Furthermore, Godfrey was an unabashed apologist for Custer, and his views of the fallen commander only became more laudatory with time.[19] Godfrey's assertion that the Seventh Cavalry could have won the day had Major Reno pressed the attack is undermined by the very simple fact that Reno's command very nearly was wiped out as well and was saved only by the intervention of reinforcements led by Captain Frederick Benteen.[20]

Sandoz, on the other hand, has no time for such excuses. Her view of Custer is that he was a talented soldier undone by his own ambition, to such an extent that his constant "go-ahead" attitude costs him, both mentally and physically. While many early fictional and nonfictional portrayals of Custer emphasize the cavalryman's stamina and dashing good looks, Sandoz's Custer is far from a physical specimen, especially in the three days leading up to his death. Sandoz paints a picture of her subject as a man worn down by his ten years serving on the western plains. His face is "wind-burned," the "sockets of his eyes deepened," and he speaks with an evident stammer indicative of his kinetic, excitable personality. Much of his life is performative, especially when the press is around. While Sandoz also describes Custer as "trapped in the confining dimensions of the scout laid out for him, as trapped as a great winged eagle forced into a cage, making wild and desperate thrusts against the confining bars, breaking plumage, talons, and beak," it is clear that Sandoz believes that the general is not on a collision course with fate due to his own ambition.[21]

Sandoz writes that Custer had been thinking about the presidency as far back as 1860, when he was still a West Point cadet, and not a particularly high-achieving one at that. At the very least, the highest office in the land was of keen interest to him. Sandoz includes a portion of a letter young Custer wrote to a friend back in his hometown of New Rumley, Ohio, wherein he states, "'I am satisfied that the [Democratic] party will yet unite on a good man and that man is destined to be the next president.'" Custer had also ridden along in support of President Andrew Johnson on his 1866 rail tour to drum up support for his policies and for his congressional candidate supporters. From the railcar platform, Custer addressed the crowds, which often displayed little enthusiasm for Johnson. Indeed, Sandoz points out that "shrill shouts demanded Grant and Custer instead of the president."[22] Sandoz illustrates that by 1876 Custer had taken this praise to heart, and she suggests that his desire for a presidential nomination is what blinded him to the overwhelming force of Indigenous warriors arrayed against him, a desire expressed to Bloody Knife and his Crow scouts. According to Sandoz,

> Custer told them this was to be his last campaign and so he must win a victory. A victory now, even if only against five or six lodges of the Sioux, would make him the President, the Great Father in Washington, and he must turn back as soon as he had won. He would take Bloody Knife to Washington with him and send him home again in a fine house built for him. All the Ree [Arikara] scouts would have plenty to eat for all time to come. . . .
> "You and all your children he had told them."[23]

From this passage, it is clear to the audience that Custer is trying to transform his goal into reality, believing, as he wrote in an 1860 letter to his hometown friend, that he is the "good man" who can unite the Democratic Party and become the next "Great Father in Washington."

A key aspect to Sandoz's thesis is, essentially, that Custer was less like Leonidas and more like Herman Melville's Captain Ahab, a flawed protagonist obsessed with an unobtainable goal and whose mania drew all close to him into its orbit until it ultimately led to catastrophe. Her view of Custer was undeniably pathbreaking and controversial in 1966, challenging the established understanding of Custer as a doomed tragic hero undone by circumstances beyond his control. Like Ahab, Custer knows what lies ahead of him. He has been warned countless times that the force of Plains Indians warriors that have converged upon the Little Bighorn is too much for him to handle, and yet he refuses to turn back; to do so would mean failure to achieve a self-imposed objective he had evidently held since he was a very young man. Sandoz's Custer is an eagle, trapped, yes, but trapped by *himself*, not the circumstances or the physical environment surrounding him.

Having taken the reader through the three days leading up to the battle, emphasizing the sense of inescapable doom that permeates the command, Sandoz comes to the battle itself. She first narrates the plight of Major Marcus Reno, one of Custer's subordinate officers, who was sent to attack the east end of the giant village on the Little Bighorn. Among writers and historians sympathetic to Custer, Reno is a human jinx, an incompetent coward who basically failed his way upward through the army's ranks until his poor behavior on the battlefield resulted in the death of a national hero and 264 others. However, Sandoz emphasizes that Reno did at the very least try to do his duty during the battle but was overwhelmed by an unprecedented fighting force after practically being abandoned by Custer. Sandoz writes, "Reno glanced back anxiously for Custer, for his support, as he worked the command across the Little Bighorn and out upon the bottoms. [First Lieutenant William] Cooke and [Captain Myles] Keogh were all that was visible of the Custer battalion. They sat their horses, watching awhile. Then they shouted, 'Good luck!' and turned back."[24] The implication is that Custer sent Reno off to attack the village and continued on, hoping that Reno would do his duty with little to no support from Custer's men. From that point on, Sandoz suggests, Reno and his troops were on their own and outnumbered. Her description of Reno's fight at the east end of the village emphasizes Sandoz's sympathies for Reno's battalion.

According to Sandoz, both Reno and Captain Frederick Benteen resented Custer for his treatment of Major Joel Elliott during the Washita Massacre eight years earlier, on November 27, 1868, an event that eerily foreshadowed Custer's behavior at the Little Bighorn. During the Washita Massacre, Major Elliott of the Seventh Cavalry had led several dozen men against the fleeing Southern Cheyennes, allegedly shouting, "Here goes for a brevet or a coffin!" as he did so. When he did not return, Custer refused to organize a rescue party, citing a Southern Cheyenne, Kiowa, and Comanche force amassing near the site of the massacre. Elliott and all his men were later found to have been killed and mutilated, leading to a surge of resentment for

Custer among the enlisted ranks.²⁵ As Sandoz writes, Custer's alleged abandonment of Elliott would have absolutely been on Reno's mind as he and his men struck the east end of the great encampment. "Even with his left flank collapsed," Sandoz writes, "Reno realized that the Sioux should be fighting harder than this so near their standing village, and he dared not proceed without strong reinforcement. There was no support anywhere in sight, Benteen probably fifteen miles up the river and Custer—who could guess where Custer was now? Certainly not any man who knew that he did not support Major Elliott and his men on the Washita, had not even tried to rescue their bodies."²⁶ By including reference to the incident involving Major Elliott, Sandoz simultaneously casts aspersions on Custer while somewhat vindicating Reno. This would have been a radical path to take in the 1960s, challenging the prevailing narrative that Reno's incompetence, cowardice, and even possible drunkenness had all contributed to the death of Custer and his men.

Sandoz portrays Reno as a capable if massively overwhelmed career soldier who did his best to save his own life and the lives of the men with him on the battlefield. Unlike Custer, who continues to lead his men stubbornly and maddeningly into the leviathan's mouth, in Sandoz's narrative Reno sees that the game is up and that to remain on the river, fighting the highly motivated Native force opposing his battalion, would be tantamount to suicide. Sandoz captures the moment when Reno truly realizes that he needs to pull his men back, writing, "Reno caught a glimpse of interpreter Isaiah Dorman, and then of the sooted, resigned face of Charley Reynolds. . . . Methodically Charley Reynolds thrust cartridges into the breech of his rifle, and . . . watched with his customary patience for a warrior charging in close or for the slow, gentle shake of brush that revealed a stealthy Sioux approach. Then he pulled the trigger. . . . Bloody Knife too had the calm face of the resigned, bending forward, peering through the brush and smoke, his gun ready."²⁷ Sandoz's prose is apocalyptic in its intensity. Through her portrayal of Reynolds and Bloody Knife, she emphasizes that the heroes among the cavalrymen that day were these civilian and Indigenous scouts, led into a dire situation by Custer's ambition and knowing they could neither survive nor retreat. They are fighting here not for glory, not so that Custer can win the presidency, and not so that the United States of America can realize its divine right to Manifest Destiny. They were fighting for their very lives.

When the book was published the late 1960s, the war in Vietnam was beginning to intensify and many enlisted men found themselves fighting against a foreign enemy in a conflict they did not always understand and in which they had no personal investment. With that context in mind, the following passage resonates powerfully as Sandoz brings readers to Reno's moment of decision:

> A new burst of bullets ripped through the torn foliage. One of them struck Bloody Knife, blowing his skull open and spattering the handsome black silk kerchief that Custer had given to his once-favorite scout—spatterings that reached Major Reno standing beside the Ree [scouts]. For a moment the hardened campaigner was as sickened as the rawest recruit. Plainly the Indians were everywhere, penetrating everywhere, so many of them that even two–three times the number of his battalion would not hope to hold out in this patch of timber. . . . Plainly he must act fast if he was to save any of his deserted force, save any at all, even at the sacrifice of leaving the dead behind. Waving his pistol, the major shouted his orders to repair to a new position beyond the river, on the bluffs.[28]

The imagery of Bloody Knife's death is telling. Not only does he die fighting against his father's people, but his blood soils the mark of his servitude, the neckerchief that was a gift from Custer himself. Later in the text Sandoz describes how the scout's corpse is found by his "Sioux half-sister . . . his head was cut off in the ancient manner of the tribe, the custom long before they learned about scalping from the warriors who had gone east to fight in the French and Indian Wars." Bloody Knife is punished harshly for his perceived betrayal; by mutilating him in this manner, Bloody Knife's own family has prevented him from joining his ancestors in the afterlife. This not only serves as a final, brutal rejection from the Lakota side of his family side of his family but also an example of how the northern plains peoples visited retribution on those who betrayed them.[29]

Finally, Sandoz takes the reader to Last Stand Hill, to Custer's battalion and his failed attack upon the big village. Previously, the tendency among authors and scholars had been to describe the battle from the point of view of the Seventh Cavalry troops. A great deal of supposition would of course have to take place, because at that point it was believed that no man, either white or Native, riding with Custer on the day of the battle had lived to tell the tale. For that reason, Sandoz makes a dynamic structural decision for her text; rather than view Custer's fall through the lens of supposition and white martyrdom, Sandoz uses the accounts of Indigenous veterans to present the Last Stand not as a national tragedy in which heroes died while covering themselves in glory but as a thrilling victory for a people who had spent the previous two centuries being steadily pushed west by the arrival of European settlers and who now had the opportunity to push back with a vengeance.

It is no coincidence that Sandoz inhabits Reno's point of view while eschewing Custer's; Reno is a victim of Custer's folly and thus deserves vindication, while Custer has placed himself in the predicament that he is in. Sandoz appears to inhabit only the personalities of the historical figures who have earned her sympathies. During Reno's attack, she tells the story through Reno's eyes. During the Last Stand, she shifts to the Indigenous viewpoint. The result is a narrative account of the battle that emphasizes Indigenous bravery while refusing to acknowledge the cavalrymen as heroic martyrs. Sandoz rightly points out that the Native men were protecting their families, present in the village, and were motivated by decades of massacres and broken promises. "This was not a day for mere coups and honors," Sandoz writes, "as in wars far from the villages and the helpless women and children. This day they must strike hard, strike to destroy this enemy who dared attack their great summer conference, something that had never happened before. No army had ever come against a Sioux camp of any size except upon the band . . . under the peace chief Little Thunder, twenty years ago. For that, too, there must be punishment today."[30] By including the reference to Little Thunder, a peace-keeping Sicangu (Brule) Lakota chief whose village had been massacred by U.S. Army troops under General William Harney in the summer of 1856, Sandoz places the Little Bighorn within the broader spectrum of imperialistic atrocities committed by the U.S. military against the Indigenous peoples of the Great Plains.[31] In doing so, she strips the Battle of the Little Bighorn of its nationalistic aura, recontextualizing it not as a tragedy but as a victory. Rather than stand with Custer, his brothers, his fellow officers, and the enlisted men under them atop Last Stand Hill, Sandoz asks her audience to ride with the Lakotas, Cheyennes, and Arapahos.

After Custer's battalion has been pushed to the ridges bordering the river, Sandoz shows the Lakotas, Cheyennes, and Arapahos behaving with remarkable cohesion and organization, signaling "to those behind the ridges for crossfire, safe for the warriors, with the troops on the backbone [ridgeline] above them, the few bullets whistling overhead." Meanwhile, Custer's soldiers are scattered and disorganized, "trying to make little stands, not only to hold the enemy, but to keep the troopers who had never fought whooping warriors from breaking into a run that could not be stopped." The Native fighters themselves charge "whooping through the dust, particularly the Cheyennes with Lame White Man from the Reno fight, leaving the troopers little time to untie their horses or even cut the leather, so that some fell still reaching for the rein, the gut-shot horses screaming."[32] While Sandoz acknowledges that "there were some good men on that hill, some trying to shoot carefully from the knee even as the Indians closed in," she does not mention any of them by name, let alone Custer, who ostensibly fell atop the hill; the specifics of how Custer died have never really been clear, and Sandoz does not continue the trend of speculating about his demise. Instead, she describes the final moment of the Last Stand as the moment when a Native fighter named No Flesh killed the standard bearer and tore the banner from his faltering hand, while another bold warrior rode straight through the little circle of troopers, his pony jumping the dead horses and men. He was followed by a whole charge, and so the soldiers went down under hoof and spear and war club until nobody could be alive in that bloody pile. But there were a few. Jumping up together, they headed off through the haze of smoke and dust down the slope . . . the whooping warriors running them down like newborn buffalo calves, striking them to the ground, looking for more, until suddenly there were no more.[33]

This would forever be the Indigenous view of the Last Stand—not a blaze of glory but rather a fast, bloody, and thoroughly inglorious end for Custer and the men of his battalion. His death is not mentioned. It does not need to be. At this point in the text, Sandoz chooses to focus not on him and the tragedy of his death but rather on the Lakota forces and the scale of their victory.

In his book *The Journey of Crazy Horse: A Lakota History*, Lakota historian Joseph M. Marshall III depicts the final moments on the ridge similarly, devoting no more than a few paragraphs to the Last Stand in his cultural biography of Crazy Horse. Like Sandoz, Marshall shows a last ragged group of soldiers attempting to flee from the ridge to the safety of the river, but by then "the Lakota and Shahiyela (Cheyenne) seemed to be rising out of the earth itself, avenging spirits flying through the dust that hung low over the slopes and ridges, and made the soldiers pay a terrible price."[34] The fact that Sandoz's book was published in 1966 and preceded Marshall's by nearly forty years illustrates just how deeply Sandoz tapped into Indigenous oral history and chose to honor that history with her portrayal of the battle itself.

In his pathbreaking biography of Custer, *Cavalier in Buckskin: George Armstrong Custer and the Western Military Frontier*, historian Robert M. Utley writes, "Clearly, the Custer of legend and symbol is a different person from the Custer of reality. For each generation of Americans since 1876, the mythic Custer tapped deep into revealing intellectual and emotional currents. He was what they wanted him to be, and what they made him told more about the creators than the created."[35] The truth of this assessment cannot be denied, and Sandoz certainly played a part in the more negative view of Custer, based on her background in the Sandhills of Nebraska and in tune with the civil rights movement of the 1960s. Her work, together with both the novel and the film *Little Big Man* and later works like Dee Brown's *Bury My Heart at Wounded Knee*, helped usher Custer and his status as a tragic hero atop Last Stand Hill into the rogue's gallery of historical villains. However, what Sandoz accomplished with *The Battle of the Little Bighorn* is more than just another revisionist view of an iconic event within the greater context of American history. By presenting the Last Stand from the point of view of the Indigenous force that killed Custer and his men, Sandoz did not simply follow a trend and keep up with what was in vogue at the time. She challenged the grand narrative of Manifest Destiny, giving voice to a people whose greatest victory had been refashioned into a national tragedy in which their enemy had been sanctified and martyred. Through this slim volume, her last book, Mari Sandoz had finally paid tribute to the old Lakota man who noticed her sneaking up to listen to stories of the old days, and to He Dog, who thought of her as a granddaughter. Not only did she bring the rain to the parched prairies of her childhood, she shared with her audience a people's truth, the truth of a people whom she had long admired.

NOTES

Epigraph: From the University of Nebraska Press edition (1978), 20–21.

1. Arthur Penn, dir., *Little Big Man*, starring Dustin Hoffman (Los Angeles: Paramount Pictures, 1970).
2. Vine Deloria Jr., introduction to *Crazy Horse: The Strange Man of the Oglalas*, by Mari Sandoz, 3rd ed. (Lincoln: University of Nebraska Press, 2004), xv.
3. Mari Sandoz, *Crazy Horse: The Strange Man of the Oglalas*, 3rd ed. (1942; Lincoln: University of Nebraska Press, 2004), xx.

4. Sandoz, *Crazy Horse*, xxi.
5. Joseph M. Marshall III, *The Journey of Crazy Horse: A Lakota History* (New York: Penguin Books, 2005), 299.
6. Evan S. Connell, *Son of the Morning Star: Custer and the Little Bighorn* (San Francisco: North Point Press, 1984), 353.
7. Michael A. Elliott, *Custerology: The Enduring Legacy of the Indian Wars and George Armstrong Custer* (Chicago: University of Chicago Press, 2007), 30.
8. Larry McMurtry, introduction to *Little Big Man*, by Thomas Berger, 50th anniversary ed. (New York: Thomas Dunne Books, 2015), xi.
9. Raoul Walsh, dir., *They Died with Their Boots On*, starring Errol Flynn and Olivia de Havilland (Los Angeles: Warner Bros. Pictures, 1941).
10. Johnny Cash, vocalist, "Custer" by Peter La Farge, recorded March 1964, track 3 on *Bitter Tears: Ballads of the American Indian*, Columbia Records, digital recording.
11. Mari Sandoz, *The Battle of the Little Bighorn* (1966; Lincoln: University of Nebraska Press, 1978), 7, 11.
12. George A. Custer, "Battling with the Sioux on the Yellowstone," in *The Custer Reader*, ed. Paul Andrew Hutton (Norman: University of Oklahoma Press, 2004), 215–16.
13. Connell, *Son of the Morning Star*, 15–18.
14. Sandoz, *Battle of the Little Bighorn*, 15.
15. Sandoz, *Battle of the Little Bighorn*, 16.
16. Edward S. Godfrey, "Custer's Last Battle," in *The Custer Reader*, ed. Paul Andrew Hutton (Norman: University of Oklahoma Press, 2004), 311–12.
17. Godfrey, "Custer's Last Battle," 312.
18. Godfrey, "Custer's Last Battle," 313.
19. Paul Andrew Hutton, ed., *The Custer Reader* (Norman: University of Oklahoma Press, 2004), 230. Godfrey also proudly participated in the massacre at Wounded Knee, an act seen by many as a brutal revenge killing for the army's losses at the Little Bighorn. See Nathaniel Philbrick, *The Last Stand: Custer, Sitting Bull, and the Battle of the Little Bighorn* (New York: Penguin Books, 2010), 298–99. The defect Godfrey is referring to involves the Springfield carbines carried by the troops. Evidently, the copper-jacketed rounds became so overheated during the battle that they softened and jammed in the carbine's breech, forcing the soldier to clear the jam with a penknife. This naturally made them an easy target for an Indigenous fighter armed with a repeating rifle, bow and arrow, or a war club.

20. Philbrick, *Last Stand*, 190–205; Sandoz, *Battle of the Little Bighorn*, 94.
21. Sandoz, *Battle of the Little Bighorn*, 22.
22. Sandoz, *Battle of the Little Bighorn*, 27–28.
23. Sandoz, *Battle of the Little Bighorn*, 31.
24. Sandoz, *Battle of the Little Bighorn*, 70.
25. Connell, *Son of the Morning Star*, 192–95.
26. Sandoz, *Battle of the Little Bighorn*, 74.
27. Sandoz, *Battle of the Little Bighorn*, 82.
28. Sandoz, *Battle of the Little Bighorn*, 82–83.
29. Sandoz, *Battle of the Little Bighorn*, 115.
30. Sandoz, *Battle of the Little Bighorn*, 120.
31. Marshall, *Journey of Crazy Horse*, 63–69.
32. Sandoz, *Battle of the Little Bighorn*, 122–23.
33. Sandoz, *Battle of the Little Bighorn*, 128.
34. Marshall, *Journey of Crazy Horse*, 228.
35. Robert M. Utley, *Cavalier in Buckskin: George Armstrong Custer and the Western Military Frontier*, rev. ed. (Norman: University of Oklahoma Press, 2001), 12.

5

Writing against Empire

Mari Sandoz and the Fog of War

KENT BLANSETT

The Indians slipped into ravines or cut banks or washouts, mostly leaving the horses hidden, creeping in upon the enemy. A few did charge boldly in the open, but not in the usual single recklessness against which Crazy Horse, Gall, and others harangued. This was not the day for mere coups and honors, as in wars far from the villages and the helpless women and children. This day they must strike hard, strike to destroy this enemy who dared attack their great summer conference, something that had never happened before. No army had ever come shooting against a Sioux camp of any size except upon the band of Brules under the peace chief, Little Thunder, twenty years ago. For that, too, there must be punishment today.
—Mari Sandoz, *The Battle of the Little Bighorn*

On a cold New York City evening in 1966, one month before Mari Sandoz passed away, she met with David Lowe, an associate editor from *American Heritage* magazine, at her apartment. Her building was located on Hudson Street in the heart of Greenwich Village, a stone's throw away from the nearest subway station. As Lowe glanced around the celebrated author's home, he noticed a large living room window that faced west, a far cry from the beloved Nebraska Sandhills of Sandoz's youth. The young editor paused for a moment and allowed his eyes to dance along the bookshelves and home decor that told the literary story of Sandoz's life. Her dark hair now silver, she took Lowe on a short tour of her residence and acknowledged a set of file cabinets that contained all the research from her last book, *The Battle of the Little Bighorn*. Not long after the tour, the two westerners exited the apartment building, locked arms, and braved the chill of the New York streets as they hurried to the warmth of a nearby restaurant.

At dinner, their conversation drifted toward one critical subject, the war in Vietnam—a subject that Lowe later recalled had served as the most pressing issue for Mari Sandoz at this stage in her career. A controversial topic of that era, the war in Vietnam provides a unique and critical lens through which to contemplate the significance of Sandoz's final book. Throughout her writing career, Sandoz had championed an antiwar stance in a number of books, including *The Tom-Walker* (1947) and *Cheyenne Autumn* (1953), to name a few. Several years later, Lowe published a short article in *Prairie Schooner* detailing his dinner meeting with Sandoz: "As she spoke . . . , a passion which had not been there came into her voice. She was not dogmatic, not absolutely certain where the truth of the situation lay, but she wondered what the truth was, whether or not our Government was telling it to the people, most importantly, whether or not our Government itself knew the truth of the situation in Southeast Asia."[1] Lowe's statement echoed the nation's uncertainty about the Vietnam War. This fog of war provides a critical perspective from which to view Sandoz's last major publication and a context for seeing it as a significant antiwar novel.

Sandoz's passion for literary hell-raising is well noted in her correspondence. Writing to Blanche Knopf, president of the Alfred Knopf publishing house, in 1944, she stated, "Speaking up in times of stress has always been the premise of the serious novelist, it shall always be mine." Through inspired storytelling in her provocative account of the Battle of the Little Bighorn, Sandoz connects a powerful moment in the history of America's colonization and military conquest of Indigenous nations to both the anti-Vietnam and Red Power movements. In the book, Sandoz transforms the central character of the story, George Armstrong Custer, from a frontier hero into a symbol of antiwar protest and Red Power for a new generation of readers grappling with the fog of war.[2]

By 1966 the United States had accelerated its commitment to provide military aid to South Vietnam in an effort to prevent its fall to communism. As a result, more American soldiers engaged in direct military encounters with troops from North Vietnam. American intervention in Vietnam had begun in the 1950s, when President Harry S. Truman offered diplomatic and fiscal support to French military forces in their struggle to thwart North Vietnam's attempt to unify all of Vietnam and end France's colonial rule in Indochina. Shortly after the 1954 slaughter of French forces at the battle of Dien Bien Phu, Truman's containment mission quickly began to unravel under President Dwight D. Eisenhower's administration, when anticolonial campaigns forced France to end its sixty-year colonial reign over Indochina. Ultimately, France's defeat in Vietnam propelled the United States to accelerate its involvement in promoting a democratic and capitalist Vietnam.[3]

In 1961 President John F. Kennedy deployed American military advisors to aid South Vietnam's armed forces, who struggled to maintain their strategic and ideological missions against communist North Vietnam. In August 1964, less than a year later after Kennedy's assassination, the Gulf of Tonkin incident provided his successor, President Lyndon Johnson, with enough political capital to deploy over two hundred thousand more American ground troops. Shortly after Mari Sandoz's passing in 1966, the United States deployed over half a million soldiers to Vietnam. Soon thereafter, U.S. military leaders and soldiers rebranded Vietnam with the new name "Indian Country" and likened the Vietnam campaign to the historic struggle to colonize the American West. Anthropologist Stephen Silliman likened this rebrand of the Vietnam War to a heritage metaphor crafted by a sixties generation raised on a steady diet of Hollywood Westerns.[4] With this metaphoric link—between Vietnam and Indian Country—America's long history of colonization has arguably made Mari Sandoz's *The Battle of the Little Bighorn* one of the most significant antiwar, social justice, and Indigenous rights books of the mid-twentieth century.

Sandoz wrote her book between 1960 and 1965, just as America was ramping up its commitment to South Vietnam, and her portrayal of

Custer's defeat offers a symbolic warning about the costs of marching headstrong into colonial wars. *The Battle of the Little Bighorn* offers a stark warning for a nation that never attempted to reconcile itself with the truly brutal legacy of violence perpetrated against Indigenous peoples. In Sandoz's literary treatment of the battle, the U.S. military failed to complete its sole military objective—the complete subjugation or annihilation of all Indigenous nations. In essence, the Lakota and allied Indigenous nations fought collectively in defense of their families, homes, villages, lifeways, and territory and against the real threat of genocide that had claimed Indigenous lives at the Sand Creek (1864), Washita (1868), and Marias River (1870) massacres, just to name a few.[5] While present throughout Sandoz's narrative, the themes of defense and genocide are prominent in the following passage:

> The Indians slipped into ravines or cut banks or washouts, mostly leaving the horses hidden, creeping in upon the enemy. A few did charge boldly in the open, but not in the usual single recklessness against which Crazy Horse, Gall, and others harangued. This was not the day for mere coups and honors, as in wars far from the villages and the helpless women and children. This day they must strike hard, strike to destroy this enemy who dared attack their great summer conference, something that had never happened before. No army had ever come shooting against a Sioux camp of any size except upon the band of Brules under the peace chief, Little Thunder, twenty years ago. For that, too, there must be punishment today.[6]

In June 1876 the United States celebrated the centennial of its independence from Britain, and it also represented a critical time of ceremonial significance, as the Lakotas, Cheyennes, Arapahos, and other allies gathered for their annual ceremonies of renewal and Sun Dance. Collectively this Indigenous peoples' mass movement west or "great summer conference" had followed the buffalo away from the territorial boundaries of the Great Sioux Reservation and represented a treaty obligation for the continuation and exercise of their treaty hunting and religious rights. Sandoz's account capitalizes on the larger-than-life events of the battle in a high suspense and thrilling narrative. She understood that most of her readers were already aware of Custer's fate, so she built upon her audience's anticipation. Like Alfred Hitchcock plotting a thriller, she crafted a suspenseful narrative while documenting the key historical events that led to Custer's death.

Beyond her gripping prose, Sandoz's account effectively exposed the links between war, colonization, and empire, a historic prescription that conceptually intertwined the fates of rolling prairies in Montana with the dense jungles of Vietnam. Beyond her portrayal of the Little Bighorn battle, she left readers with an unresolved question about the cost of the conflict. The appendix to Sandoz's book lists the names and ranks of those U.S. Army soldiers killed under Custer's command, and with that list Sandoz offers a final moment of reflection on the real cost of ignorance and warfare as she constructs a dark memorial to the fallen men. In a bold move, Sandoz raised a couple of stark questions about the contemporary situation: What memorial would be built to commemorate the Vietnam War? Was Vietnam destined to become another Little Bighorn?

Loyal to their uniform and country, U.S. soldiers under Custer's problematic leadership suffered a humiliating end. The marching pace of Sandoz's prose offers both conflict and empathy for those who served under Custer, and yet in the end she challenges her audience to rid themselves of any mythic sympathy for the fallen Boy General. Her narrative refutes Custer's historical legacy as the martyred darling of American western expansion. As a guide, Sandoz offered her audience a more complicated understanding about Lakota, Cheyenne, and Arapaho lifeways and the military defense of their homelands. She depicted a sophisticated Indigenous military response and a proven strategy that had, eight days earlier, defeated General George Crook's advance at Rosebud Creek, a major factor in the near total annihilation of Custer's forces at the Little Bighorn. Each of these historic battles called into question America's colonial strategy and its justifications for Manifest Destiny and westward expansion.[7] Sandoz's interpretation of the Little Bighorn battle aligns with these points, as she challenged her audience to weigh the enormous costs of western expansion against the long-term benefits of a war fueled by political ambition, conquest, and greed.[8]

Not long after bone cancer had claimed Sandoz's life in March 1966, *The Battle of the Little Bighorn* appeared in American bookstores. Critics quickly launched their own vicious attacks to discredit Sandoz. Several reviews criticized Sandoz's research and lack of source citations; many more took greater offense at her antiheroic portrayal of Custer. Published in 1967, a review by Jack Burrows in *Arizona and the West* went so far as to wrongly accuse Sandoz of outright plagiarism. Burrows's review sought to completely discredit Sandoz by pointing out phrases he claimed had been stolen from Frederic Van de Water's 1934 book *Glory-Hunter: A Life of General Custer*—Van de Water is credited with having authored one of the first antihero Custer accounts.[9] Likewise, Wisconsin historian Paul Hass in his review of *The Battle of the Little Bighorn* referred to Sandoz's book as "polemical." In Hass's view, Sandoz's interpretation of the historic event held little to absolutely zero historiographical value in the literature of what he termed the "Custer fight."[10] Hass's label "Custer fight" begs the question, whose fight was it?

Several academic reviews further dismissed Sandoz's contention that Custer's ambitions went far beyond a major military victory over the Lakota nation and stretched all the way to the White House. Sandoz encouraged her audience to contemplate Custer's true motives and even the prospects of an alternative history. What if Custer had succeeded at the Little Bighorn and earned the Democratic Party nomination for the presidency? In such a historical twilight zone, one must wonder what the legacy of a Custer presidency—especially in relation to Indian policy, wars of conquest, and the ongoing task of Reconstruction—might have looked like. Custer's death perhaps saved America from a Custer presidency. However, although Custer died on the battlefield, the patriotic idea of Custer continued to influence nearly every facet of American popular culture.

Many reviewers of *The Battle of the Little Bighorn* took offense at Sandoz's lack of source citations throughout the book. It's not that Sandoz lacked evidence. Recall that file cabinet of sources located in her New York apartment. The problem was that many of her sources had vanished.[11] For a historical source to be reputable, it must be both accessible and easily reproducible for other scholars to scrutinize. In Helen Winter Stauffer's authoritative biography *Mari Sandoz: Story Catcher of the Plains*, she notes that many of the sources related to the Custer fight, which Sandoz had initially accessed in the late 1930s, had disappeared from the official War Department Records housed at the National Archives. Stauffer speculated that these missing Custer documents had vanished when the federal government relocated the war records to a new facility. Stauffer also notes significant gaps that appeared in the microfilm collections, reels of which had been created only after the official documents had been moved. Stauffer, in further defense of Sandoz, noted that these significant and sizable source gaps had delayed the publication of *The Battle of the Little Bighorn*.[12] Regardless of the status of Sandoz's source materials, unlike her previous works that had referenced the battle, she authored this account for a popular war series, a book series for which the editors strove to limit unwieldy endnotes so they could market the book to a mainstream audience. Interestingly, some scholars, including Alvin M. Josephy Jr., rushed to Sandoz's defense, calling her book a literary masterpiece and "literature of the highest order."[13]

Beyond the critics, much of the success of Sandoz and the appeal of her writing are bound by her lived experience, an experience deeply rooted in and interconnected with the American West and its past. For Sandoz, the answer to America's most pressing contemporary issues, whether political scandal, the Great Depression, World War II, the Red Scare, the civil rights movement, or Vietnam, could all be resolved in a national reckoning with an unflinching historical examination of the American West. Sandoz embraced a bold literary form of historical relativism as she relied upon the vibrant history of the American West to inspire progressive reforms, from Indigenous rights and equality to challenging military conquest. Sandoz's treatment of history was both a method of study and a process designed to address the most complicated issues of her own day.

A child of Swiss settlers, Mari Sandoz's talent as a storyteller offers a compelling challenge to historian Frederick Jackson Turner's argument that by 1890 the frontier had officially closed. Throughout her writings, the history of the American West remained unresolved and conflicted. Her prose took on popular myths and revealed the traumatic legacies of war and colonization. She posited that settlement remained an ongoing process, that the frontier remained an immeasurable experience that carried the legacy of conquest and colonization far beyond her own lifetime. Her intimate connection to the American West also meant that Sandoz's life story often remained inseparable from her subjects. From *Old Jules* (1935) to *Crazy Horse* (1942), she never abandoned the memory of that little girl who sat next to the roar of a campfire and listened to old Lakota buffalo hunters share their stories about an Indigenous West. These early life experiences had branded Sandoz with a *true* western perspective.

Uniquely, her identity as an American citizen and as a westerner never departed from a connection to American Indian history, lifeways, and experience. In 1965 Nebraska television host Rita Shaw interviewed Mari Sandoz. Halfway through the interview, Sandoz spoke about the significance of Native American history, stating that you "can't conquer anything without absorbing something of the conquered." Her provocative and insightful statement offered an interesting critique to American modernity, character, and civilization. Sandoz expanded on her statement:

> They had managed to live in a way, we might think about . . . here you had a society without locks, so they couldn't tolerate a thief, you had a society without paper, a record of man's word, so you couldn't tolerate a liar, you had a society without jails so you couldn't have any troublemakers. . . . We broke up . . . their . . . whole system of life and gave them nothing to fit their environment

in turn. We gave them no philosophical pattern, we gave them no economic pattern . . . so now we have a . . . transitory people.[14]

In Sandoz's view, a perspective that later came to be identified with the Red Power movement, America had much to learn from Indigenous civilizations. Toward the end of her interview by Shaw, she offered a plea for greater rights and justice for Indigenous peoples. Throughout her writing career, Sandoz mastered the craft of storytelling to champion Native voices, peoples, cultures, and rights as a staunch advocate for more Americans to accept the truths that emanate from the study of American Indian history.

Mari Sandoz, like her dear friend and contemporary John G. Neihardt, the author of *Black Elk Speaks* (1932), relied upon Native oral histories as the major primary source that informed her literary works. Their shared experiences in utilizing early Indigenous research methodologies served as the foundation for other critical works, including Sandoz's *Cheyenne Autumn* (1953), which documented the Northern Cheyenne Exodus and Custer's command in the brutal Washita Massacre. Their bold prose and storytelling pace mimicked their encounters with Native storytelling, as each of their exchanges in collecting Native oral histories forever changed them as writers.

From a young age Sandoz had listened to Indigenous storytellers, and these oral histories impressed upon her the value of Indigenous knowledge systems and storytelling structures. While her research often incorporated a myriad of different sources, ranging from military records to oral histories, she also explored various nontraditional sources, such as ledger art, a Lakota history as told through a visual record. A prime example would be the drawings by Amos Bad Heart Bull, which Sandoz considered an invaluable historical source in the 1940s. From Bad Heart Bull's images Sandoz gained a Lakota perspective about Crazy Horse's appearance, such as what paint he used in battle, the color of his pony, and the care he took to dress his horse, as well as how Lakota warriors remembered or memorialized the fall of U.S. soldiers at the Little Bighorn. From such experiences,

Sandoz became an early advocate for documenting Native voices and perspectives. In addition to preserving Bad Heart Bull's ledger art, Sandoz also recovered an 1893 autobiography dictated by Lakota leader Red Cloud, a monumental project that Sandoz completed in the early 1930s for the Nebraska State Historical Society.

In 1965 a young anthropology student at the University of Chicago wrote to Mari Sandoz and inquired about Lakota history in between offering his sincere praise for her scholarship. In his letter, the student inquired about the differences between the Lakota words "hunka" and "kola" and if the hunkapi and alowanpi ceremonies referred to the same ceremony. Mari Sandoz replied seven days later: "Dear Raymond DeMallie: You will have to look through the Oglala Societies and relationships yourself. I'm at St. Lukes Hospital with incurable bone cancer. Sorry."[15] Of course, this young student went on to become an incredibly influential anthropologist in the field of Indigenous studies scholarship and to write the book *The Sixth Grandfather: Black Elk's Teachings Given to John G. Neihardt* (1985). Ahead of her time in scholarly technique and methodology, Sandoz engaged in scholarship that helped to amplify the fields of ethnography and then ethnohistory as well, as she combined both traditional anthropological and historical sources to elevate Indigenous sources and allocate greater agency to Indigenous voices throughout her long career.[16]

While Mari Sandoz's scholarship influenced the early foundations of ethnohistory, her literary contributions helped spark another academic movement—the advent of Native American studies (NAS). Before 1970 only a handful of Native American studies departments and programs existed in the United States. With some exceptions, most Native American studies programs and departments were established in the late 1960s and early 1970s.[17] Many university history departments in this era lacked any course offerings devoted to the teaching, writing, and methods of American Indian history. Far fewer still were the number of Indigenous scholars who earned their doctorate degrees; only a few individuals held this degree, among them Cherokee anthropologist Robert K. Thomas, Salish Kootenai scholar D'Arcy McNickle, Ponca historian Roger Buffalohead, Lakota anthropologist Beatrice Medicine, Lenape/Renape historian Jack Forbes, and Okay Owingeh Pueblo anthropologist Alfonso Ortiz. Despite this sparse representation of Indigenous scholars in academic circles, countless books had been authored on or about Native peoples, but only a handful of these publications engaged with Native sources. A growing interest in ethnographic methods and the legal research that informed tribal cases before the Indian Claims Commission (ICC; established in 1946) inspired growth in literature on Native histories. The ICC legal cases produced forty-three volumes of court opinions and sourcing. In these cases, tribes had relied upon a diverse assortment of government, church, pioneer, and military records, as well as Native oral histories and other sources, to attest to their deep historical connections with their homelands. Of course, there were exceptions. For instance, Angie Debo, Grant Foreman, and other scholars had utilized a myriad of Native and non-Native sources to construct their sophisticated studies. These works, alongside Sandoz scholarship, served as the cornerstones for a pedagogy and methodology that still informs modern Native American studies scholarship. Sandoz's books appeared not only in classrooms but also on a book list for San Francisco State College's first Native American studies program, which produced some of the leaders of the Alcatraz occupation between 1969 and 1971. Since then, several generations of college students have looked to Sandoz's works, including *The Battle of the Little Bighorn*, as authoritative accounts. In this way, Sandoz served as an early champion of an interdisciplinary methodology that is still at the core of Native American studies historiography.[18]

In addition to being a foundational scholar for Native American studies, Sandoz used her fame as a staunch advocate for Native rights to challenge destructive federal policies. By the early 1950s, Sandoz had joined the Association on American Indian Affairs, an organization instrumental in lobbying Congress to repeal relocation and termination policies.[19] During the McCarthyism turmoil of the 1950s, some U.S. senators likened American Indian reservations to communist states that needed to be broken up and integrated into the rest of American society, in either of two ways: relocate Native peoples to one of six major American cities (i.e., individual termination) or legislatively terminate the federal trust relationship with specific Native nations (i.e., tribal termination). Sandoz, vehemently opposed to the federal government's second adoption of an assimilation doctrine, wrote strong letters and urged all politicians to repeal and reject all such policies. Sandoz, through her lobbying and letter writing, became an early supporter of Native nationalism and self-determination. Unfortunately, her life ended before she could witness the meteoric rise of the Red Power movement.[20]

As a writer, Sandoz also understood the important functions of heroes in literature, and she wrote during a time when a new generation was only beginning to challenge the Custer myth. While Sandoz's book is not explicitly a book about Red Power or the antiwar movements, she wrote it against the backdrop of these movements, and the societal fog of war from that historical context elicits new dialogues that speak to the greater significance of *The Battle of the Little Bighorn*. Destroying the heroic frontier icon of Custer garnered new meaning in this pivotal era when Custer emerged as the ultimate symbol for the failures of U.S. colonial and imperial wars. His was an image that emboldened the commitment of both antiwar and Red Power activists to greater action. As historian Brian Dippie suggested, "Destroy the Custer myth, the biggest one of all, and you'll start getting an understanding of everything that happened and an end to the bias against the Indian people."[21] Sandoz's book represents a literary turning point: the previously heroic Custer came to be viewed, largely through the activism of the antiwar and Red Power movements, as the ultimate antihero of the American West. Her treatment of Custer laid the foundation for other Indigenous and allied writers, musicians, artists, and scholars to reimagine Custer's memorialization.

George Armstrong Custer holds a unique place of villainous notoriety throughout Indian Country, which helped to cultivate a different version of the Custer myth, or what I term the Indian Custer myth.

Much of the disdain for Custer stems from his dark historical legacy and an overall resistance to the prevalence of Americans' obsession with treating Custer as the ultimate martyr and hero of western expansion. The Custer myth is so prominent in American popular culture that it has been marketed and consumed by countless generations and often found in art, political cartoons, comics, film, music, and a host of other critical media.[22] Custer's earlier heroic image inspired two large statues created to honor his legacy—one at his birthplace in New Rumley, Ohio, and another at his childhood hometown of Monroe, Michigan, where they sponsor an annual celebration to honor him. At the Little Bighorn National Battlefield in Montana, more than three hundred thousand people a year continue to visit the site of his defeat and learn more about the fate of the Seventh Cavalry.[23]

Despite the Battle of the Little Bighorn's place in American society and its heritage tourism appeal, few scholars have documented how Indigenous peoples began to transform the Custer myth into a symbol of antiwar resistance to advance Indigenous sovereignty and self-determination.[24] The most notable example of an Indian Custer myth is tied to Dakota intellectual Vine Deloria Jr.'s book *Custer Died for Your Sins: An Indian Manifesto* (1969), which provided an important scholarly foundation for the Red Power movement. Deloria, like Sandoz, promoted a future that sought reconciliation with the Custer myth. With a dash of humor and fate, Deloria is noted for having gained the inspiration for his book's title from a popular bumper sticker that circulated throughout Indian Country. It is little wonder that Deloria, a former student of theology and the law, had picked up on the power of this political statement. *Custer Died for Your Sins* was so influential, the book inspired an album recorded by Dakota musician Floyd Red Crow Westerman, whose songs served as a soundtrack to the Indigenous rights movement.[25]

Like the appeal of the album, Deloria's *Custer Died for Your Sins* chapter on Indian humor references how Native peoples employ humor as a strategy to confront the violent past and generational trauma of American colonization. The ability to laugh at oppression

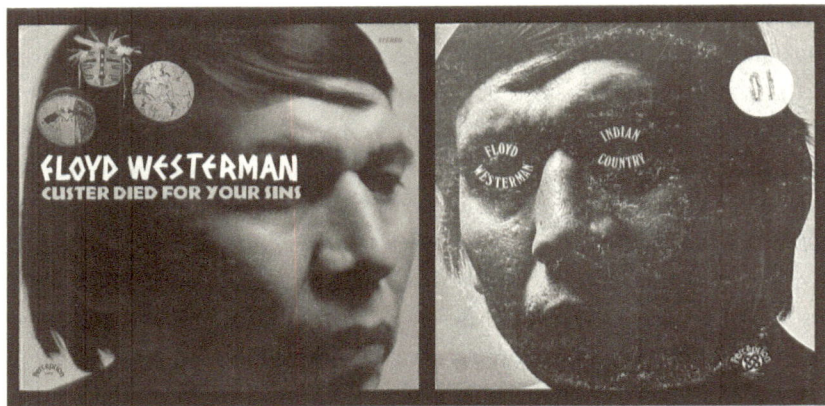

14. TOP: Album covers for Floyd Westerman, *Custer Died for Your Sins*, cover design by J.C., photograph by Stan Moldoff (Denver CO: Perception Records, Inc., 1969), and *Indian Country*, cover design uncredited on album, photograph uncredited but attributed to Stan Moldoff (Denver CO: Perception Records, 1970). Author's collection.

15. BOTTOM: Album covers for Peter La Farge, *Iron Mountain and Other Songs*, cover design by Ronald Clyne, photograph by David Gahr (New York: Folkways Records & Service Corp., 1962), and *On the Warpath*, cover design by Ronald Clyne, photograph by David Gahr (New York: Folkways Records & Service Corp., 1965). The *Iron Mountain and Other Songs* album preceded La Farge's 1963 album *As Long as the Grass Shall Grow* and features an often-replicated portrait of La Farge. *On the Warpath* featured "Ira Hayes (The Ballad of Ira Hayes)." Author's collection.

and break the chains of continued repression is a strategy for determining a different Indigenous future. Deloria, inspired by such an idea, devoted a large section of his Indian humor chapter to the "Custer joke," or a "last saying," as he termed it. A popular joke from the text reads, "Custer['s] on top of the hill looking at a multitude of warriors charging up the slope at him. He turns resignedly to his aide and says, 'Well, it's better than going back to North Dakota.'"[26]

Well before Deloria's challenge to the Custer myth, in 1963 self-identified Narragansett descendant folk artist Peter La Farge had released the song "Custer" on his second album, *As Long as the Grass Shall Grow.*

Today La Farge is most recognized for his chart-topping 1962 single "Ira Hayes," but only after the song's popularity skyrocketed when it was covered by country music legend Johnny Cash. Prior to this success, La Farge's voice had dominated folk music. A contemporary of Pete Seeger, Bob Dylan, Phil Ochs, and Cree musician Buffy Sainte-Marie, his music, like theirs, emerged from the early 1960s New York Greenwich Village folk scene. Prior to Deloria's manifesto, La Farge's music prompted a fascinating intervention, a challenge to whoever told Custer's story and owned Custer's legacy and memory. Indian Country is not monolithic, as Blackfeet author James Welch has noted, and "the Battle of the Little Big Horn, that relatively small event in this country's war history, continues to create division among Indian people, as well as tensions between Indians and whites, over a century later. Custer seems to be alive and well and riding in our midst."[27] If history was written and owned solely by the colonizer, then what part of the Custer story can Native peoples truly claim? Such logic sought to upend previous scholarship that upheld a distorted and often one-dimensional view of Native peoples. This strain of musical performative resistance remains an essential quality of La Farge's art. He composed his "Custer" track in the lyrical style of an Indian forty-nine dance or social song—songs and their performance that originated in the afterhours of a powwow—and his song represents one of the first forty-nine songs ever recorded by a popular label.

Old Custer split his men,
Well he won't do that again
'Cause the general he don't ride well any more. . . .

He got eliminated
And his legend uncreated
And the general he don't ride well any more.

The iconic song demonstrates another facet of the Indian Custer myth: a sonic futurism composed in the tradition of "We Shall Overcome," a song also championed as a political chant by Red Power activists. Deeply rooted in this Indian Custer myth is a rallying cry, a "Remember Custer" slogan that U.S. soldiers were rumored to have shouted after Custer's death but that here spoke to the strength of Native nationalism and an intertribal unity that remains at the heart of modern American Indian politics. Central to La Farge's "Remember Custer" anthem is also a rejection of the conquered and a rejection of wardship, control, and paternalism. This decolonized process of reframing the Custer myth sought reconciliation with American colonization and fostered a greater vision of Indigenous sovereignty and self-determination.[28]

Although there is no evidence of a direct encounter between the musician Peter La Farge and Mari Sandoz, one fascinating connection did emerge through Sandoz's own active membership in the Association on American Indian Affairs. Sandoz's letters revealed a working relationship with Peter La Farge's father, Oliver La Farge, who served as president of the association. In 1929 Oliver La Farge had won a Pulitzer Prize for his book *Laughing Boy*.[29] Considering the association, it is highly probable that Sandoz may have met Peter La Farge or attended a performance by him at the Gaslight or Café Wha or may possibly have purchased or listened to Peter La Farge's 1963 album, which featured the popular song "Custer."[30] The probability of this association is high for one simple reason. Greenwich Village was home to thousands of New Yorkers, but for those working on furthering Native rights, it amounted to a small world, a world shared by both Sandoz and the young musician. The vivacious singer-songwriter also had much in common with Mari Sandoz. Peter La Farge, like Sandoz, had grown up in the West. In his early years, without his father's presence, he spent time on a cattle ranch in Fountain, Colorado. As a cowpuncher, La Farge collected cowboy and ranching ballads—western stories told through song. Later, he traded his cowboy skills for a life on the rodeo circuit and traveled across America as a professional bronc rider. Like Sandoz, he relocated to Greenwich Village, where he took up songwriting and performed in folk music venues. In the absence of a direct link between Sandoz and La Farge, they each told western stories through literature and music to inspire change in audiences often far removed from the American West.

Throughout the second half of the twentieth century, Native writers, artists, and activists each channeled Red Power as a call for progressive social and political reform. Like Mari Sandoz accomplished in *The Battle of the Little Bighorn,* each work as part of a collective promoted a path toward decolonization and a national reconciliation by dismantling the Custer myth as a powerful symbol. Western historian Brian Dippie argues that "Red Power activists have exploited him [Custer], making him the center of their own mythology. In this capacity, as a symbolic rallying point for modern Indian dissent, Custer is not just useful, but essential."[31] Over time Indigenous peoples have created their own Custer myth. The Indigenization of the Custer myth is a process that reimagines the national narrative alongside a very different, very Indian Custer myth. Through such a process, Custer's memorialization in popular culture eventually served as a critical battleground for the ideological foundations that define the Red Power movement.

A quick sampling of the Indian Custer myth through popular culture has Custer turning up in the most unexpected of places throughout Indian Country. Custer's image appeared on countless Red Power bumper stickers and political buttons, sporting slogans like the infamous "Custer Wore an Arrow Shirt" or "Custer Had It Coming." The

16. Slogans referencing Custer: (*top*) "Custer Had It Coming!" bumper sticker from Checkers Enterprises, St. Louis, Missouri, no date; (*bottom center*) "Custer Wore an Arrow Shirt" political button by Discovery Corp., Rapid City, South Dakota, no date. Political statements from the Alcatraz Island occupation by Indians of All Tribes (IAT), 1969–71: (*bottom left*) "Custer Was Here" (located in the dungeon or basement of Alcatraz's main cellblock, which contains Civil War–era cells; occupiers used lighters or candles to make the markings on the ceiling); (*bottom right*) "Custer had it Comeing [*sic*]" (located in a cell in the main cellblock of the former prison). Author's collection.

organization Indians of All Tribes replicated these same slogans for use as political statements that appeared in red paint on the prison walls and structures of Alcatraz during the nineteen-month Native occupation of the island (1969–71).[32]

Throughout the 1960s and well into the 1970s, an Indigenous rewriting of the Custer myth transformed the popular image of George Armstrong Custer from tragic hero into the universal antihero, a dark symbol of American exceptionalism and imperialism.

Sandoz's final years of research and writing *The Battle of the Little Bighorn* coincided with the dawn of a new movement of Indigenous modernism in the art world, many champions of which had an asso-

17. Custer posters: (*left*) "Let's Win This War and Get Out!" Gen. George Armstrong Custer, June 25, 1876, No. 4, IDEAS Inc. (Little Bighorn Veterans Association, 1970); (*right*) "Custer Died for Our Sins," poster art by Norman Orr, 1970. Orr's poster was inspired by Dakota scholar Vine Deloria Jr.'s monumental book *Custer Died for Your Sins: An Indian Manifesto* (1969). These posters inspired greater public sympathy for Indigenous rights as well as the anti–Vietnam War movement. The Custer poster was Orr's first commercial poster, and he was later one of several popular artists who garnered mass acclaim for creating psychedelic concert posters. Author's collection.

ciation with the Institute of American Indian Arts (IAIA) in Santa Fe, New Mexico. One group that specifically engaged with reimagining the Custer myth comprised Indigenous painters. Throughout the Red Power era, American Indian artists ranging from Luiseño painter Fritz Scholder to Kiowa/Caddo sensation T. C. Cannon explored the power behind confronting the Custer myth.[33] Their artistic interventions influenced world-renowned pop artist Andy Warhol, who employed modernism as a tool to force his audiences to confront and reflect upon the pervasiveness of the Custer myth as well as America's glorification of genocide. For Warhol and other pop artists,

Custer represented a powerful American icon that by the mid-1970s had fractured due to the corruption and scandal associated with President Richard Nixon's resignation. Like Mari Sandoz, Warhol sought to highlight this moral outrage by placing the Custer myth into a national conversation and critique within his classic *Cowboys and Indians* portfolio of paintings (1986).[34]

Long before Warhol's American West critique, transforming the Custer myth represented powerful subject matter for Native artists. The most potent manifestation of an Indigenized Custer myth can be located in Kiowa/Caddo citizen T. C. Cannon's provocative interpretations of Custer and a painting simply titled *Soldiers*.

From 1964 to 1966, Cannon attended the Institute for American Indian Arts and then enlisted in the army. He served as a helicopter gunner in the 101st Airborne Division during the height of the Tet Offensive in the Vietnam War from 1967 to 1968.[35] After his tour of duty, Cannon returned stateside with two Bronze Stars, and the worlds on his canvas exploded with vibrant color. Thick brushstrokes of paint as bright as a napalm burst outlined his sophisticated subjects. His 1970 painting *Soldiers* features a conjoined human figure that is half Indigenous warrior and half yellow-bearded bluecoat settler soldier. The figure has outstretched arms on the canvas, reminiscent of either a crucified Jesus or Leonardo da Vinci's famous 1490 ink drawing *Vitruvian Man*, a vision of the ideal human proportions. Some have suggested that *Soldiers* represents the effect of military training on Indian soldiers and the generational trauma inherited from the Indian Wars. There are even more meanings that can be gleaned from Cannon's provocative vision. With striking colors of red (day/fire) and blue (night/water), Cannon referenced the same color sequence that appears on Kiowa gourd dancers' peyote blankets. Typically made from trade cloth, these blankets are worn draped over the shoulders of a gourd dancer. A reflection of Native veterans and their service, Cannon's painting honors both their conflict and sacrifice.[36]

Often interpreted literally as a split between two opposites—a conjoined Native warrior and white U.S. soldier—the painting presents an

18. T. C. Cannon (1946–78, Caddo/Kiowa), *Soldiers*, 1970. Oil on canvas. Collection of Arnold and Karen Blair. © 2017 Estate of T. C. Cannon. Photo by Scott Geffert. Collection identification number TCC-076 24-1. Special thanks to Joyce Cannon Yi and Karen Kramer at the Peabody Essex Museum, Salem, Massachusetts.

alternative perspective on assimilation. Who is doing the assimilating? Who is being sacrificed? *Soldiers* represents two halves of the same body, like two separate forces that have merged into one, a colonial conflict connected only through their shared humanity. In addition, Cannon's painting reflected his own personal struggle with post-traumatic stress disorder (PTSD). After their return from the war, most Vietnam veterans never received any official diagnosis, assistance, or therapy to help them deal with the aftermath of living through and with the war, and Cannon used his canvas as a biographical and therapeutic tool to expose injustice and challenge his audience to question the social and colonial constructs of inequality and to confront a simple truth: *we have all been colonized.* As art historian Karen Kramer has argued, this painting points to Cannon's internal struggle as a Vietnam veteran, the conflict of wearing the dual hats of colonized and colonizer.[37]

One year later, Cannon continued to employ Custer as a subject, this time for a woodcut print titled *Zero Hero*, which was included in a three-part linocut series he completed at Central State College in Oklahoma. In its title alone, this image speaks to Custer's antihero status and use as a provocative symbol of empire and colonization. Cannon further enriched the background of *Zero Hero* with what appears to be a symbolic rising sun that is hidden behind a stream and high, almost mountainous Black Hills.

The landscape hints at a Custer looking toward the East with his back up against the West; multiple signs of empire collide between the negative and positive spaces that complete the image. Often what is missing in a work of art can be just as compelling as what is present. The rising sun image and the Zero (the common name for a Japanese fighter plane) are artifacts forever linked to Japan's vast military empire during World War II, the last fascist dictatorship that only fell as a result of two atomic blasts. While the United States had won the war, it never escaped the haunting legacy of killing hundreds of thousands of people at Hiroshima and Nagasaki in the flash of two artificial suns. In a subsequent edition of the *Zero Hero* artwork, Cannon replaced the imperial flag of Japan in the background with one of the most frightening images of the Cold War: a mushroom cloud from an atomic blast. With dark irony, Cannon offers a powerful association between U.S. aggression in the Indian Wars and Japan's surprise military attack on Pearl Harbor, which serves as a critique on how villains are manufactured. While the image lacks any Native peoples, it leaves an unresolved question: where is the moral outrage over Indigenous erasure, dehumanization, and genocide? Cannon's *Zero Hero* linocut offers its viewers a highly charged political subject.[38]

In 1971, several months after the linocut series, Cannon painted a full-color interpretation of *Zero Hero*. In this colorful new edition, Cannon removed any hint of directionality, a comedic take on Custer's horrible sense of direction. The painted version of *Zero Hero* erased any indication of nature beyond the sky. All that remains is the shape of an enormous atomic blast's mushroom cloud. To help his audience make the connection, he inserted a replica of the Seventh Cavalry military flag (without the U.S. inscription) banded in red and white horizontal stripes, the banner hovering above Custer. Cannon quite deliberately allowed the red band to encroach or bleed into the white space of the flag. For this image, Custer's uniform, in this case his

19. T. C. Cannon (1946–78, Caddo/Kiowa), *Zero Hero*, 1971. Woodcut. Anonymous. © 2017 Estate of T. C. Cannon. Photo by Addison Doty. Collection identification number TCC-076 24-1. Special thanks to Joyce Cannon Yi and Karen Kramer, Peabody Essex Museum, Salem, Massachusetts.

hat, displays a single star, whereas the earlier linocut version featured two stars, a historical transition that spoke to Custer's reduction in rank.[39] Cannon's alternative perspective provides a postmodern window through which to view his clash of time, space, subjects, and politics. His take on Custer screamed antihero and antiwar sentiment.

A hallmark of T. C. Cannon's paintings is that he often blended history with an everyday experience or action as his brush voiced both the testimony and duty of a modern Native warrior. The intense and deeply personal perspective found in Cannon's paintings stems from his belonging to the Kiowa Black Leggings Society. His participation in this society provided Cannon with a unique perspective on the roles and duties of a warrior upon return from war. As a part of the Black Leggings Society, Cannon inherited a sacred duty, a responsibility that arises from taking the life of another human being. In many Native lifeways, an enemy's life or spirit becomes a part of you, so taking a life has the power to transform a warrior physically, emotionally, intellectually, and spiritually. Part of Indigenizing the Custer myth means that the taking of Custer's physical life created a new relationship. Custer had been absorbed into an Indigenous story, and his experience became as much a responsibility for Indigenous peoples as the conflict had.[40]

Indigenous artists challenged the prevalence of the Custer myth in a concerted effort to highlight the true legacy of the Battle of the Little Bighorn in much the same way that Sandoz sought to clarify it in her 1966 book on the battle. In 1969 the prominent Luiseño artist Fritz Scholder painted *Custer and 20,000 Indians*, which isolated Custer in the middle of the canvas, as the lone obsession or target.[41] With his pistol drawn toward the east, Custer raises his sword high over his head, as if ready to slay an empty space. To keep the balance of this last desperate action, Custer stands with one leg raised, steadying his boot on top of a large boulder (maybe Scholder's own nod to the occupation of Alcatraz, popularly known as the Rock). Custer's entire buckskin-clothed body is frozen midway, paused and unable to complete one singular action of violence. Through Scholder's

20. T. C. Cannon (1946–78, Caddo/Kiowa), *Zero Hero*, 1971. Oil. Private collection. Courtesy Estate of T. C. Cannon. Special thanks to Joyce Cannon Yi and Joan Frederick, author of *T. C. Cannon: He Stood in the Sun* (Flagstaff AZ: Northland Publishing, 1995).

deconstructed historical lens, it appears that no other soul mattered more in this battle than Custer's. Scholder isolated Custer on his canvas as if he were suspended in time, his death imminent. He stands beneath a crimson sky at a crossroads between light and dark and before an unknown, nonexistent, fill-in-the-blank enemy. Scholder, who was a former instructor of Cannon at the Institute of American Indian Arts and a controversial painter who once vowed that he would never paint the Indian, was known for his altering of historical images of the Indian.[42] His Custer painting drew inspiration from an 1876 newspaper illustration, *The Death Struggle of General Custer*, by William de la Montagne Cary.

Seven years later, Scholder revisited the same subject matter for his lithographic adaptation of Edgar S. Paxson's 1899 painting *Custer's Last Stand*. Paxson's painting was unveiled to the public at the conclusion of the Spanish-American War, a war inflamed by yellow journalism and imperial expansion that erupted in Cuba and expanded west to the Philippines.

Ironically, Scholder unveiled his own reinterpretation only a year after the fall of Saigon and the end of America's involvement in Vietnam. Scholder elected to reverse the original image and have Custer face east as he became completely engulfed by the chaos of war.[43] In this context and during the height of Red Power, Scholder's reversal of Custer's traditional position protested the use of Custer's death as an acceptable form of American patriotism for western expansion.

As one of the most celebrated of all Custer paintings, Paxson's image remains essential to the Custer myth. Part of the celebratory nostalgia for Paxson's memorial involves the artist's own penchant for

21. (*Top*) Edgar S. Paxson, *Custer's Last Stand*, 1899. Oil on canvas. Courtesy of the Buffalo Bill Center of the West, Cody, Wyoming; Whitney Western Art Museum; 19.69. (*Bottom*) One of the first artistic depictions of the battle, by William de la Montagne Cary, *The Battle on the Little Big Horn River—The Death Struggle of General Custer*, 1876. Courtesy of the Buffalo Bill Center of the West, Cody, Wyoming; McCracken Research Library; MS062—Don Russell Collection; MS62.1.0.3.27.01.

THE BATTLE ON THE LITTLE BIG HORN RIVER—THE DEATH STRUGGLE OF GENERAL CUSTER.

research; after 1877 he visited the battlefield multiple times, interviewed prominent Lakota military leaders, and collected the testimonies of at least ninety-six veterans who had some connection to Custer's former command.[44] Often referenced as one of the more accurate interpretations of Custer's last moments, Paxson's image is laced with nationalist symbols, as the flags and banners of the Seventh Cavalry never fall and the tattered but upright American flag appears in the foreground along the "western" edge of his canvas. He placed Custer near the top of the hill in a gallant stride, poised to confront his fate. In Scholder's deconstructed and reimagined interpretation of Paxson's vision, the distorted dark silhouettes of the bluecoats claim a vast proportion of the negative space while the overwhelming presence of an Indigenous military closes in upon Custer within the same positive space. Scholder minimized the celebratory nationalism in *Custer's Last Stand*, completely removing the American flag from his own rendering and leaving only one blank flag within the positive space and thus signifying the uncertainty of and hope for a different America. Once again, Scholder's willful use of negative and positive blocking demonstrates Indigenous ownership of and a significant reframing of the Custer myth. By placing both Cannon and Scholder in conversation with Sandoz, their collective struggle to reimagine the Custer myth elevates *The Battle of the Little Bighorn* to the first of an emerging array of antiwar and Red Power artistic works.

Collectively, the intersection of music, brushstrokes, and prose of the Indigenous Custer myth positions Sandoz's methodology and collected works as an influential contributor to the historiographical development of two critical academic fields.

The pivotal event in the Indigenized Custer myth, where life interpreted art, occurred ten years after Sandoz's death. During the one-hundredth anniversary commemorations of the Battle of the Little Bighorn, Red Power activists interrupted the National Park Service's official event. It was a rare cold and overcast day on June 24, 1976, when the American Indian Movement (AIM) arrived in a caravan of cars to demonstrate at what was then called the Custer Battlefield in

Montana. The National Park Service had spent months planning an elaborate ceremony for this anniversary, though the main event was scheduled the day before the actual anniversary date. National Park Service officials elected to move up the official ceremony to thwart any potential protests by Indigenous leaders. In the wake of the 1973 AIM takeover of Wounded Knee and a bloody shootout in 1975 on the Pine Ridge Reservation that had ended in the deaths of two Federal Bureau of Investigation (FBI) agents and one AIM member, officials felt it was necessary to assemble a small army of heavily armed park rangers and enlist help from a larger force of Montana Highway Patrol officers, FBI agents, and federal park police, who stood on full alert alongside their security dogs. Fearful of protesters looting precious historical artifacts, National Park Service organizers ordered the removal of Custer's uniforms and key battlefield artifacts to a secure storage facility located over thirty hours' drive away, in West Virginia.[45]

Park service officials had reason to fear. At Wounded Knee in 1973 the Oglala Sioux Civil Rights Organization (OSCRO) leaders had asked for representatives from the American Indian Movement (AIM originated out of Minneapolis, Minnesota, in 1968) to act as a security force and to help them publicize issues of corruption, scandal, and abuse that Pine Ridge citizens experienced under the contested regime of tribal chairman Dick Wilson. Before they arrived at Wounded Knee, AIM leaders had gained notoriety for their support of the 1972 BIA building takeover in Washington DC—the first time since the War of 1812 that a federal building had been taken by another sovereign power. The following year AIM led a protest in the reservation border town of Custer, South Dakota, which erupted into a violent clash with local law enforcement officers over the brutal lynching of Lakota citizen Wesley Bad Heart Bull. After the Custer protest, they arrived at Wounded Knee, where in 1890 the remnants of Custer's Seventh Cavalry had massacred 146 Lakota men, women, and children and then received Medals of Honor for their role in this massacre. What transpired eighty-three years later led to a seventy-one-day armed standoff that pitted the two Indigenous organizations against a combined force of federal marshals, FBI agents, well-armed supporters of a corrupt tribal chairman, and local vigilantes. This ragtag assortment of local law enforcement and vigilantes received military aid and equipment consisting of armored patrol carriers that had been used in Vietnam. By the end of the standoff and after enduring countless days of taking heavy gunfire from federal forces, two activists lost their lives: Cherokee descendant Frank Clearwater and Lakota Vietnam veteran Buddy La Monte.

In the aftermath of Wounded Knee, several highly publicized trials led to the assassination of Lakota activist Pedro Bissonette at the hands of BIA police. Overzealous supporters of Dick Wilson retaliated against everyone who supported OSCRO or AIM, unleashing a bloody reign of terror that forever changed the lives of nearly every Pine Ridge citizen. Throughout this dark period, countless people disappeared or were murdered outright, and there were few arrests or convictions, eerily echoing the conflict in Vietnam. Two years into this violence, on June 26, 1975, two FBI agents in vehicular pursuit of a wanted suspect trespassed onto the Jumping Bull Compound (a private family residence that sheltered a large AIM encampment) on the Pine Ridge Reservation. What transpired after their arrival is still a mystery; after a massive gun battle, two FBI agents and Coeur d'Alene activist Joseph Stuntz, a graduate of IAIA, were dead.[46] In the wake of those events, any AIM demonstration, especially in 1976, drew an enormous law enforcement presence. The violent response by law enforcement to initially nonviolent Indigenous actions had effectively stripped the Red Power movement of its nonviolent principles in the public mind and falsely painted all Native activism as militant.

As a result of the high frequency of these militant and violent images of Native peoples within the mainstream media, the National Park Service made its decision to request extra security before it hosted the Little Bighorn centennial event. On the day of the ceremony over five hundred spectators gathered at the site and listened as a crescendo of horns and sharp drum taps from a uniformed military band played Custer's battle hymn, "Garry Owen." As soon as the band started, they were drowned out by the strong voices of an Indigenous delegation consisting of several Lakota singers carrying a large honor drum as they led several hundred AIM protesters to the ceremony site.[47]

This delegation composed of Lakota and Cheyenne leaders emerged just over a hill that overlooked the official ceremony. The marchers walked in the footsteps of their ancestors as they approached the ceremonial stage. They were led by Lakota elder and World War II veteran Oscar Bear Runner, who carried a sacred pipe. A small group of marchers carried an upside-down American flag, a position that honored U.S. military protocols signaling a unit under distress. Its vailing provided a poignant and provocative message about the failure of the United States to honor its commitments to Indigenous treaties and human rights. The marchers themselves represented the living descendants of a powerful confederacy that had completely overwhelmed Custer's command only a century ago. Once the procession had reached the speaker's stand, Lakota AIM leader Russell Means, dressed in a colorful Seminole-design jacket, climbed up the stairs and walked across the event stage. After Means took over the podium, a few members of the crowd found it difficult to conceal their uneasiness as they awkwardly repositioned themselves in their chairs. Others in the crowd grew more agitated and offended. Some attendees went so far as to request that park officials seize the American flag from the marchers. Standing alongside Means at the podium was Bear Runner, who offered the stem of his pipe up toward the sky. To commemorate this day, Indigenous activists arrived unarmed and carried symbols of peace and progress to memorialize this space as hallowed ground. Means took a moment to gather his thoughts as he looked out over the crowd, and then he began to speak: "In 1876 we were invited to a similar gathering. In 1976 we were not invited. We would like you to observe with due respect our sacred pipe. One hundred years ago there was not time to present that pipe to the invaders. Tomorrow is our day of celebration. In your Bicentennial year, we, the Indian people have a centennial year to celebrate—a year that gives us pride and dignity. We bear no ill will."[48] Much to his surprise the crowd applauded. Means then proclaimed that a victory dance would commence at the Last Stand marker and feature the Floyd Red Crow Westerman song "Custer Died for Your Sins."

The fog of war, more specifically over both Vietnam and the Little Bighorn, had shadowed the centennial planning. The National Park Service also received criticism from spectators angry over the lack of any uniformed military presence at the event except for the band. In fact, one of Custer's descendants, Colonel George Custer, was prohibited from sitting on the stage, and only at the end of the ceremony was he allowed to present a memorial wreath to commemorate his ancestors. The recent fall of Saigon and the antiwar movement, fresh on the minds of most Americans, muted the atmosphere planned for that day, for the ceremony held that day was not a celebration of the U.S. military but rather an official commemoration of what had been lost and who was still missing.

After Russell Means spoke (a tough act to follow), noted western historian Robert M. Utley, a former NPS employee whose service had begun in 1947, addressed the crowd as the formal keynote speaker. His speech, summarized by the *New York Times*, attempted to dismantle a new myth, one impacted by the Vietnam War, and offered a singular view of Custer's forces and the frontier military as the real savages, hell-bent on exterminating all Native peoples. Utley's interpretation was a version of what Sandoz had penned in *The Battle of the Little Bighorn*. It was decidedly not along the lines of the recent best-selling book by Dee Brown, *Bury My Heart at Wounded Knee*. Utley's comments targeted Dee Brown's book, in which Brown had reduced the Native experience to an exclusive role—that of the iconic "end of the trail" victim or declension narrative.[49] This was a moment when the Indian Custer myth found a national stage.

Contrary to Dee Brown's powerful but exploitive account, Sandoz's book had proved a far more potent symbol for the Red Power movement, as Native peoples emerged as victors and survivors rather than as victims. Her research and writing criticized Custer's military career while it also challenged and signaled the changing nature of

22. (*Top*) On June 24, 1976, American Indian Movement (AIM) members demonstrated at the Little Bighorn centennial anniversary event. (*Bottom, left to right*) Oglala Lakota activist and AIM leader Russell Means with activists and dancers at Last Stand Hill. All photos are by and courtesy of Clifford Oliver, cliffordoliver.zenfolio.com/NativeAmerica. Special thanks to artist Thom Ross, who also attended the event.

the Custer myth. In this context, Sandoz should be remembered as a staunch supporter of Native rights, a foundational scholar for the establishment of Native American studies, and an early anti–Vietnam War voice and Red Power advocate. Other historians agreed with Utley. It was time the Custer myth passed. Writing in preparation for the centennial celebration, historian Paul Hutton authored an essay that helps to detangle the significance of the Custer myth: "Heroes are not born, they are created. Their lives so catch the imagination of their generation, and often the generations that follow, that they are repeatedly discussed and written about. The lives of heroes are a tes-

tament to the values and aspirations of those who admire them. If their images change as time passes they may act as a barometer of the fluctuating attitudes of society. Eventually, if certain attitudes change enough, one hero myth may replace another. Such is the case with George Armstrong Custer."[50]

The potential for an Indian Custer myth is on full display in one of the most overlooked details of Sandoz's *The Battle of the Little Bighorn*. She was cognizant of the major events taking place in her last days, and for the back cover of the first edition of the book Sandoz selected a black-and-white photograph that represents the last image she wished to show the world, a photo that she wanted her audience to remember. Sandoz selected this photo as she confronted her own mortality and battled to complete her final book. In a way, it was her own last stand, taking place in her own fog of war. Out of all the photos she could have selected, she picked one that was snapped only four years after the official end of World War II, a period bookended by the communist revolution in China and the first successful test of an atomic bomb in Russia. Hundreds of miles away from these historical events, former Custer Battlefield National

23. Major E. S. Luce, superintendent of the Custer Battlefield National Monument, and Mari Sandoz, 1949, as featured on the back cover of the first edition of Sandoz's *The Battle of the Little Bighorn* (Philadelphia: J. B. Lippincott, 1966). Image 2003.001.00270, Caroline Sandoz Pifer Collection, Mari Sandoz High Plains Heritage Center. Courtesy of the Mari Sandoz Society.

Monument superintendent Major E. S. Luce, himself a former captain of the Seventh Cavalry, and Mari Sandoz stood on opposite sides of Custer's memorial marker.[51] The two stood as if staged, as they faced one another, each with their hands in their pockets and a marked but empty grave between them. Sandoz seems to stare beyond the uniformed authority of Major Luce. This photo represents a symbolic changing of the guard over the memory and memorialization of America's most infamous unknown soldier.

Mari Sandoz sought to change the symbolic landscape of this battlefield and invite a new generation—one that would protest the Vietnam War and advocate for Red Power—to change the course of history.[52] Sandoz championed the power of story to promote reform in her own time. As future generations will continue to wrestle over control of and responsibility for the Custer myth, we have an opportunity to discover new heroes and recover stories that, in the spirit of Sandoz, speak to a brighter tomorrow of reconciliation and freedom.

NOTES

This chapter was originally delivered as a lecture for the Mari Sandoz Society annual meeting on October 14, 2016, at the Sandoz High Plains Heritage Center located on the campus of Chadron State College in Chadron, Nebraska.

Epigraph: From the J. B. Lippincott edition (1966), 120.

1. David Lowe, "A Meeting with Mari Sandoz," *Prairie Schooner* 42, no. 1 (Spring 1968): 24.
2. Sandoz to Knopf, March 15, 1944, quoted in Kathy Bahr, "Collateral Damage: Veterans and Domestic Violence in Mari Sandoz's *The Tom-Walker*," *Great Plains Quarterly* 30, no. 2 (Spring 2010): 94. For more on Mari Sandoz's antiwar stance, see Bahr, "Collateral Damage," 83–96. The phrase "fog of war" is usually attributed to Carl von Clausewitz, who used it to describe the uncertainty in situational awareness experienced by participants in military operations. The term speaks to insecurities in one's own abilities, the enemy's skill, and the objectives in battle—the unknown variables that can alter any war-games scenario. The phrase may also be construed more

broadly, in relation to a society's turmoil during wartime, and in that sense it is an appropriate descriptor of the antiwar and protest ferment that may be the true muse behind Sandoz's last book.

3. John Prados, *Vietnam: The History of an Unwinnable War, 1945–1975* (Lawrence: University Press of Kansas, 2009), 26–36, 148–65. See also Neil Sheehan, *A Bright Shining Lie: John Paul Vann and America in Vietnam* (New York: Vintage Books, 1988); David Halberstam, *The Best and the Brightest* (New York: Ballantine Books, 1992); and George C. Herring, *America's Longest War: The United States and Vietnam, 1950–1975* (New York: McGraw Hill Education, 2002).

4. The first public record that referenced Vietnam as "Indian Country" came in the form of General Maxwell Taylor's testimony before the Senate Foreign Relations Committee, known popularly as the Vietnam Hearings, in January 1966. Taylor stated, "'We have always been able to move in the areas where the security was good enough. But I have often said it is very hard to plant the corn outside the stockade when the Indians are still around. We have to get the Indians farther away in many of the provinces to make good progress.' In Vietnam American officers like to call the area outside GVN [Government of (South) Vietnam] control 'Indian Country.'" Quoted in Frances FitzGerald, *Fire in the Lake: The Vietnamese and the Americans in Vietnam* (Boston: Little, Brown, 1972), 367–68. General Taylor's testimony occurred a few weeks before David Lowe visited with Mari Sandoz. For more on the origins of the term in military jargon, see Stephen W. Silliman, "The 'Old West' in the Middle East: U.S. Military Metaphors in Real and Imagined Indian Country," *American Anthropologist* 110, no. 2 (June 2008): 237–47; and David Espey, "America and Vietnam: The Indian Subtext," *Journal of American Culture and Literature*, January 1994, 128–36. For more on victory culture, see Tom Engelhardt, *The End of Victory Culture: Cold War America and the Disillusioning of a Generation* (Amherst: University of Massachusetts Press, 2007). See also Richard Slotkin, *The Fatal Environment: The Myth of the Frontier in the Age of Industrialization, 1800–1890* (Middletown CT: Wesleyan University Press, 1986), 16–18. Scholars argue that the origins of the term "Indian Country" deserve further research in nineteenth-century war records and correspondence to locate its first military use as a signifier of conquest and elimination.

5. For biographical treatments of Custer, see also T. J. Stiles, *Custer's Trials: A Life on the Frontier of a New America* (New York: Knopf, 2015); and Robert M.

Utley, *Cavalier in Buckskin: George Armstrong Custer and the Western Military Frontier* (Norman: University of Oklahoma Press, 1988).

6. Mari Sandoz, *The Battle of the Little Bighorn* (Philadelphia: J. B. Lippincott, 1966), 120.

7. Cherokee historian Tom Holm argued that the continued use of a savagery or primitive lens to interpret Indigenous military engagements "painted European military conquest as a civilizing action. . . . [Only with] this view of Native American warfare, depicting it as functional only in terms of revenge, gaining access to new hunting grounds, obtaining booty and women, or providing warriors with the opportunity to demonstrate their individual prowess . . . did Indian people rise above the 'military horizon,' becoming actual states with real political aspirations." Tom Holm, "American Indian Warfare: The Cycles of Conflict and the Militarization of Native North America," in *A Companion to American Indian History*, ed. Philip J. Deloria and Neal Salisbury (Malden MA: Blackwell, 2004), 155.

8. In conversation with Sandoz's political rhetoric, H. Richard Nielson Jr. states that she tried "drawing a connection with her audience for she based her challenges on anger at social ills, against which she sought to arouse . . . her readers. . . . She expressed a more overt political agenda . . . yet this agenda often . . . causes her work to fall short of her revolutionary goals. . . . Mari Sandoz always insisted on the writer's need for . . . emotional commitment in social responsibility." H. Richard Nielsen Jr., "Articulating Protest: The Personal and Political Rhetorics of Clifford Odets and Mari Sandoz in the 1930s" (PhD diss., University of Nebraska–Lincoln, 1991), 43–44. In her March 1944 letter to Blanche Knopf, Mari Sandoz stated that "characters symbolize a society which is wounded by the power of war, with its corruption and greed." Quoted in Bahr, "Collateral Damage," 94.

9. Jack Burrows, review of *The Battle of the Little Bighorn*, by Mari Sandoz, *Arizona and the West* 9, no. 1 (Spring 1967): 65–67. See also Frederic F. Van de Water, *Glory-Hunter: A Life of General Custer* (Indianapolis: Bobbs-Merrill, 1934).

10. Paul H. Hass, review of *The Battle of the Little Bighorn*, by Mari Sandoz, *Wisconsin Magazine of History* 50, no. 3 (Spring 1967): 268–69.

11. See Elaine Marie Nelson, "Draft by Draft: The Battle of Sandoz and Her Bighorn Manuscript," *Great Plains Quarterly* 39, no. 2 (Spring 2019): 131–58.

12. Helen Winter Stauffer, *Mari Sandoz: Story Catcher of the Plains* (Lincoln: University of Nebraska Press, 1982), 248–49. Another factor missing from the literature on disappearing documents involves the 1972 occupation of

the Bureau of Indian Affairs building by protesters affiliated with several Indigenous organizations. Several of the documents removed from the BIA on that occasion dealt with the assassination of Crazy Horse. Many of these government documents ended up being spread throughout Indian Country or were also destroyed in the weeks following the takeover. It is also rumored that out of fear of receiving a harsher sentence, Native activists buried or destroyed these documents at the 1973 Wounded Knee occupation. More recently, some documents, including those that reference the assassination of Crazy Horse, have turned up on social media posts by veterans of the American Indian Movement.

13. Stauffer, *Mari Sandoz: Story Catcher*, 261.
14. Mari Sandoz, interview by Rita Shaw, 1961, for *Past, Present & Future*, excerpt at Nebraska Public Media, January 16, 2011, http://netnebraska.org/interactive-multimedia/none/past-present-future-mari-sandoz.
15. Mari Sandoz to Raymond DeMallie, April 14, 1965, Folder 10, Box 38, Mari Sandoz Collection, Archives and Special Collections, University of Nebraska–Lincoln Libraries.
16. Helen Stauffer, "Two Authors and a Hero: Neihardt, Sandoz, and Crazy Horse," *Great Plains Quarterly* 1, no. 1 (January 1981): 54–66; and J. O. Brew, "From the Brush of Bad Heart Bill: A Pictographic History of the Oglala Sioux," *New York Times*, February 25, 1968, BR7.
17. See Russell Thornton, ed., *Studying Native America: Problems and Prospects* (Madison: University of Wisconsin Press, 1998); and Clara Sue Kidwell and Allan Velie, *Native American Studies* (Lincoln: University of Nebraska Press, 2005).
18. "Book List," Folder: Ethnic Studies-NAS, Hayakawa Papers, San Francisco State University Archives, San Francisco, California.
19. "Advocacy for American Indians did not just entail writing a few letters to legislators. . . . The Association on American Indian Affairs (AAIA) . . . focused on assisting tribes in seven focused areas: education, health, land tenure, industry, irrigation, religion, and autonomy. . . . Sandoz began her affiliation with AAIA in 1950. . . . This group . . . was one of the most adamant and vocal proponents for Native American rights during the termination years." Kimberli A. Lee, *"I Do Not Apologize for the Length of This Letter": The Mari Sandoz Letters on Native American Rights, 1940–1965* (Lubbock: Texas Tech University Press, 2009), 17.

20. For more information on termination and relocation, see Donald Fixico, *Termination and Relocation: Federal Indian Policy, 1945–1960* (Albuquerque: University of New Mexico Press, 1986); Laurie Arnold, *Bartering with the Bones of Their Dead: The Colville Confederated Tribes and Termination* (Seattle: University of Washington Press, 2012); and Douglas K. Miller, *Indians on the Move: Native American Mobility and Urbanization in the Twentieth Century* (Chapel Hill: University of North Carolina Press, 2019).
21. Brian Dippie, *Custer's Last Stand: The Anatomy of an American Myth* (1976; Lincoln: University of Nebraska Press, 1994), 134.
22. For instance, Custer or a version of the frontier hero featured in at least nineteen movies between 1912 and 1966, from *Custer's Last Fight* (1912) to *The Plainsman* (1936 and again in 1966). Even a young actor and future U.S. president, Ronald Reagan, starred as Custer in the 1940 film *Santa Fe Trail*.
23. Scott Kirkwood, "One More Casualty at Little Bighorn?" *National Parks*, Summer 2012, https://www.npca.org/articles/1070-one-more-casualty-at-little-bighorn.
24. For a more information on the origins and production of the Custer myth, consult Dippie, *Custer's Last Stand*; Slotkin, *Fatal Environment*; Hutton, *Custer Reader*; and Michael A. Elliott, *Custerology: The Enduring Legacy of the Indian Wars and George Armstrong Custer* (Chicago: University of Chicago Press, 2008). Two of the more recent Indigenous interpretations of the Battle of the Little Bighorn include James Welch and Paul Stekler, *Killing Custer: The Battle of the Little Bighorn and the Fate of the Plains Indians* (New York: Norton, 1994); and Joseph M. Marshall III, *The Day the World Ended at Little Bighorn: A Lakota History* (New York: Viking Press, 2007).
25. Floyd Westerman, *Custer Died for Your Sins* (New York: Perception Records, 1969).
26. Vine Deloria Jr., *Custer Died for Your Sins: An Indian Manifesto* (New York: Macmillan, 1969), 41.
27. Welch and Stekler, *Killing Custer*, 226.
28. Peter La Farge, *Peter La Farge Sings of the Indians: As Long as the Grass Shall Grow* (New York: Folkways Records, 1963).
29. For more on Oliver La Farge, see Robert A. Hecht, "Oliver LaFarge, John Collier, and the Hopi Constitution of 1936," *Journal of Arizona History* 26, no. 2 (Summer 1985): 145–62.

30. Johnny Cash covered many of La Farge's songs, including "Custer," on the 1964 release of his Columbia Records album *Bitter Tears: Ballads of the American Indian*. Later in 1969, Johnny Cash and Buffy Sainte-Marie performed "Custer" on television for *The Johnny Cash Show*. Buffy Sainte-Marie continued to perform La Farge's "Custer" to live audiences throughout the 1970s.
31. Dippie, *Custer's Last Stand*, 135.
32. For more on the Alcatraz occupation, see Kent Blansett, *A Journey to Freedom: Richard Oakes, Alcatraz, and the Red Power Movement* (New Haven: Yale University Press, 2018); Troy Johnson, *The Occupation of Alcatraz Island: Indian Self-Determination and the Rise of Indian Activism* (Urbana: University of Illinois Press, 1996); Robert Warrior and Paul Chaat Smith, *Like a Hurricane: The Indian Movement from Alcatraz to Wounded Knee* (New York: New Press, 1996); and Sherry Smith, *Hippies, Indians, and the Fight for Red Power* (New York: Oxford University Press, 2012). For more information on the political symbols on Alcatraz, see Dean Rader, *Engaged Resistance: American Indian Art, Literature, and Film from Alcatraz to the NMAI* (Austin: University of Texas Press, 2011).
33. Interestingly, Custer as a subject is missing from many of the paintings by early Native women painters, including Cherokee artist Kay WalkingStick, Muscogee Creek and Cherokee painter Joan Hill (who used Vietnam and scenes of traditional life to present an Indigenous comment on the war), and the explosive paintings of Hopi/Choctaw painter Linda Lomahaftewa. In my research, the first Native woman to paint Custer was Salish artist Juane Quick-to-See Smith. Her painting of Custer appears in 1993, the year after the quincentenary anniversary of Columbus's invasion. It is also important to acknowledge that these themes of the Custer myth and Vietnam transcend the period and continue to be revisited by more contemporary artists. As one scholar notes, "'Resistance to (neo)colonial hegemony' is clearly one of the most salient characteristics of Indian art since the 1960s.... Indians themselves now have taken the power of the image and begun to use it for their own enjoyment as well as for its potential power as a political weapon.... Artists have also used art as an effective tool to rewrite their histories, understanding that images are often more powerful and memorable than high school history texts that marginalize or ignore the place of American Indians in historical rhetoric." Nancy Parezo, "Indigenous Art: Creating Value and Sharing Beauty," in *A Companion to American Indian History*, ed. Philip J. Deloria and Neal Salisbury (Malden MA: Blackwell, 2004), 227.

34. For more on Warhol and the West, see Heather Ahtone, Faith Brower, and Seth Hopkins, *Warhol and the West* (Oakland: University of California Press, 2019); and Alexxa Gotthardt, "Why Andy Warhol Was Enthralled with the West," *Artsy*, August 15, 2019, https://www.artsy.net/article/artsy-editorial-andy-warhol-enthralled-wild-west. Interestingly, in 1976 Warhol did a painting of American Indian Movement leader and Lakota activist Russell Means for his *The American Indians* series. It was released in time for the hundredth anniversary of the Little Bighorn battle.
35. According to one scholar, "The average age of Native Americans in the . . . Vietnam War was between 19 and 21 [and] . . . more than 42,000 Native Americans served in Southeast Asia either as advisors or as combat troops between 1960 and 1973. More than 250 American Indians died there." Tom Holm, *Strong Hearts, Wounded Souls: Native American Veterans of the Vietnam War* (Austin: University of Texas Press, 1996), 10–11.
36. See Benjamin R. Kracht, "Kiowa Powwows: Tribal Identity through the Continuity of the Gourd Dance," *Great Plains Research* 4, no. 2 (August 1994): 257–69; Clyde Ellis, *A Dancing People: Powwow Culture on the Southern Plains* (Lawrence: University Press of Kansas, 2003); and Jenny Tone-Pah-Hote, *Crafting an Indigenous Nation: Kiowa Expressive Culture in the Progressive Era* (Chapel Hill: University of North Carolina Press, 2019).
37. Karen Kramer, ed., *T. C. Cannon: At the Edge of America* (Salem MA: Peabody Essex Museum, 2018), 132; Joan Frederick, *T. C. Cannon: He Stood in the Sun* (Flagstaff AZ: Northland, 1995), 81. The only other split art that Cannon produced is a possible untitled self-portrait study pencil sketch that appears on the cover of his published works of poetry. The split image features T. C. Cannon in sunglasses against a dark background, and the opposite side is a portrait of historic Kiowa leader Satanta (ca. 1820–78)—who used an army bugle in battle to confuse U.S. troops as to their positions and commands. As a side note, Satanta was held hostage by Custer for several months (this occurred after Custer led the massacre of Black Kettle's Cheyenne peoples in the 1868 Battle of the Washita River). Custer threatened to hang the Kiowa leader as a tactic to force a Kiowa surrender and their acceptance of a life confined to their assigned treaty reservation lands. Joyce Cannon Yi, ed., *My Determined Eye: Writings of T. C. Cannon* (La Mirada CA: Cannon Yi, 2006).
38. Kramer, *T. C. Cannon*, 211–12.
39. Frederick, *T. C. Cannon*, 127.

40. Kramer, *T. C. Cannon*, 37–43.
41. As fate had it, Fritz Scholder's mother, Elle Mae Haney, worked as the official typist for the novelist Oliver La Farge, who was also leader of the Association on American Indian Affairs. Lowery Stokes Sims, Truman T. Lowe, and Paul Chaat Smith, *Fritz Scholder: Indian/Not Indian* (New York: Prestel, 2011), 27.
42. Sims, Lowe, and Smith, *Fritz Scholder*, 46–50.
43. Christine C. Brindza, "Truth, Myth, and Imagination: Art of the Battle of Little Bighorn," *Points West*, Summer 2010, 4–9.
44. Brindza, "Truth, Myth, and Imagination."
45. Russell Means and Marvin J. Wolf, *Where White Men Fear to Tread: The Autobiography of Russell Means* (New York: St. Martin's Press, 1995), 357–58; Robert M. Utley, "Custer and Me," *True West* 48 (May–June 2001): 59–64.
46. For more on the history of the Wounded Knee occupation, see Akim D. Reinhardt, *Ruling Pine Ridge: Oglala Lakota Politics from the IRA to Wounded Knee* (Lubbock: Texas Tech University Press, 2007).
47. Robert M. Utley, *Cavalier in Buckskin: George Armstrong Custer and the Western Military Frontier* (Norman: University of Oklahoma Press, 2001), 11, 67. The Irish folksong "Garry Owen" is attributed to a drinking song that Custer adopted and then played before the Washita Massacre (November 27, 1868), when eight hundred soldiers under his command attacked and killed survivors of the Sand Creek Massacre (November 29, 1864). The title of the song is a corruption of Irish words meaning Garden of Owen, a garden located near King John's castle, constructed in 1200 to control maritime commerce; today it's a popular tourist destination in Limerick, Ireland. "Garryowen: Regimental Song," 1st Cavalry Division Association, accessed April 12, 2022, https://1cda.org/history/garryowen/#:~:text=Local%20traditions%20and%20folk%20lore,means%20%E2%80%9CGarden%20of%20Owen%E2%80%9D. See also Robert M. Utley, "Robert Utley Memoirs," presented at a symposium of the Friends of the Little Bighorn Battlefield, June 26, 2001, https://www.friendslittlebighorn.com/utleyreflections.htm.
48. Grace Lichtenstein, "Custer's Defeat Remembered in Entreaties of Peace," *New York Times*, June 25, 1976, 24.
49. Lichtenstein, "Custer's Defeat Remembered," 24; Dee Brown, *Bury My Heart at Wounded Knee: An Indian History of the American West* (New York: Henry Holt, 1970).
50. Paul Andrew Hutton, "From Little Bighorn to Little Big Man: The Changing

Image of a Western Hero in Popular Culture," *Western Historical Quarterly* 7, no. 1 (January 1976): 19.

51. One year after the battle, in 1877, the remains of Custer, his fellow officers, and the troops they commanded were removed from the battlefield. Custer's body was sent to its final resting place at the United States Military Academy, located at West Point, New York. After the battle most of the bodies had been only lightly covered with earth or vegetation, their remains destined to be scattered by coyotes or the occasional tourist who wanted a keepsake from one of America's most infamous battles. For more information, see Bob Reece, "Interment of the Custer Dead," Friends of the Little Bighorn Battlefield, accessed April 24, 2022, https://www.friendslittlebighorn.com/dusttodust.htm.

52. Interestingly, the battlefield site has undergone significant changes since it was first designated the Custer Battlefield National Monument in 1946. The impromptu first attempt to establish an Indian memorial at the site occurred in 1972, when the Trail of Broken Treaties caravan passed through the area. Seventeen years later the first Native woman superintendent of the site, Barbara Boocher, who is Cheyenne/Northern Ute, received her official appointment. Two years later, in 1991, Congress elected to change the name of the official site to the Little Bighorn Battlefield National Monument and to create an Indian memorial. Between 1999 and 2006, a total of eight markers were erected to honor the fallen warriors who engaged in the military defense of their homelands and people: Lame White Man (Southern Cheyenne), Noisy Walking (Northern Cheyenne), Closed Hand (Northern Cheyenne), Cut Belly (Northern Cheyenne), Limber Bones (Northern Cheyenne), Black White Man (Lakota), Bear With Horns (Lakota), and an unknown Lakota warrior. One year later, Russell Means led a Sun Dance at Medicine Tail Coulee to demonstrate against the quincentenary of Columbus's invasion. Finally, on June 25, 2003, there was a dedication ceremony for a sculpture by Oglala Lakota artist Colleen Cutshell depicting three warriors riding off into the battle to aid their people. Her art utilized both the positive and negative space of the landscape in a style reminiscent of Indian ledger art, like that of Amos Bad Heart Bull.

6

All That We Cannot See

The Little Bighorn Battlefield Then and Now

LEISL CARR CHILDERS

On either side the earth fell away; the slopes of gray rock, sage, and sparse grass were dotted with the green-black of cedar and jack pines coming out of the foggy morning haze. Far down the eastern slopes there was the bluer drift of smoke from the regimental fires creeping up across the daybreak. . . . [The battlefield] was like a great leaf, dead and fading in its straggly and browned June grasses and, sagebrush, like a leaf crumpled into ravines and shallow gorges of dry waterways, with slopes rising along the ridges that were the broken midrib.
—Mari Sandoz, *The Battle of the Little Bighorn*

The sun bakes the grasslands of southern Montana incessantly in June and July. In 2014 temperatures at the end of July ranged from lows in the upper 60s to highs in the lower 90s Fahrenheit. The humidity hovered around 40 percent, and both grasses and shrubs, as well as highway asphalt and concrete, took in the heat. At the end of June 2015, temperatures ranged from the upper 50s to the mid-70s Fahrenheit, but the nearly 60 percent humidity made it feel much warmer, just like it had the previous July.[1] At more than three thousand feet above sea level, though not the high altitude of the nearby mountains, the Little Bighorn Battlefield National Monument bakes under intense sunlight that can burn human skin quickly, which makes touring the battlefield at this time of year a sweaty, dehydrating affair. The site commemorates the Battle of the Little Bighorn, the victory of the

Tituwaŋ (Lakotas) and Tsis tsis'tas (Northern Cheyennes), and the defeat of George Armstrong Custer and the Seventh Cavalry, fought in the sweltering weather of June 25–26, 1876.[2]

Tourists flock to the battlefield in all seasons but especially in June and July. Between 120,000 and 150,000 visitors drive their cars along the five-mile route, stopping to take in the view, visit the memorials, read the red-and-white markers naming the dead, and take photos of the landscape and interpretive signs.[3] Some take in the battlefield experience from the Little Bighorn Visitor Center, located just to the south of the entrance gate at the west end of the monument, and gaze southeast along the ridge where the battle took place. Some spend their time at the Seventh Cavalry Memorial and the graves on Last Stand Hill overlooking the visitor center or the Indian Memorial across the road, looking north, away from the battlefield across the grassy hills of the northern plains. The more ambitious visitors drive their cars on a ten-mile out-and-back journey along the ridgeline between Last Stand Hill and Reno Hill. Those visitors who want to experience the battle as it unfolded across the landscape drive to Reno Hill and slowly make their way from the geographic starting point of the fight to the culminating battle at Last Stand Hill, taking in each interpretive sign along the way.

What visitors feel under the blaze of the summer sun as they move between their air-conditioned vehicles and the open-air memorials is an approximation of the expansive heat combatants suffered under nearly 150 years ago. What visitors see as they gaze out on the landscape of the battlefield, on the ridge, down in the coulees, and along the Little Bighorn River plain is a sea of grass, punctuated by small bunches of sagebrush rising among narrow forests of trees, that looks nothing like the terrain in which combatants fought. This disjunction of the historic and current environment poses an interesting problem for interpreters articulating the historic moment of the battle and visitors seeking to understand the physical context in which it took place. The green and gold vegetation that blankets the battlefield suggests a lushness and abundance of grass that did not exist in 1876. The lack of shrubs suggests a dearth of places to hide during the battle. The ready accessibility of water and lack of dust belies the desperate situation faced by the Seventh Cavalry.

The battlefield has changed subtly yet significantly since the late nineteenth century, but many of those changes have come about since the mid-1990s. Strikingly, until the 1990s the battlefield remained much like it had in 1876—a dry, rolling set of hills covered in sagebrush and some grasses overlooking a lusher river plain with dense clusters of trees along the riverbank. Not much of this landscape appears in most accounts of the Battle of the Little Bighorn. For most writers, the landscape is setting, but for author Mari Sandoz the environment of the Little Bighorn is as much a character in the story as the people engaged in violence. On the back cover of the first edition of *The Battle of the Little Bighorn*, published in 1966, is a 1949 photo showing Sandoz with the battlefield's superintendent, Major E. S. Luce. Between them is a white marble tablet marking the place where George Armstrong Custer died. The area surrounding them is punctuated by small tufts of bunchgrasses, and beyond a fence line are the bushy bundles of sagebrush. Kent Blansett, in his chapter in this volume on Sandoz and the fog of war, contextualizes this image in terms of the violence of warfare. In the present chapter, the image of Sandoz and Luce marks a moment in time in which she is seen on the battlefield observing its vegetation and form. Her visits to the battlefield and her observations, as recorded in her account of the battle, alongside her reading of historical accounts of the event pull together the most accurate picture of what the environment of this place was like and what it was like for combatants to be there.

Historian David Lowenthal reminds interpreters of history that the past can be a veritable foreign country, a different world. In his revised examination of how the past is remembered and memorialized, he writes, "The past is a foreign country reshaped by today, its strangeness domesticated by our own modes of caring for its vestiges."[4] Lowenthal's emphasis on the contemporary influences impacting interpretations of the past is a reminder that visitors at sites where we commemorate historical events view these places from their position in the present. Lowenthal points out that "some traces of antiquity are so faint that only contrivance makes them visible. Minus signposts, how many early battlefields would be recognized as such or seen as 'historic'? But for markers, people would pass by most monuments unaware of their antiquity."[5] In a place such as the Little Bighorn Battlefield, the large Seventh Cavalry Memorial, Indian Memorial, and Reno-Benteen Memorial bookend the linear space of where the battle took place. The smaller red-and-white markers in between, delineating where combatants fell, provide a sense of the violence and death. The record of the battle is visible through these markers on the land. According to Lowenthal, "All markers unavoidably alter what we see. Awareness of the past is reshaped as well as sharpened by signs that tell where it is and what it was."[6] Without the memorials, markers, and interpretive signs at the Little Bighorn Battlefield, the events of June 1876 would be subsumed in the grassy plains of southern Montana. But these very grassy plains obfuscate the actual environmental conditions under which the battle took place.

Lowenthal addresses one aspect of the distance that can exist between historic and contemporary environments at commemorative sites. In his discussion of the pitfalls of restoring landscapes to so-called pre-human conditions, he writes that "landscapes have no 'original state'; they ceaselessly evolve."[7] Indeed, the Little Bighorn Battlefield has changed significantly since 1876. Neil Mangum, former superintendent of the Little Bighorn Battlefield, commented in an article written for a group affiliated with the national monument that "Last Stand Hill is always changing." Mangum meant that the memorialization of the battle, first known as Custer's Last Stand and now known as the Battle of the Little Bighorn, has changed and will likely change again, but he just as easily could have meant the battlefield itself is always changing.[8] Its shape and geography are the same, but the passage of a century and a half has radically altered the vegetation that covers the hills, coulees, and river valley.

Exploring these changes provides a nuance to our understanding of the differences between what visitors see today and what combatants experienced then. The 1876 battlefield itself constitutes an unknown land, and a greater consciousness of the environmental differences between then and now can greatly affect the interpretation of the battle itself and the visitor experience at the national monument. In visitor interpretation "the setting is crucial," according to public historians Debra Reid and David Vail. In their recommendations on interpreting the environment at museums and historical sites, these historians write, "One takes the audience back in time to a particular environment—a place and a time" with interpretive signs and experiences.[9] Immersing audiences in specific environmental moments enriches the experience and brings greater understanding to the choices made and actions taken by historical actors. The National Association for Interpretation emphasizes that public-facing interpretation should consist of a "communication process that forges emotional and intellectual connections" between visitors and the sites they visit.[10] Immersing visitors in not just the story but the place of the Little Bighorn battle creates empathy and understanding for those in the past.

The Little Bighorn Battlefield National Monument covers a little over one square mile and comprises two separate sections: a larger section, the Custer Unit, encompassing the place where the Tituwaŋ and Tsis tsis'tas annihilated Custer and his men, and a smaller section, the Reno-Benteen Unit, three miles away to the southeast and encompassing the site where Major Marcus Reno and Captain Frederick Benteen nearly met a similar fate. Designated the Little Bighorn Battlefield National Monument on December 19, 1991, Congress had originally declared the 600-acre site around Last Stand Hill the Custer Battlefield National Cemetery on August 1, 1879, and tasked the War Department with its management. In 1891 the battlefield was fenced off (most likely by order of the War Department) to prevent livestock grazing.[11] In the century in between, Congress directed the Interior secretary, who oversaw the Bureau of Indian Affairs, to acquire the 162-acre Reno-Benteen Battlefield from the Apsáalooke (Crows) on April

14, 1926, as part of the fiftieth anniversary commemoration of what was then known as Custer's Last Stand.[12] After four years of negotiation, the Apsáalooke transferred the second section on April 15, 1930. The National Park Service (NPS) took over the responsibility of managing the monument from the War Department in 1940, and on March 26, 1946, Congress redesignated the site as a national monument. The National Park Service kept the moniker Custer Battlefield, reflecting the continued emphasis on Custer's demise, until 1991, when protest of the continued portrayal of the battle as a massacre of the Seventh Cavalry prompted the name change, though the memorial sites on the national monument still privilege the perspective of the U.S. military.

The battle took place on territory that has had other names more descriptive of the actual environment. The Tsis tsis'tas called it É'komo'éo'hé'e (Greasy Grass River) and the Apsáalooke called it Bikkaatashisée (Big Greasy Grass), referring to the shiny grass, which was high in protein and looked as if it had been dipped in fat, that lined the waterway of what the NPS now calls Lodge Grass Creek.[13] The É'komo'éo'hé'e (Greasy Grass River) met the Tšéške'kósáeo'hé'e (Little Bighorn River) southeast of the Tituwaŋ and Tsis tsis'tas encampment in 1876.[14] This area was part of the region contested among the Apsáalooke, designated in the 1851 Treaty of Fort Laramie; the Tituwaŋ, designated in the 1868 Treaty of Fort Laramie; and the U.S. government, which ultimately intended it as a settlement for white migrants. Custer had six Apsáalooke scouts with the Seventh Cavalry, which comprised seven hundred troops before the battle. The Tituwaŋ and Tsis tsis'tas encampment contained perhaps seven to eight thousand individuals, an unusually large congregation of Indigenous people. The massive number of horses, an estimated twenty thousand head, brought to the area by both groups, likewise required massive amounts of forage.[15]

Grass is ubiquitous at the national monument today. Varieties of native bunchgrasses predominate, including wheatgrass (*Agropyron smithii* and *Agropyron spicatum*), green needlegrass (*Nassella viridula*), and needle-and-thread grass (*Hesperostipa comata*). Non-native grasses,

24. Memorial markers at the Little Bighorn National Battlefield site near the Crow Agency community in the U.S. state of Montana, memorializing fallen members of the U.S. Army's Seventh Cavalry and the Lakotas and Cheyennes in one of the Plains Indians' last armed efforts to preserve their way of life. LC-DIG-highsm-71523, Library of Congress, Carol M. Highsmith Archive.

such as crested wheatgrass (*Agropyron cristatum*), smooth brome (*Bromus inermis*), Kentucky bluegrass (*Poa pratensis*), and cheatgrass (*Bromus tectorum*) are also present. Today this mixed-grass community covers nearly 80 percent of the battlefield, especially along the ridgeline. The remaining 20 percent is covered for the most part by eastern cottonwood and green ash forest along the Little Bighorn River, with some minor shrubland in between.[16] It is a lush landscape, grazed by small herds of Apsáalooke horses and cattle that wander along the battlefield's ridgeline road.

When visitors to the Seventh Cavalry Memorial and Indian Memorial cast their gaze over the grassy hills, they likely wonder how the Tituwaŋ and Tsis tsis'tas encampment of thousands could have been obscured. They are likely appalled at how exposed those on the hills and ridgeline were. At the top of Last Stand Hill, they likely draw

25. TOP: Memorial markers and tombstones at the Little Bighorn National Battlefield site near the Crow Agency community. LC-DIG-highsm-71524, Library of Congress, Carol M. Highsmith Archive.

26. BOTTOM: Last Stand Hill, April 1984 (in the aftermath of the 1983 fires). Keith Ewing, *Tombstone of G. A. Custer,* Flickr, https://flickr.com/photos/kewing/51287268093/in/album-72157719260668039/.

in a breath as they realize, looking down toward the Little Bighorn River, how clear the line of sight is toward the trees on the banks of the river. Looking up toward the top of the hill, they probably realize what obvious targets men and horses made, without any shrubs to hide behind.

But the battlefield today is not the battlefield on which the Tituwaŋ and Tsis tsis'tas fought Custer and the Seventh Cavalry. Although the topography has changed only a little, the vegetation is radically different. Instead of the grasses we see today, the battlefield was once covered in sagebrush, with far fewer grasses. Plains silver sagebrush (*Artemisia cana*) and Wyoming big sagebrush (*Artemisia tridentata*) plants are still present on the battlefield, but in far smaller numbers and far fewer areas.[17]

On August 11, 1983, a massive and intense conflagration burned over 90 percent of the battlefield, incinerating the vegetation across the entire Custer Unit, including Last Stand Hill and the cemetery, and most of the rest of the battlefield. The fire obliterated the sagebrush and other shrubs.

It also "helped to fend off encroaching shrubs and invasive species, and allowed for a reseeding of native grasses." The National Park Service credits the fire and a second large-scale burn, on August 22, 1991, at the Reno-Benteen Unit, with allowing the battlefield to resume "much of its historic and natural character."[18]

What the NPS official making this statement meant by "historic and natural character" is that the battlefield had once had a proliferation of native grass species facilitated by historic fire, and, in the wake of these recent fires, it had these native grasses again. The decades in between the historic fires, either naturally caused or set by Indigenous peoples, and the recent fires, one caused by a cigarette and the other of unknown human origin, featured near-total fire suppression.[19] Federal land management agencies have a long history of enforcing fire suppression, which began after 1910, when catastrophic fires in the American West prompted the Department of Agriculture's Forest Service to launch its fire suppression policy, which was then emulated by the NPS.[20] In addition, federal removal and confinement of Indigenous peoples onto reservations ended Indigenous burning practices, and expanding white settler and settler descendant agricultural operations precluded any use of fire.[21]

Without small, frequent fires to suppress sagebrush growth, grasses struggled to find purchase between the more dominant shrubs. The scattered sagebrush sucked moisture from the soil, leaving sandy stretches in between the small shrubs. This was the state of the battlefield that writer Mari Sandoz encountered in her trips to Montana and the battlefield at Little Bighorn.

According to her biographer, Helen Winter Stauffer, Sandoz took trips to the sites of significance for her writing. Stauffer argues, "Physical contact with the region was essential for [Sandoz's] creativity." Being on site and experiencing places firsthand "helped her begin recreating in her mind the actions that had taken place there."[22] She traveled to the Little Bighorn battlefield in 1949, 1963, and again in 1964 expressly for this purpose.[23] For Sandoz, the environment was more than just a setting; it was a character in the story. Her rich, descriptive prose immerses readers in the landscape and the experiences of the battle as she reconstructed it from archival records and personal accounts. Sandoz's view of the battlefield was very different from what visitors see today and much closer to what participants experienced in 1876. She saw more sagebrush and sand, less grass, except near waterways, and fewer structures and people. It is difficult, if not impossible, for today's visitors to the battlefield to truly understand the roughness of the terrain, the heat and scarcity of water away from the river, and how much even the smallest bush provided in terms of protection.

Historians, journalists, and other writers have penned plenty on the Battle of the Little Bighorn. In 1976 Fort Worth museum curator and visual culture specialist Michael A. Sievers published a centennial historiography of the literature on the battle. Situating works by such noted historians of the American West as Robert M. Utley, Robert Athearn, Alvin M. Josephy, Donald Jackson, George E. Hyde, Dee Brown, and Paul A. Hutton, Sievers tackled a series of questions that

27. A. L. Nash, Plastichrome postcard, site of General Custer's Last Stand, circa 1960. Author's collection.

contextualized the event and provided an overview of the decisions made by Custer and others before and during the battle, beyond the so-called technicalities. Sievers devotes little attention to Sandoz's work in answering these questions and instead places particular emphasis on the work of Utley, a prominent historian of that era.[24]

Utley knew the battlefield landscape intimately, having spent seven summers there between 1946 and 1952, first as a visitor and the rest as a park ranger for the National Park Service, but he rarely mentioned much about the environment except to provide some sense of setting.[25] In a 1949 booklet he wrote, plus the various battlefield brochures provided to visitors, and his short 1969 book about the monument, geography is central, but the environment is absent. Utley wrote prominently of the battle, how it unfolded across the landscape, and the people who participated in it but little of the place itself.[26] Of his observations of the battlefield, he only wrote that the Little Bighorn River was surrounded by cottonwood trees where the Tituwaŋ and Tsis tsis'tas encampment had been, and he described

Custer Hill rising above the manicured green grass of the national cemetery, which stood in contrast "to the dry plains grass dappled with blue-gray clumps of sagebrush."[27] Perhaps Utley assumed visitors to the battlefield did not need the landscape in front of them described in print. Perhaps, having been at the battlefield for multiple years and having examined numerous reports and photographs, he recognized that very little of it had changed in the decades since 1876. Utley's assumption that the battlefield's environment was static is an important reflection of the fire suppression policy that dominated during his lifetime, as well as a signal of the impact of that policy. It is nearly impossible for landscapes to remain the same for long and yet this one did for more than a century.

Though Sandoz featured only peripherally in Sievers's discussion, her work is far more important in this conversation because of the attention she gave to describing the place where the battle unfolded. Sandoz's account provides a glimpse into the physical situation of the battlefield. Her descriptions of the heat of the day and aridity of the season, the dearth of forage for the horses, and the minimal but important cover provided by the sagebrush draws readers into a landscape not readily apparent to visitors at the national monument.

Of the heat, Sandoz writes, "The windrows of thin clouds cut off the direct scorch of the sun but not the heat, so the men sweltered under the sultry, whitish sky," and the "thermometer often went above 110 degrees."[28] Battlefield historian Jerry L. Russell inferred that temperatures at the time of the fight were at least in the mid-90s based on inference from the 91-degree temperatures recorded by U.S. Army Corps of Engineers personnel on the Yellowstone River more than thirty miles to the north on June 25, 1876.[29] The heat caused troops to be "desperate for water," the dust "gritty and burning the dry mouths of the able as well as the burning and delirious wounded."[30] The minimal rain that fell the evening of the first day of the battle, "the raindrops making light running sounds over the dry earth, like timid mice . . . was not enough to wet one parched tongue or to soak the grass piles of the Indians watching the way to water. Besides, there was repeated heat lightning, revealing all the ridge and its bluffs in rosy glare" and threatening to ignite the grasslands.³¹

The Tituwaŋ and Tsis tsis'tas lit fires along the riverbank in the dead rushes and in the undergrowth of the cottonwood and ash trees to obscure their village and movements, thus igniting the grass and sagebrush.³² The fires, according to Sandoz, "reached straight ahead into the higher, drought-withered weeds and burned more rapidly, making a great smoke as it crept along the dusty, dried brush tops in the light northeast wind, blazing up in the tent caterpillar webs, leaving the green wood smoldering, the fire smoke setting even the seasoned, gun-broken cavalry horses wild."³³ Many of the Seventh Cavalry likely never saw much of the encampment because of these fires, the village below them "still largely hidden by the rise of brush- and grass-fire smoke on the bottoms, although the dust down there was drifting away over the prairie."³⁴ Sandoz writes, "The river valley was full of dust and smoke from the powder, and from the grass that the Indians had fired."³⁵

Some Tituwaŋ and Tsis tsis'tas continued to light fires throughout the battle, leading "smoke to rise behind them from patches of grass and sagebrush, the smoke pearling upward."³⁶ But there was little grass and sagebrush to burn, and what was there was scattered and sparse; due to lack of fuel, the prairie along the ridgeline did not catch fire, although the Seventh Cavalry certainly feared it would.³⁷ In the aftermath of the battle, Sandoz explains, "with their adjutants close behind, the men rode across the bottoms that had been grazed by the village horses of the Indian, the earth torn now by all the bare-hoofed charges of two days ago, the grass roots so cut up that the Indian fire had barely crept out of the dead rushes and timber patches."³⁸ In addition, the Tituwaŋ and Tsis tsis'tas had ignited some of the vegetation west of the Little Bighorn River and the battle, intending to cover their retreat and discourage any troops following them.³⁹

It was so dry, according to Sandoz, that Tituwaŋ and Tsis tsis'tas war leaders cautioned their people: "'Nobody is to be reckless and get hurt. The soldiers can all be killed by no water.'"⁴⁰ "Several times the next day," Sandoz writes, "Reno tried to get a detail to water, but the Indians were most watchful along the river bluffs."[41] When those who survived into the next day on what became known as Reno Hill were able to get their horses to water, the animals drank frantically and were difficult to move because they desperately needed to drink their fill.[42]

Sweltering temperatures were only the beginning. The forage available to both the Tituwaŋ and Tsis tsis'tas encampment and the Seventh Cavalry was lean to begin with, except in the river bottom, and had largely been consumed by the time the battle began. Sandoz writes that on June 22, the Seventh Cavalry "made camp in a patch of timber at the foot of a steep shielding bluff only eleven or twelve miles out [in the Rosebud Valley], but this, as Reno had reported, was one of the last lush stretches of grass before they reached the deserted campsites of the Sioux, where the valley, the bluffs, and the upland were cropped bare by the vast pony herds of the Indians, the lodgepole trail leading up the creek wide and deeply worn."[43] On June 23, Sandoz writes, "the scouts out ahead reported that the grass was eaten off short for miles around, the earth dotted with the droppings of thousands of horses, droppings beetle-worked and dry."[44]

The lack of grass only became more of a problem. Sandoz writes, "The terrain along the breaks of the Rosebud and the Wolf Mountains was unfailingly rough and rocky, largely bare of grass, sage, or weeds."[45] In the Seventh Cavalry's journey up the Rosebud Valley, on June 24, "the stable sergeants had their constant worries over forage for the stock of the command, well over eight hundred head, not counting the horses of the various civilians, and this with the grass eaten into the ground. The Indians and other scouts were worried too: their horses had to cover substantially more miles than those of the regiment. Six Indians were sent out to hunt up remote low spots and bottoms for grass for their hungry ponies, grass preferably rich in seed to be gathered into their blankets and bundled tight with the lariats."[46]

As the Seventh Cavalry progressed, according to Sandoz, "The greenness of the broken branches around the camps, the growing freshness of the pony droppings, and the windblown ashes of the fires told the scouts and even some of the troopers how swiftly Custer was overtaking the Indians. Finally the column reached a large, grazed-over stretch, the grass eaten bare for many miles out over the low hills and along the pretty valley of the Rosebud."[47] At the end of the twenty-six-mile march that day, Sandoz writes, the Seventh Cavalry's horse handlers had a difficult time maintaining control of the animals trying to feed on the stubble of grass that was left, "the first real grass they [the Seventh Cavalry] had found."[48]

By midnight of Sunday, June 25, the horses were still hungry. Sandoz describes them "grabbing hungrily for a mouthful of grass or weed through bitted teeth."[49] As the Seventh Cavalry continued their progress, stopping periodically to rest the horses, they let the animals "eat the little grass available."[50] When dawn broke, the Indian scouts and Seventh Cavalry officers, including Custer, gazed over what Sandoz describes as "the slopes of gray rock, sage, and sparse grass . . . dotted with the green-black of cedar and jack pines coming out of the foggy morning haze" toward the valley of the Little Bighorn.[51] She writes, "When Custer first climbed the peak of the Crow's Nest, Charley Reynolds pointed to a spot for observation. With field glasses to his eyes, the colonel stared a long time into the bluish haze that was creeping over much of the lightly shadowed heights and hollows. He looked and said he was unable to distinguish what others called lodge smoke or even the movement of the enormous pony herds, probably on the way to water or returning to the grassy hills beyond the Little Bighorn."[52]

As the fight progressed from Sunday to Monday, Seventh Cavalry troops observed Tituwaŋ and Tsis tsis'tas horses moving en masse such that "the gradual slopes of grassy prairie looked as though fire had scorched the foliage of a vast stretch of brush . . . heading perhaps to water or to new pasture."[53] Sandoz explained, "Then someone expressed the disturbing possibility that the Indians might just be short of meat and grass—very convincing in such a vast camp—and were moving the families to some buffalo range the hunters had located, the horses to fresh pasture."[54] The battle ended, in her estimation, not so much from Tituwaŋ and Tsis tsis'tas giving up the fight as from the need for their leaders to break up the encampment and move to where there was feed for their tens of thousands of horses.

Grasses, especially in the short- and mixed-grass prairies, generally do not provide much protection or cover in a battle, and there were fewer bunches of grass in which either the Tituwaŋ and Tsis tsis'tas or the Seventh Cavalry could hide. Sandoz notes that the men, particularly veterans of previous battles, crawled and dodged "from hollow to weed to sage clump to prairie-dog mound" and used the cover of gunfire smoke and dust.[55] According to the NPS, late nineteenth-century photos indicate "an abundance of big sagebrush on the battlefield at this time."[56] In Sandy Barnard's multiple studies of the historic photographs of the Little Bighorn site, the prominence of sagebrush is striking. According to Barnard, photographer John Fouch took the first photo of the place where Custer fell in 1877, a photograph that prominently displays far more sagebrush than grass.[57] Around a decade later, the battlefield still featured sagebrush as the dominant vegetation on much of the battlefield.

On the battle's fiftieth anniversary in 1926, photographs taken indicate far more sagebrush than grass on the battlefield, with patches of loose earth in between the shrubs.

Kenneth Roahen, a prolific photographer of the battlefield, "shot and reshot the Little Big Horn battlefield every year or two" from the 1940s until the early 1970s, and his images similarly reveal a much greater amount of sagebrush than we see today.[58] In subsequent decades the landscape changed little, with sagebrush the predominant feature of the rolling hills.

Sandoz saw this same sagebrush in her time at the Little Bighorn Battlefield. Writing her account based on what she saw as much as on what she read in the historical record, she detailed the dust and the "sturdy sagebrush" against which troops propped the Seventh Cavalry standards and in which they hid as best they could.[59] Sandoz writes, "As the firing sharpened, every man hugged the dry, dusty earth, making himself as thin as possible, none with the time to dig

28. TOP: "The battle of Custer's last charge, 2 miles from Crow Agency, Montana," circa 1880–1910. Image x-31645, Denver Public Library Special Collections.

29. BOTTOM: Little Bighorn Battlefield National Monument, Last Stand Hill, 1926. National Park Service, Little Bighorn Battlefield National Monument.

in if there had been more shovels, those flattened down behind sagebrush hoping that it was neither transparent or bullet-welcoming, the whole command—particularly Reno's battalion—in no condition for hard work or for a protracted wait without dozing off in the desperate need for sleep."[60]

After the fighting ended and the remnant of the Seventh Cavalry surveyed the battlefield, Sandoz writes, "It was like a great leaf, dead and fading in its straggly and browned June grasses and sagebrush, like a leaf crumpled into ravines and shallow gorges of dry waterways, with slopes rising along the ridges that were the broken midrib."[61] One of the troops "noticed a movement in a small brush patch nearby—a horse. It turned out to be [Captain Myles] Keogh's favorite, called Comanche, with seven wounds but still alive," and they searched "through hollows and clumps of sagebrush" for other survivors.[62]

In their 2006 survey report on the battlefield's vegetation and birds, Jane H. Bock and Carl E. Bock write that although we cannot know exactly what the appearance of the battlefield was in 1876, descriptions provided by Indigenous participants highlight the predominant presence of sagebrush on the hills.[63] In 2015 historian Gregory Smoak concurred but noted that the sagebrush shrubs were "relatively small," and there were other shrubs such as greasewood (*Sarcobatus vermiculatus*) and even species of cactus, likely prickly pear (*Opuntia polyacantha*).[64] Whatever their size and variation, these shrubs were scattered across the dusty hills and along the ridgeline, with few grasses in between. This was the state of the ground on which the Tituwaŋ and Tsis tsis'tas and the Seventh Cavalry fought. Little protection was to be found anywhere, but the sagebrush provided some minimal cover, and the lack of grass forage heightened the stakes. Custer and his men made decisions based on these factors. But this is not what visitors see on the battlefield today.

The drastic difference between the Little Bighorn Battlefield today and its condition in 1876 speaks to the ways in which landscapes change over time and how those changes must be interpreted alongside the events that take place in those landscapes. Knowing that Seventh

Cavalry troops were not entirely exposed in the mixed-grass prairie we see today but took cover in the denser sagebrush highlights an advantage Custer and his men actually had and makes their actions more sensible. Understanding the hot, dry weather, the lack of water, and the limited forage for their horses makes their desperation more pronounced.

The disjunction also points to a conundrum for battlefield managers. What then is the so-called natural state of the battlefield? Should it conform to conditions in 1876? Should it undergo regular ecological succession based on the application of fire? The answer depends on the purpose for which the battlefield is managed and whose stories it is designed to tell. Perhaps it can tell a few stories that intentionally incorporate this knowledge.

First, the battlefield's current condition highlights the fundamental role fire has played and continues to play in the health of ecosystems. Fire promotes mixed-grass prairie health, and the transformation of the battlefield into a healthy, lush grassland showcases its effect. Second, the story of the battlefield's transformation speaks to the human decision-making involved in land management. Fire suppression practices maintained the battlefield much as it had been during the conflict for more than one hundred years, and visitors then tacitly understood the physical situation of the conflict more specifically than they do today because of that practice. This is an important part of the battlefield's story beyond the battle itself.

Finally, helping visitors understand the conditions under which the battle occurred involves not only revealing the thoughts and actions of the individuals involved but also requires revealing the environment in which they operated. The environmental transformation that the Little Bighorn Battlefield National Monument has undergone between 1876 and today is subtle to the untrained eye but nothing short of astounding. Making that transformation visible and legible fundamentally enhances the visitor experience. To get to that understanding, recognizing which histories grapple with the environment of Little Bighorn intentionally and explicitly is essential. Mari Sandoz, in her

1966 book *The Battle of the Little Bighorn*, does this better than any other writer, and this history, with its rich environmental descriptions, provides a profound look at the place for those visitors generations removed from the historic fight.

NOTES

Epigraph: From the Curtis Books edition (1966), 60, 211.

1. Temperature data for July 28, 2014, and June 22, 2015, from Weather Underground, https://www.wunderground.com/history. Description is from personal experience.
2. "Očeti Šakowiŋ," Native Knowledge 360° (Smithsonian Institution), accessed April 22, 2022, https://americanindian.si.edu/nk360/plains-belonging-nation/oceti-sakowin; Northern Cheyenne Tribe, Montana Governor's Office of Indian Affairs, accessed April 22, 2022, https://tribalnations.mt.gov/northerncheyenne.
3. Little Bighorn National Battlefield attendance statistics from 2012 to 2016, National Park Service, accessed February 26, 2024, https://www.nps.gov/libi/learn/management/statistics.htm.
4. David Lowenthal, *The Past Is a Foreign Country—Revisited* (New York: Cambridge University Press, 2015), 4.
5. Lowenthal, *Past Is a Foreign Country*, 429.
6. Lowenthal, *Past Is a Foreign Country*, 434.
7. Lowenthal, *Past Is a Foreign Country*, 475.
8. Neil Mangum, "Changing Faces [of] Last Stand Hill," Friends of the Little Bighorn Battlefield, June 23, 2002, https://www.friendslittlebighorn.com/little-bighorn-changing-faces.htm.
9. Debra A. Reid and David D. Vail, *Interpreting the Environment at Museums and Historic Sites* (Lanham MD: Rowman & Littlefield, 2019), 73.
10. "Mission, Vision, and Core Values," National Association for Interpretation, accessed April 22, 2022, https://www.interpnet.com/nai/interp/About/About_NAI/What_We_Believe/nai/_About/Mission_Vision_and_Core_Values.aspx?hkey=ef5896dc-53e4-4dbb-929e-96d45bdb1cc1.
11. Jane H. Bock and Carl E. Bock, "A Survey of the Vascular Plants and Birds of Little Bighorn Battlefield," Department of Ecology and Evolutionary Biology, University of Colorado, Boulder, July 2006, 23.

12. Crow Nation, Montana Governor's Office of Indian Affairs, accessed April 22, .2022, https://tribalnations.mt.gov/crow.
13. George Bird Grinnell, "Cheyenne Stream Names," *American Anthropologist* 8, no. 1 (January–March 1906): 19; spelling from the Cheyenne Dictionary, accessed April 22 2022, http://www.cheyennelanguage.org/dictionary/index.html; Gregory E. Smoak, "An Environmental History of Little Bighorn Battlefield National Monument," December 10, 2015, 57, report housed at the Public and Environmental History Center, Colorado State University.
14. Grinnell, "Cheyenne Stream Names," 16; spelling from the online Cheyenne Dictionary.
15. Smoak, "Environmental History," 73–75, 95–98.
16. Peter Rice et al., "Vegetation Classification and Mapping Project Report, Little Bighorn Battlefield National Monument," National Park Service, Department of the Interior, October 2012, xii, 92–98, https://irma.nps.gov/DataStore/DownloadFile/583989.
17. Rice et al., "Vegetation Classification and Mapping," 101–6.
18. "Fire History," Little Bighorn Battlefield National Monument, accessed April 22 2022, https://www.nps.gov/libi/learn/nature/fire-history.htm.
19. "Fire Roared through 600 Acres of Dry Range Grass . . . ," UPI Archives, August 11, 1983, https://www.upi.com/Archives/1983/08/11/Fire-roared-through-600-acres-of-dry-range-grass/2409429422400/.
20. Hal K. Rothman, *Blazing Heritage: A History of Wildland Fire in the National Parks* (New York: Oxford University Press, 2007), 7.
21. "Fire History," Little Bighorn Battlefield National Monument.
22. Helen Winter Stauffer, *Mari Sandoz: Story Catcher of the Plains* (Lincoln: University of Nebraska Press, 1982), 82.
23. Stauffer, *Mari Sandoz: Story Catcher*, 245, 249.
24. Michael A. Sievers, "The Literature of the Little Bighorn: A Centennial Historiography," *Arizona and the West* 18, no. 2 (Summer 1976): 149–76.
25. Robert M. Utley, *Custer and Me: A Historian's Memoir* (Norman: University of Oklahoma Press, 2004), 18–44.
26. Robert M. Utley, *Custer's Last Stand: With a Narration of Events Preceding and Following* (Dayton IN: Robert M. Utley, 1949); Custer Battlefield National Monument brochure, National Park Service, 1966; Robert M. Utley, *Custer Battlefield National Monument, Montana* (Washington DC: National Park Service, 1969).

27. Utley, *Custer and Me*, 21.
28. Mari Sandoz, *The Battle of the Little Bighorn* (New York: Curtis Books, an imprint of Modern Literary Editions, 1966), 66, 192.
29. Jerry L. Russell, *1876 Facts about Custer and the Battle of the Little Bighorn* (Mason City IA: Savas, 1999), 94; John H. Sandy, "Characterization of Geographical Aspects of the Landscape and Environment in the Area of the Little Bighorn Battlefield, Montana," unpublished manuscript, University of Alabama, 2017, 11–12.
30. Sandoz, *Battle of the Little Bighorn*, 192.
31. Sandoz, *Battle of the Little Bighorn*, 183.
32. Sandoz, *Battle of the Little Bighorn*, 56, 96.
33. Sandoz, *Battle of the Little Bighorn*, 98.
34. Sandoz, *Battle of the Little Bighorn*, 107–8.
35. Sandoz, *Battle of the Little Bighorn*, 114.
36. Sandoz, *Battle of the Little Bighorn*, 195–96.
37. Sandoz, *Battle of the Little Bighorn*, 107.
38. Sandoz, *Battle of the Little Bighorn*, 209.
39. "Fire History," Little Bighorn Battlefield National Monument.
40. Sandoz, *Battle of the Little Bighorn*, 166.
41. Sandoz, *Battle of the Little Bighorn*, 174–75.
42. Sandoz, *Battle of the Little Bighorn*, 198–99.
43. Sandoz, *Battle of the Little Bighorn*, 15.
44. Sandoz, *Battle of the Little Bighorn*, 36.
45. Sandoz, *Battle of the Little Bighorn*, 110.
46. Sandoz, *Battle of the Little Bighorn*, 40.
47. Sandoz, *Battle of the Little Bighorn*, 41.
48. Sandoz, *Battle of the Little Bighorn*, 49.
49. Sandoz, *Battle of the Little Bighorn*, 55.
50. Sandoz, *Battle of the Little Bighorn*, 57–58.
51. Sandoz, *Battle of the Little Bighorn*, 60.
52. Sandoz, *Battle of the Little Bighorn*, 66–67.
53. Sandoz, *Battle of the Little Bighorn*, 128–29.
54. Sandoz, *Battle of the Little Bighorn*, 198.
55. Sandoz, *Battle of the Little Bighorn*, 91.
56. "Fire History," Little Bighorn Battlefield National Monument.
57. Sandy Barnard, *Photographing Custer's Battlefield: The Images of Kenneth Roahen* (Norman: University of Oklahoma Press, 2016), 182–83.

58. Barnard, *Photographing Custer's Battlefield*, xi–xiii.
59. Sandoz, *Battle of the Little Bighorn*, 46.
60. Sandoz, *Battle of the Little Bighorn*, 172.
61. Sandoz, *Battle of the Little Bighorn*, 211.
62. Sandoz, *Battle of the Little Bighorn*, 214.
63. Bock and Bock, "Survey of the Vascular Plants and Birds," 25.
64. Smoak, "Environmental History," 163–64.

Contributors

KENT BLANSETT (PhD, University of New Mexico) is the Langston Hughes Associate Professor of Indigenous Studies and History at the University of Kansas, the author of *A Journey to Freedom: Richard Oakes, Alcatraz, and the Red Power Movement* (Yale University Press, 2018) and multiple essays on Red Power in various anthologies, and curator of the exhibit *Not Your Indians Anymore: Alcatraz and the Red Power Movement, 1969–71*, displayed at Alcatraz Island through 2021.

LEISL CARR CHILDERS (PhD, University of Nevada, Las Vegas) is an associate professor of history at Colorado State University, a member of the Public and Environmental History Center, and the author of *The Size of the Risk: Histories of Multiple Use in the Great Basin* (University of Oklahoma Press, 2015), which won the Western Writers of America 2016 Spur Award for contemporary nonfiction, as well as multiple essays in anthologies on public history and the American West.

CATHRYN HALVERSON (PhD, University of Michigan) is a senior lecturer in English at Södertörn University in Huddinge, Sweden, and she was the 2021–22 Distinguished Fulbright Chair at the Swedish Institute of American Studies at the University of Uppsala. She is the author of three monographs about western women. The most recent, *Faraway Women and the "Atlantic Monthly"* (University of Massachusetts Press, 2019) was the 2019 winner of the Thomas J. Lyon Award for best single-author monograph in western literary and cultural studies.

TAYLOR G. HENSEL (MA, University of Wyoming) is a writer and high school teacher from Denver, Colorado. Hensel's thesis, "Men of Notoriously Vicious Intemperate Disposition: The Role of the Gunfighter in American History, Popular Culture, and Masculinity, 1865–Present Day," examined the distinctly human lives of the men who had been mythologized by years of fiction. He has published articles on famous western personalities in the *Epoch Times* and *American Essence* magazine.

MARGARET HUETTL, a Lac Courte Oreilles Ojibwe descendant, is the director of Indigenous studies at the University of Wisconsin Oshkosh. She is a scholar of Native American history and North American Wests, and her research examines the continuities of Ojibwe sovereignty in the western Great Lakes region, centering Ojibwe ways of knowing. Her research has been published in several places, including the *Journal of Ethnohistory* and in *Understanding and Teaching Native American History* from the University of Wisconsin Press.

PAUL ANDREW HUTTON (PhD, Indiana University) is Distinguished Professor of History and Emeritus Professor of History at the University of New Mexico, a past executive director of the Western History Association, and the author of numerous award-winning histories of the American West, including *The Apache Wars: The Hunt for Geronimo, the Apache Kid, and the Captive Boy Who Started the Longest War in American History* (Crown, 2016).

RENÉE M. LAEGREID (PhD, University of Nebraska–Lincoln) is the Andrew Allen Excellence Fellow in Western History at the University of Wyoming. Her research includes women and gender in the nineteenth- and twentieth-century U.S. West, and she has authored, edited, and published works in numerous places. She also researches and publishes on the cultural and social analysis of western iconography, examining how symbols of the West have been created and shaped over time and across international boundaries.

ELAINE MARIE NELSON (PhD, University of New Mexico) is an assistant professor of history at the University of Kansas, where she teaches courses on the American West, women and gender, and the Great Plains. Her published work appears in the *Great Plains Quar-*

terly, South Dakota History, and various anthologies. Nelson's book on the history of the Black Hills is forthcoming from the University of Nebraska Press. Since 2017 she has served as the executive director of the Western History Association.

CHERYL A. WELLS (PhD, University of South Carolina) served as an associate professor of nineteenth-century U.S. history at the University of Wyoming and as a visiting professor at the University of New Brunswick Saint John. Her work dealt with time and temporality, Civil War and Reconstruction, and Indigenous history. She is an independent scholar currently working for an Ottawa-based historical consulting firm focused on Indigenous affairs.

DR. JOHN WUNDER (PhD, University of Washington) (1945–2023) was an emeritus professor of history at the University of Nebraska–Lincoln and former director of the Center for Great Plains Studies. He is the author of multiple books on the Great Plains, Indigenous peoples, and Mari Sandoz. He was the founding editor of the Sandoz Studies series at the University of Nebraska Press, and in 2021 he was the recipient of the Sower Award in the Humanities for his significant contributions to the public's understanding of the humanities in Nebraska.

Index

Page numbers in italics refer to illustrations.

AAIA. *See* Association of American Indian Affairs (AAIA)
Abbot, Mary Squire, 13, 30, 31
Adams, Cassilly, xviii
Adjutant General's Office (AGO), 12, 17, 18
Adventures of Huckleberry Finn (Twain), 72
Ahab, xxviii, 101
AIM. *See* American Indian Movement (AIM)
Alamo, xix, 97
Alcatraz, 121, 128, 134
Alfred Knopf (publishing house), 112
American Bureau of Ethnology, 31
American Heritage, 32, 111
American Indian Movement (AIM), 93, 138, 139, 140, 141, *143*, 148n12, 151n34
American West, 3, 93, 118, 122, 127, 130, 164; examination of, 117; Indigenous perspective on, 94–95; story of, 6; writing about, 9, 15
Anderson, Mary Ann Pifer, 7–8, 26, 36, 41n38, 43n69; birth of, 22; graduation of, 25; letter from, 1, 32–33; on literature, 2; Mari Sandoz and, 2, 3, 21, 24, 27, 28, 42n69
Anheuser-Busch Company, xviii
antiwar movement, xxviii, 112, 134, 142, 146n2
Apsáalooke (Crows), 159, 160, 161
Arapahos, 56, 88, 97, 106, 114, 115
The Arikara Narrative of the Campaign against the Hostile Dakotas (Libby), xxii
Arikaras, 58, 86, 98, 101, 104
Arizona and the West, 116
Asbury, Edith Evans, 25
As Long as the Grass Shall Grow (La Farge), *124*, 125
assimilation, 122, 132
Association of American Indian Affairs (AAIA), 121, 126, 148n19, 152n41
Athearn, Robert, 164
Atlantic Monthly, 75
Austin, Louise, 10

Bad Heart Bull, Amos, 19, 40n35, 119, 153n52; ledger art by, 120
Bad Heart Bull, Wesley, 139
Baldwin, Hanson, xxi, xxvi, 29; Mari Sandoz and, 12–13, 16

183

Bancroft, Caroline, 6, 27, 28
Barnard, Sandy, 170
Barnett, Louise, xxv
Battle of the Greasy Grass. *See* Battle of the Little Bighorn
Battle of the Little Bighorn: centennial of, 143, 151n34; commemorations of, 138, 155–56; documentation for, 56; interpretation of, 115–16, 149n24; legacy of, 134 research on, 16, 17, 21; writing about, 12, 62
The Battle of the Little Bighorn (Sandoz): Custer legend and, xxi; environmental descriptions in, 174; impact of, xxvi; military engagement and, 36; publication of, xvii, 35, 45, 92, 116, 117; as rebuttal, 87; researching, 19, 111–12, 128–29; reviews of, 46, 47–48, 116–17; sensory world and, 49, 62–63; sympathies of, 73; warning from, 114; writing of, xxvii, xxviii–xxix, 2–3, 53, 82, 142
The Battle of the Little Bighorn River (Cary), xviii, 136, *137*
Battle of the Washita River (1868), xxiv, 71, 151n37
Bear Runner, Oscar, 141
Bear With Horns, 153n52
The Beaver Men (Sandoz), 9, 16
Becker, F. Otto, xviii
Bennett, James, xxiii
Benteen, Frederick, xxv, 35, 100, 102, 103, 159
Berger, Thomas, xxi, 91
BIA. *See* Bureau of Indian Affairs (BIA)

Big Greasy Grass, 160
Billy the Kid, 92
Bird by Bird (Lamott), 2
Bissonette, Pedro, 140
Bitter Tears (Cash), 96, 150n30
Black Elk Speaks (Neihardt), 119
Black Hills, 51, 96, 132
Black Kettle, 151n37
Black White Man, 153n52
Blakemore, Carolyn, 30, 31
Blansett, Kent, xxiv, xxviii–xxix, 157
Blish, Helen, 19, 40n35
Bloody Knife, xxii, 58, 87, 98, 101, 103; death of, 104
Bob Hampton of Placer (movie), xviii
Bobtail Bull, xxii
Bock, Carl E., 172
Bock, Jane H., 172
Boocher, Barbara, 153n52
Boots and Saddles (Custer), xx, 71, 72, 74, 75, 77, 79, 81, 82, 83, 86; Custer's political nature and, 85; landscape of, 84; vantage point of, 76
"Boots and Saddles" (song), 57, 82
Brady, Cyrus Townsend, xviii
Britton of the Seventh (movie), xviii
Brodie, Fawn, xxv
Brooks, Bill, 46
Brown, Dee, xvii, 97, 108, 142, 164
Brules, 111, 114
Buel, J. W., xviii
Buffalohead, Roger, 121
The Buffalo Hunters (Sandoz), 9
Bull Run, 76
Bureau of Indian Affairs (BIA), 40n33, 140, 147n12, 159

Burrows, Jack, 45, 46, 116
Bury My Heart at Wounded Knee (Brown), xvii, 97, 108, 142
Butte of the Crouching Bear, 59

Café Wha, 126
Calhoun, James, 78
Calhoun, Margaret, 78
Camp Carlin, 18
Cannon, T. C., 129, 130, 131, 133, 134, 135, 136, 138, 151n37; PTSD and, 132
Carnegie Institution, 40n35
Carr, Jim, 21
Carr Childers, Leisl, xxii, xxix
Cary, William de la Montaigne, xviii, 136
Cash, Johnny, 96, 97, 125; Peter La Farge and, 150n30
The Cattlemen (Sandoz), 9, 12
Cavalier in Buckskin (Utley), 107
Central New Jersey News, 55
Cherokees, 97
Cheyenne Autumn (Sandoz), xvii, xxii, xxiv, xxv, xxviii, 2, 83, 112; research for, 119
Cheyenne Depot, 17
Cheyennes, xix, 35, 46, 71, 83, 91, 93, 97, 106, 107, 114, 115, 141, 161; Custer and, 18; massacre of, 151n37. *See also* Northern Cheyennes; Southern Cheyennes
civil rights movement, 96, 108, 117
Civil War, xviii, xxiv, 76, 83
Clark, Ben, xxv
Clark, LaVerne Harrell, 48
Clearwater, Frank, 140
Closed Hand, 153n52

Clyne, Ronald, 124
Cody, William F., xix, xx
colonization, xxviii, 6, 112, 113, 115, 118, 126
Columbia Records, 150n30
Columbus, Christopher, 150n33, 153n52
Comanches, 102
A Complete Life of George A. Custer (Whittaker), 76
Connell, Evan S., 95
Cooke, William W., 18, 102
Crazy Horse, xxv, 22, 24, 30, 51, 83, 93, 94, 96, 107, 111, 114; appearance of, 119; assassination of, 148n12
Crazy Horse (Sandoz), xvii, xxv, xxviii, 2, 22, 30, 36, 73, 93, 118; publication of, 94–95, 96; reprinting of, 24
Crook, George, 18, 95, 115
Crow Agency, 161, 162
Crow Nation, 98
Crow's Nest, 169
"Custer" (La Farge), 96, 126, 150n30
Custer (Monaghan), xxi
Custer, Boston, 60, 71, 78, 98
Custer, Elizabeth Bacon, 82; Mari Sandoz and, xx–xxi, xxvii, 71–72, 73, 86, 87; marriage of, 83; pen pictures and, 76; Phil Sheridan and, xxvi; portrait by, xxviii, 86; self-identification of, 78; works of, xx, xxv, 72, 77
Custer, George Armstrong: ambitions of, 116; as antihero, 122, 128, 134; antiwar protest and, 112;

Custer, George Armstrong (*cont.*)
character of, 74, 80, 88, 97; criticism of, 142–43; death of, xxiv, 95, 106, 107, 115, 116, 126, 157, 160; depiction of, 98, 100, 101, 116; emotional state of, 87; family of, 71; image of, xvii, xviii; infidelity of, 83; legacy of, 115; letters from, 81, 82; martyrdom of, 105; memorialization of, 122; political nature of, 85; portrait of, 73, 96; pranks by, 79; presidential plans of, xxiii, xxiv, 98

Custer, Tom, 71, 78, 80, 86, 98

Custer and 20,000 Indians (Scholder), 134

Custer Battlefield National Cemetery, 159

Custer Battlefield National Monument, 144, 153n52

Custer Died for Your Sins (Deloria), xvii, 123–24

Custer Died for Your Sins (Westerman), *124*, 142

"Custer Had It Coming" (slogan), 127, *128*

Custer Hill, 166

Custer legend, xxi, 72, 73, 125

Custer Luck (Stewart), xxi

Custer myth, xxi, xxiv, xxvii, 35, 128, 136, 149n24, 150n33; challenging of, 122, 125, 129; Indian, 122–23, 126, 127, 130, 134, 138, 142, 144; prominence of, 123, 127, 134; reframing of, 138; responsibility for, 145; significance of, 143; transformation of, xxviii–xxix

The Custer Myth (Graham), xxi

Custerology (Elliott), 95

Custer's Fall (Miller), xxiii

Custer's Last Fight (Adams), xviii

Custer's Last Fight (movie), 149n22

Custer's Last Stand, xviii, 92, 105, 158, 160; Indigenous view of, 107

Custer's Last Stand (Paxson), 136, *137*, 138

Custer Unit, 159, 163

"Custer Wore an Arrow Shirt" (slogan), 127, *128*

Cut Belly, 153n52

Cutshell, Colleen, 153nn52

Danker, Donald, xxv

da Vinci, Leonardo, 130

Davis, Laura, 47

Deadwood Gulch, 59

Debo, Angie, 6, 121

Declaration of Independence, 91

de Haviland, Olivia, 96

Deloria, Vine, Jr., xvii, 123–24; Custer jokes and, 125; Custer myth and, 125; Mari Sandoz and, 24, 93–94

DeMallie, Raymond, 120

Democratic National Convention, xxiii, xxiv

Democratic Party, 98, 101, 116

Department of Agriculture, 163

Department of the Interior, 17, 39n28

DeVoto, Bernard, 48

Dippie, Brian, 122, 127

Dorman, Isaiah, 103

Doubleday, 39n21

Downey, Betsy, 82
Drago, Henry Sinclair, xxi
Dylan, Bob, 125

Eagle Plume, Charles, 23, 24
Earp, Wyatt, 92
Eisenhower, Dwight D., 113
Elliott, Joel, 102, 103
Elliott, Michael A., 95
Empires of the Senses (Rotter), 49
environmental conditions, 158, 159, 173, 174
ethnohistory, 6, 120

Farnum, Dustin, xviii
Federal Bureau of Investigation (FBI), 139, 140
Ferril, Thomas, xix
Fetterman, William, 83
Fifth Cavalry, xix
Fisher, Clay, xxi
The Flaming Frontier (movie), xviii
Flynn, Errol, xviii, 96
Following the Guidon (Custer), xx, xxv, 72
Forbes, Jack, 121
Foreman, Grant, 121
Fort Lincoln, 78, 79, 85
Fouch, John, 170
Frame, John, xxv
Freedom of Information Act, 39n30
French and Indian Wars, 104

Gall, 30, 59, 111, 114
Garden of Owen, 152n47
Garfield, James, xxiv
"Garry Owen" (song), 140–41, 152n47

Gaslight, 126
gender roles, Native American, 80
genocide, 96, 114, 129, 133
Gerard, Fred, xxii
Gesterfield, Mrs. Arnold, 28
Gibbon, John, 71, 86, 91, 95, 98, 99
Gilded Age, xxiii
Gipson, Fred, 39n21
"The Girl I Left behind Me" (song), 81
Glory-Hunter (Van de Water), xxi, 116
Godfrey, Edward S., 99–100, 109n19
Gondos, Victor, 40n33
Government Information Subcommittee, 17
Graham, W. A., xxi
Grant, Ulysses S., xxiii, 101
grasses, 160–61, 167, 170, 173
Greasy Grass River, 160
Great American Desert, 84
Great Depression, 117
Great Plains, 28, 50, 77, 106; history of, 2, 29; interpreting, 3–4, 6–11, 84–85; writing about, 11, 15
Great Sioux Reservation, 114
Great Sioux War, xix
Greene, Jerome, xxv
Greenwich Village, 25, 111, 125, 126, 127; Mari Sandoz and, 8, 55

Haley's Garage, 17, 19, 39n28, 40n33
Half Yellow Face, 58
Halverson, Cathryn, xxi, xxvii–xxviii
Hancock, Winfield Scott, xxiv
Haney, Elle Mae, 152n41
Harney, William, 106

Index 187

Harper and Brothers, 11, 13, 14, 16, 39n21
Hass, Paul H., 56, 116
Hat Creek, xix
Haycox, Ernest, xxi
Hayward, Barton M., 46
Healy, Amanda, 74
He Dog, 51, 94, 108
Hemings, Sally, xxv
Hendricks, Thomas, xxiv
Hensel, Taylor G., xxiv, xxviii
Hickok, Wild Bill, xx
Hill, Joan, 150n33
Hinman, Eleanor, 23, 94
history, American Indian, 118, 120, 121
Hitchcock, Alfred, 115
Holm, Tom, 147n7
Hull, Ron, 28–29
Hutton, Paul A., 143, 164
Hyde, George E., 164

IAIA. *See* Institute of American Indian Arts (IAIA)
Illustrated Police News, xviii
imperialism, 122, 128
Indianapolis Star, 46
Indian Claims Commission (ICC), 121
Indian Country, 24, 113, 122, 123, 127, 146n4, 148n12
Indian Memorial, 158, 161
Indians of All Tribes (IAT), 128
Indian Wars, xvii, xxiii, 40n33, 79, 130, 133
Indigenous peoples, 3, 101, 105, 106, 114, 163, 164; future of, 125; responsibility for, 134; rights and justice for, 123; violation of, 59
Indigenous rights movement, 123
Institute of American Indian Arts (IAIA), *129*, 130, 136, 140
In the Footsteps of Crazy Horse (Marshall), 24
"Ira Hayes" (La Farge), 125

Jackson, Donald, 164
James Carr's Books, xxi
J. B. Lippincott Company, xxi, xxvi, 12, 18, 29, 46
Jefferson, Thomas, xxv
Johnson, Andrew, 100, 101
Johnson, Dorothy, 6
Johnson, Lyndon, 113
jokes, 79; Custer, 125
Josephy, Alvin M., Jr., xxiii, 35, 36, 43n71, 43n73, 46, 117, 164
The Journey of Crazy Horse (Marshall), 107
Jumping Bull Compound, 140

Kahn, Roger, 39n21
Keller, Douglas, 45
Kelsey, D. M., xviii
Kennedy, John F., 113
Keogh, Myles, 172
Keyes, Sarah, 56
Kiowa Black Leggings Society, 134
Kiowas, 102
Knopf, Blanche W., 53, 112, 147n8
Kocks, Dorothee E., 48
Kraft, Louis, 74
Kramer, Karen, 132

La Farge, Oliver, 126, 152n41
La Farge, Peter, 96, 97, 124, 126; Johnny Cash and, 125, 150n30; Mari Sandoz and, 127
Lakotas, xxviii, 35, 56, 88, 93, 94, 97, 98, 105, 106, 107, 114, 115, 116, 118, 119, 120; Black Hills and, 96. *See also* Tituwaŋ
Lame White Man, 106, 153n52
La Monte, Buddy, 140
Lamott, Anne, 2
Last Stand Hill, 95, 105, 106, 108, *143*, 156, 158, 159, 161, *162*, 163, *171*
Laughing Boy (La Farge), 126
Leavenworth Weekly Times, 97
Leckie, Shirley, 74
Le Guin, Ursula, 39n21
Levi Strauss Golden Saddleman Award, 34
Libby, Orin G., xxii
Life, xxiii
Limber Bones, 153n52
Lincoln Star Journal, 7
Little Bighorn, 95, 96, 99, 101, 102, 106, 115, 116, 119
Little Bighorn Battlefield National Monument, xxix, 123, 153n52, 155, 159, *171*; description of, 159; environmental transformation of, 172–73; memorial markers at, *161*, *162*; visiting, 164, 170
Little Bighorn River, 156, 160, 161, 163, 165, 167
Little Bighorn Visitor Center, 43n73, 156
Little Big Man (movie), xxiii, 91, 92, 96, 97, 108

Little Killer, 94
Little Thunder, 106, 111, 114
Lomahaftewa, Linda, 150n33
Louisiana Purchase, 15
Love Song to the Plains (Sandoz), xx, 9, 11; publication of, 13, 16; writing of, 14, 15
Low Dog, 85, 97
Lowe, David, 32, 51, 111, 112, 146n4
Lowenthal, David, 157, 158
Luce, E. S., *144*, 145, 157
Lundeen, George, xxvi

Macmillan, 39n21
Mangum, Neil, 158
Manifest Destiny, 92, 96, 104, 115; challenging narrative of, 108; Mari Sandoz on, 94
Marias River Massacre (1870), 114
Mari Sandoz (Stauffer), 117
Mari Sandoz High Plains Heritage Center, xxvi, 22
Mari Sandoz Society, xxvi, 72
Marshall, Joseph M., III, 24, 94, 107
McDougall, Thomas Mower, 62
McIntosh and Otis (agency), Mari Sandoz and, 13
McKenna, Richard, 39n21
McMurtry, Larry, 95
McNickle, D'Arcy, 121
Means, Russell, 141, 142, *143*, 151n34, 153n52
Medicine, Beatrice, 121
Medicine Tail Coulee, 153n52
Melville, Herman, xxviii, 101
memorial markers, *161*, *162*
Miles, Nelson, 95

Index 189

Miller, David H., xxiii
missing files, case of, 16–19
Miss Morrissa (Sandoz), 9
mixed-grass prairie, 161, 170, 173
Moby Dick (Melville), xxviii
modernism, 118–19, 128–29
Moldoff, Stan, 124
Monaghan, Jay, xxi, 17, 39n29
Monahsetah, xxiv, xxv, 83
Montana Highway Patrol, 139
Morrison, Frank, 25
Moss, John E., 17, 39n30
My Life on the Plains (Custer), xxiv–xxv, 76

Nagle, Kathleen, 28
National Archives, xxv, 4, 17, 18, 40n33, 117
National Association for Interpretation, 159
nationalism, Native, 122, 126
National Park Service (NPS), 138, 139, 140, 160, 163, 164, 165, 170; criticism of, 142
Native Americans, 3, 4, 29, 92; childhood experiences with, 23; genocide of, 96; injustices faced by, 58; relocation of, 122; self-identity of, 97
Native American studies (NAS), 120
Nebraska Educational Television (NET), 28
Nebraska Public Broadcasting System, 29
Nebraska State Historical Society, 120
Neihardt, John G., 119

Nelson, Elaine Marie, xxi, xxvii
Newell, Quincy D., 56
New York City, 49, 53, 55, 60; Mari Sandoz and, 8, 49–51, 52, 54, 57, 62; Mary Ann Pifer Anderson in, 21, 25, 28; scents and sounds of, 57; society of, 68n59
New York Daily Graphic, xviii
New York Herald, xxiii
New York Times, xxvi, 8, 12, 25, 26, 142
Nicoll, Bruce, 14, 39n22
Niobrara River, 3, 4, 92
Nixon, Richard, 130
No Flesh, 106
Noisy Walking, 153n52
North Dakota Historical Collection, xxii
Northern Cheyenne Exodus, 119
Northern Cheyennes, 56, 83, 88, 119, 156. *See also* Tsis tsis'tas
NPS. *See* National Park Service (NPS)

Ochs, Phil, 125
Oglalas, 22, 24, 51, 83–84, 85, 88, 97
Oglala Sioux Civil Rights Organization (OSCRO), 139, 140
Oglala Societies, 120
The Oilcloth Bag (Thiessen), 26, 52
O'Kieffe, Charley, 48, 65n23
Old Jules (Sandoz), 22, 75, 118; reception for, 93
Old Jules Country (Sandoz), 33
oral histories, 30, 76, 119, 121; Cheyenne, xxv; gathering, 23; Lakota, 24
Ortiz, Alfonso, 121

OSCRO. *See* Oglala Sioux Civil Rights Organization (OSCRO)
Owen Wister Award for Lifetime Achievement in Western Writing, 34

Palmer, Robert, 46, 62
Parrish, Randall, xviii
Paxson, Edgar S., 136, *136*, 138
Penn, Arthur, xxiii, 91
pen pictures, 76
Pifer, Caroline Sandoz, 10, 21, 22, 25, 33
Pilster Great Plains Lecture, xxvii
Pine Ridge Reservation, 22, 23, 93, 139, 140
Plains Indians, 8, 51–52, 56, 101
The Plainsmen (movie), 149n22
Playing House in the American West (Halverson), 74–75
Plimpton, George, 39n21
Porter, Henry R., 61
Prairie Schooner, 112

Quarter Master Files, 18, 40n31
Quick-to-See Smith, Juane, 150n33
Quinn, Anthony, 96

Reagan, Ronald, 149n22
Red Cloud, 120
Red Cloud Agency, xix
Red Feather, 94
Red Power movement, xxviii, xxix, 112, 119, 122, 123, 126, 127, 129, 136, 138, 142, 143, 145; nonviolent principles of, 140
The Red Right Hand (Cody), xix

Red Scare, 117
Red Star, xxii–xxiii
Ree. *See* Arikaras
Reed, Autie, 60, 98
Reed, Emma, 78
Reed, James, 78
Reid, Debra, 159
"Remember Custer" (La Farge), 126
Reno, Marcus, 35, 36, 46, 61, 86, 100, 106, 159, 172; Custer and, 102; incompetence of, 103; Mari Sandoz on, 103, 104, 105, 168; panic route of, 99
Reno-Benteen Battlefield, 159
Reno-Benteen Memorial, 158
Reno-Benteen Unit, 159, 163
Reno Court of Inquiry, xxii
Reno Hill, 156, 168
Revere, Paul, xix
Reynolds, Charley, 103, 169
Reynolds, Joseph, 83
Richardson, Stewart "Sandy," 18, 29, 30, 46
Roahen, Kenneth, 170
Rocky Mountain Herald, xix
Rosebud, 58, 87, 91, 115, 168, 169
Rotter, Andrew, 49
Russell, Jerry L., 166

sagebrush, 157, 163, 164, 170, 172, 173
Sainte-Marie, Buffy, 125, 150n30
Sand Creek Massacre (1864), 114, 152n47
Sandhills, xxvi, 27, 28, 48, 49, 50, 52, 53, 108, 111; Mari Sandoz and, 4; nature of, 61; scents and sounds of, 55, 57; visiting, 24–25

Index 191

"Sandoz, Custer, and the Indian Wars" (lecture), xxvii
Sandoz, Jules, 22, 41n40, 53; biography of, 92–93
Sandoz, Mari, 5, 6, 7, 9, *10*, *11*, *12*, *16*, *20*, *26*, *34*, *144*; cancer of, xxvi, 3, 19, 21, 25, 26, 27, 28, 30, 31, 32, 33, 49, 116, 120; career of, 6–7; criticism of, xvii, 46, 48; death of, xxvi, 28, 33, 42n69, 43n70, 111, 116; interpretive approach of, 4; legacy of, 22; letter from, 33; literary strategies and devices of, 85, 114; plagiarism accusation against, 116; reputation of, 14–15; research by, 16–17, 19, 23, 93, 112, 119; storytelling by, 118; writing of, 11–16, 29, 35–36, 47, 48–49; youth of, 4, 60, 111
Santa Fe Trail (movie), 149n22
Satanta, 151n37
scents. *See* smells
Scholder, Fritz, 129, 134, 136, 138, 152n41
Seeger, Pete, 125
self-determination, 122, 123, 126
Senate Foreign Relations Committee, 146n4
Seventh Cavalry, xviii, 46, 56, 58, 59, 81, 83, 85, 91, 95, 97, 98, 99, 100, 102, 105, 123, 133, 138; Custer Clan and, 78; expedition of, 72; massacre by, 139; massacre of, 160; partisanship of, 73
Seventh Cavalry Memorial, 156, 158, 161
Shaw, Rita, 118

Sheridan, Phil, xxvi
Shipp, Etta, 28
Short Bull, 94
short-grass prairie, 170
Sievers, Michael A., 164–65, 166
sights, xxvii, 29, 46, 48, 50, 52, 61, 62
Silliman, Stephen, 113
Sioux, 36, 46, 58, 94, 96, 103, 104, 168
Sitting Bull, xix, xx, xxv, 56
The Sixth Grandfather (Neihardt), 120
Smedley, Agnes, 53–54
smells, xxvii, 29, 46, 48, 50, 52, 55, 56, 57, 58, 60, 61, 62
Smith, Jane F., 39n28, 40n33
Smith, Mark M., 47–48
Smoak, Gregory, 172
Soldiers (Cannon), 130, *131*, 132
Son of a Gamblin' Man (Sandoz), 9
Son of the Morning Star (Connell), 95
sounds, xxvii, 29, 46, 48, 50, 52–62, 166
Southern Cheyennes, 102
Spanish-American War, 136
Spartans, 95, 99
Stauffer, Helen Winter, 16, 35, 38n11, 48, 117, 164; on Mari Sandoz, 49
Stewart, Edgar I., xxi
Stiles, T. J., xxv
The Storycatcher (Sandoz), 16, 34
storytelling, 18, 28, 112, 118, 119
Stuart, Jesse, 50
Stuntz, Joseph, 140
Sun Dance, 114, 153n52

tastes, 46, 48, 50, 52, 55, 56, 59–60, 61, 62

Taylor, Maxwell, 146n4
Taylor, Zachary, xxiii
Tenting on the Plains (Custer), xx, 72
Terry, Alfred, xxiv, 86, 91
textures, 47, 50, 52, 53, 61, 62
Thermopylae, 95, 97
These Were the Sioux (Sandoz), xvii, 9, 73
They Died with Their Boots On (movie), xviii, xxvi, 96
Thiessen, Leonard, 26
Thomas, Robert K., 120–21
Tilden, Samuel, xxiv
Tituwaŋ, 156, 159, 161, 163, 165, 167, 168, 169, 170, 172. *See also* Lakotas
The Tom-Walker (Sandoz), 112
tourism, 123, 156
Towner, Mary, 21
Trail of Broken Treaties, 153n52
Treaty of Fort Laramie (1851), 160
Treaty of Fort Laramie (1868), 160
Truman, Harry S., 113
Tsis tsis'tas, 156, 159, 161, 163, 165, 167, 168, 169, 170, 172. *See also* Northern Cheyennes
Turner, Frederick Jackson, 118
Twain, Mark, 72, 75

Umland, Rudolph, 36, 46
Universal, xviii
University of Nebraska, 21, 25
University of Nebraska Press, 14, 40n35
U.S. Army Corps of Engineers, 166
U.S. Supreme Court, 96
Utley, Robert M., xxv, 107, 142, 143, 164–65, 166

Vail, David, 159
Van den Bark, Melvin, 53
Van de Water, Frederic, xxi, 116
Varnum, Charles Albert, 60
Vietnam War, 32, 91, 104, 112, 113, 115, 117, 140, 142, 145, 146n4, 150n33; Native Americans in, 151n35
Vitruvian Man (da Vinci), 130
von Clausewitz, Carl, 145n2

WalkingStick, Kay, 150n33
Walsh, Raoul, 96
Warbonnet Creek, xix
War Department, 39n28, 40n33, 159, 160
War Department Records, 18, 117
Warhol, Andy, 129–30
Warner Bros., xviii, xxvi
Washington, George, xxiii
Washita Massacre (1868), 91–92, 102, 114, 119, 152n47
Welch, James, 125
Wells, Cheryl, xxii, xxvii, xxix
"We Shall Overcome" (song), 126
Westerman, Floyd Red Crow, 123, 142
Western History Association, xxvii
westward expansion, 6, 115, 116
White Clay Creek, 23
Whitman, Walt, xviii
Whittaker, Frederick, xviii, 75, 76
Whittier, John Greenleaf, xviii
"Why I Hate New York" (Sandoz file), 8
Wilson, Dick, 139, 140
Wolf Mountains, 168
World War II, 117, 132, 141, 144

Worley, E. T., 48, 65n24
Wounded Knee, 73, 109n19, 140; occupation of, 148n12, 152n46
Wounded Knee Massacre, 72, 139
Wyeth, Marion S. "Buz," Jr., 14, 16, 39n21

Yellow Hair (Yellow Hand), xix, xx
Yellowstone Expedition, 98
Yellowstone River, 61, 99, 166

Zero Hero (Cannon), 132, 133, *133*, *135*

IN THE SANDOZ STUDIES SERIES

Sandoz Studies, Volume 1: Women in the Writings of Mari Sandoz
Edited and with an introduction by Renée M. Laegreid
and Shannon D. Smith
Foreword by John Wunder

Sandoz Studies, Volume 2: Sandoz and the Battle of the Little Bighorn
Edited by Renée M. Laegreid, Leisl Carr Childers, and
Margaret Huettl
Foreword by John Wunder

To order or obtain more information on these or other
University of Nebraska Press titles, visit nebraskapress.unl.edu.

www.ingramcontent.com/pod-product-compliance
Lightning Source LLC
Chambersburg PA
CBHW022017220426
43663CB00007B/1117